Zhuangzi and the Becoming of Nothingness

SUNY series in Chinese Philosophy and Culture
―――――――
Roger T. Ames, editor

Zhuangzi and the Becoming of Nothingness

DAVID CHAI

Published by State University of New York Press, Albany

© 2019 State University of New York

All rights reserved

No part of this book may be used or reproduced in any manner whatsoever without written permission. No part of this book may be stored in a retrieval system or transmitted in any form or by any means including electronic, electrostatic, magnetic tape, mechanical, photocopying, recording, or otherwise without the prior permission in writing of the publisher.

For information, contact State University of New York Press, Albany, NY
www.sunypress.edu

Library of Congress Cataloging-in-Publication Data

Names: Chai, David, 1971– author.
Title: Zhuangzi and the becoming of nothingness / David Chai.
Description: Albany : State University of New York Press, 2019. | Series: SUNY series in Chinese philosophy and culture | Includes bibliographical references and index.
Identifiers: LCCN 2018009433 | ISBN 9781438472676 (hardcover) | ISBN 9781438472683 (pbk.) | ISBN 9781438472690 (ebook)
Subjects: LCSH: Zhuangzi. Nanhua jing. | Nothing (Philosophy) Classification: LCC BL1900.C576 C46 2019 | DDC 299.5/1482—dc23
LC record available at https://lccn.loc.gov/2018009433

10 9 8 7 6 5 4 3 2 1

To Vincent Qing-Song Shen,
a teacher unlike any other.

Contents

Acknowledgments	ix
Introduction	xi

1. Nothingness and Dao: A Time before Being — 1
   - The Nature of Nothingness — 2
   - The Language of Nothingness — 9
   - The Oneness of Dao — 18
   - Returning to Dao, Overcoming Nihilism — 25
   - Conclusion — 30

2. Dao, the One, and the Question of Being — 31
   - Original Being *qua* the Thing — 32
   - The Thing's Unveiling — 36
   - The Trace and the Traceless Sage — 40
   - Wandering in the Harmony of Dao — 48
   - Conclusion — 62

3. Dao and the Time of Nothingness — 65
   - Dao and Cosmological Time — 66
   - Human Measured Time — 76
   - Conclusion — 85

4. Zhuangzi and the Life Praxis of Being Useless — 87
   - Useless by Proxy and the Proxy of Usefulness — 87
   - Learning from the Useless Tree — 95
   - Conclusion — 104

5. Discovering Dao through Self-Forgetting ... 107
    The Mundaneness of Forgetting ... 108
    Losing Oneself in Forgetfulness ... 118
    Sitting in Forgetfulness ... 127
    A Taste of Spiritual Freedom: Composing the Heart-Mind ... 132
    Conclusion ... 137

6. Wandering Carefree in Nothingness ... 139
    Cosmological Freedom ... 140
    Three Heavenly Principles of Freedom ... 144
    Nothingness the Great Harmonizer ... 151
    Freedom as Carefree Wandering ... 161
    Conclusion ... 167

Conclusion ... 169

Notes ... 175

Bibliography ... 191

Index ... 195

Acknowledgments

I would like to express my gratitude to the staff at SUNY Press for making publication of this book a smooth and enjoyable process. I would also like to thank the two anonymous reviewers for their insightful remarks and patience in reading earlier versions of this manuscript. Part of chapter 2 appears in revised form as: "Meontological Generativity: A Daoist Reading of the Thing" *Philosophy East and West*, 64.2 (April 2014): 303–18. Chapter 3 appears in revised form as: "Zhuangzi's Meontological Temporality" *Dao: A Journal of Comparative Philosophy*, 13.3 (Sept. 2014): 361–77.

Introduction

When it comes to expounding the truth of the world, are we to speak of the beings therein in the singular or the plural? If we go one step further and ask our question of the universe, will its cosmogony be colored by constancy or flux? Should we regard the cosmos and the myriad things therein as a constant singularity, a dynamic constancy, or a multiplicity in flux? What is at issue in these questions is a particular form of dialectics, one that involves how we define what *is* and what *is not*. One cannot stop there, however, for said dialectics must also account for how the *is* and the *is not* interact with that which *is beyond*. This last point has been a source of rich debate for philosophers and theologians alike insofar as the issue of absolutism creeps into the picture once we take the *beyond* or Ultimate as an entity whose standing is removed from the *is* and *is not*. Indeed, how we prioritize the *is* and the *is not* in a cosmogony of Ultimacy directly influences the ontological status we assign them.

On this point, common sense would have us believe that what *is* exists while what *is not* does not. Accordingly, to assume that the *is not* has ontological priority over the *is* will lead to a nihilistic consumption of the *is* by the *is not*. Thus the *is* holds priority over the *is not* because it turns the latter into a thing during the act of announcing itself.[1] This line of thinking has been the standard-bearer since the time of ancient Greece and is indicative of what Nicolai Hartmann poignantly labels "old ontology." Hartmann thus calls for a "new ontology" whereby being is no longer thought of as an immobile opposite to non-being but persists in a state of flux; it is, in other words, an ontology that takes into account the being of becoming.[2] Other calls for a new ontology can be seen in the writings of David Bohm[3] and those who are beholden to an ontology of all beings in light of the destructive domination of human culture.[4]

Despite the division between old and new theories of ontology, the conundrum that belies us is how to envision the ground of the world in such a way that it is neither elusory (i.e., mystical) nor dependent upon assumptions (i.e., mythical). What is more, if we want to avoid radicalizing the relationship between being as the *is* and non-being as the *is not*, we are either forced to introduce a nihilistic supposition or simply abrogate one term in favor of the other. Western philosophy is the source of this dilemma insofar as it was the ancient Greeks who chose to nominalize the *is not* instead of seeing it as possessing normative value. The result of this decision was to define the *is not* as either an absolute nothingness—a substitute for an existent form—or an estranged otherness. The same cannot be said, however, for the philosophical traditions of Asia and, in the case of this book, ancient Chinese Daoism.

In China's high antiquity, the Shang dynasty (16th–11th centuries BCE) took the world to be under the purview of *shangdi* 上帝, the supreme deity. By the time we reach the Zhou dynasty (11th–3rd centuries BCE), however, this worldview had fallen by the wayside, replaced by a cosmology of heaven (*tian* 天). Heaven (lit. "sky") was a realm of immeasurable power and creativity while earth (*di* 地), the domain of living things, lacked such characteristics. This is why the ethical-political models of ancient China, and the individuals that epitomized them, strove to emulate the way of heaven and not that of earth. The heaven/earth dyad remained the dominant cosmological model throughout the Zhou but toward its end in the Warring States period, Daoism challenged its entrenchment by offering a cosmogonist model based upon Dao 道 (ultimate reality). Given Dao surpasses heaven and earth in terms of its creative potential, a new conceptual dyad was developed to explain this occurrence: non-being and being. Unlike the ancient Greeks, Daoism sees non-being as complimentary to being, not its negating foil; it is a belief that led to furious debates in the Wei-Jin period (3rd–5th centuries CE) over whether things are born from non-being or being.

This book examines the Daoist thinker Zhuangzi 莊子 and his cosmogonist system of Dao, *wu* 無 (nothingness), and *you* 有 (being). Its purpose is to demonstrate wherein nothingness can act as the onto-cosmological fabric of Dao while serving as the medium through which it instantiates itself in the myriad things of the world. Much philosophical ink has been spilt over the nature and limitations of human self-knowing and whether or not these claims to truth are self-derived or the result of a higher, divine source. Knowledge of Dao, however, does not reveal the being of Dao but is rather a metaphorical expression of how Dao sustains and nourishes itself. The problem is that expressions of this nature cannot be grasped or transmitted using conventional epistemological norms. All we can do is intuit, situate, and resituate them against an ever-changing reality.

Very little is known of Zhuangzi's personal life other than he hailed from the state of Song 宋 and reputedly left behind a work of one-hundred-thousand words in fifty-two chapters. According to the *Historical Records* (*Shiji* 史記), Zhuangzi lived during the time of King Hui of Liang 梁惠王 and King Xuan of Qi 齊宣王. He is also said to have turned down an offer to serve at the court of King Wei of Chu 楚威王. In light of such historical evidence, as well as other indications scattered throughout the *Zhuangzi*, we can conservatively claim that Zhuangzi lived from 375–300 BCE.[5] As for the text itself, much has been made of its redaction from fifty-two to thirty-three chapters by the Jin dynasty commentator Guo Xiang 郭象 (fl. 312 CE). Guo was responsible for collating these chapters into their current sequence, doing so according to the sectional designators of Inner, Outer, and Miscellaneous chapters in place since the Han dynasty. This, however, does not testify to the state of the *Zhuangzi* before his editorship, a period in which the text varied in terms of sectional classification and actual number of chapters.[6]

Two of the earliest known commentators to the *Zhuangzi*—Cui Zhuan 崔譔 (fl. 290 CE) and Xiang Xiu 向秀 (ca. 227–272 CE)—used a version of the text containing twenty-seven chapters, divided into Inner and Outer sections; what is more, both men differed in their opinion as to which chapters should be classified as Inner and which Outer. All of this testifies to a text whose structural framework was fluid at the time and subject to debate. And yet, many of the *Zhuangzi* commentaries referred to in this book use Guo Xiang's redacted text, not the fifty-two chapter text of Sima Biao 司馬彪 (ca. 227–272 CE), or the truncated text adopted by Cui Zhuan and Xiang Xiu. Bearing in mind such intratextual fluidity, I will refrain from making explicit references to the categories of Inner, Outer, and Miscellaneous chapters. To this end, passages and concepts attributable to Zhuangzi will not be differentiated from those written by his disciples or persons imitating his philosophical spirit; rather, I will refer to Zhuangzi and his text interchangeably.

Although only one Chinese character is translatable into non-being and nothingness (*wu* 無), this book argues that they have separate but co-dependent functions: non-being denotes the cessation of ontic being (i.e., death) while nothingness symbolizes "absentia" forms of existence (e.g., trace, shadow, void, hollow, etc.) on the one hand, and the abode of Dao on the other hand. *Wu* thus plays a pivotal role in giving the myriad things of the world their ontic and ontological value. That is, we cannot know what *is* unless we also know what *is not*, nor can we discuss the nature of being while excluding non-being. Given this, the Western definition of ontology is suddenly problematic. By rejecting human being as the authoritative form of existence, Daoism proffers a philosophy that speaks to non-being and being collectively. However, since Dao *qua* ultimate reality is neither non-being nor being but that which allows for the possibility of both, its creative potential must be actualized in a realm that permeates the universe through and through—nothingness.

Where Western philosophy sees nothingness as either an absolute negation or a path to nihilism, Daoism takes it as an integral aspect of existence as such. Using nothingness to investigate Dao *qua* ultimate reality not only articulates the metamorphosis of nothingness into being, it allows us to overcome the desire to refer to such movement as *creatio ex-nihilo* by viewing it as trans-ontological. In other words, the nothingness of Daoism is not an absolute void out of which things magically appear but is the substratum around which life is constructed. Our interpretation of nothingness thus entails viewing it not as a thing of autonomous essence but as the primal and inseparable core of being, and it is for this reason that I have taken to speaking of Daoism as a tradition of meontology.

Given that Zhuangzi lived two and a half millennia ago, the concepts and terminology he uses will at times appear unconventional. Furthermore, the topics covered in his text are not dissimilar from those seen in Western philosophy (e.g., death, time, ethics, knowledge, freedom, etc.); it is his approaching them via nothingness which makes establishing analogies of comparison less than straightforward. There are, of course, Western philosophers and theologians for whom nothingness has a role to play; however, our goal in reading the *Zhuangzi* is to illuminate the Chinese rendition of nothingness and ask whether or not it can stand as an ontological entity in its own right. No matter which tradition one aligns with, the content of this book transgresses intellectual and cultural borders, revealing the ways in which nothingness is able to extend beyond the realm of human being to that of the world at large. Only when we are willing to abandon our self-imposed status of superiority and embrace the humbleness of being one within the multitude can humanity see the profundity of the world in which we live.

To this end, chapter 1 is devoted to explicating the *Zhuangzi*'s definition and implementation of nothingness. Additionally, it is responsible for delving into the connection that binds nothingness and being to that which makes their reality possible—Dao. From this emerges a relationship in which non-being underlies being and Dao is supported by nothingness. This trio of terms is not hierarchical in the traditional sense, for they align themselves in such a way that there is movement up and down, and comingling in-between. Where this activity occurs is in the primordial One, a state of undifferentiated wholeness in which things in their original, natural state lack names and other defining attributes. The One is thus a realm from which being emerges and to which non-being returns. Without the discovery of this interweaving penetration in what is otherwise known as chaos (*hundun* 渾沌), Daoist cosmology would appear incoherent and contradictory.

Knowing what nothingness is and how it operates in the world, chapter 2 sets out to uncover the invisible traces of the One by way of discussion of the Thing. The idea behind using the Thing to elucidate the One, is to avoid any connotation of the latter in a theological sense. As the One is a state of indistinguishable unity whereby beings have yet to be divided into their myriad forms via the assignment of defining characteristics, the One acts as a holding ground for all ancestral Things. When ontological being becomes known as such, this is when it leaves the One and enters reality as ontic being. In other words, each Thing is the creational root of all lesser things in its stream and the branching-off of these lesser things is what populates the world. The chapter ends by discussing a few well-known stories in the *Zhuangzi* such as cook Ding, the catcher of cicadas, and the maker of belt-buckles, as practical applications of mastering the art of returning to Dao in order to conjoin in oneness with the world.

Chapter 3 investigates the temporal nature of Dao, arguing against the traditional conception of time as a series of static, measurable points, as well as the notion that time is bound to the being of man. These arguments can be made because the *Zhuangzi* neither subscribes to the notion that death renders time impermanent nor that time is restricted to a so-called lived time of the here and now. For the *Zhuangzi*, Dao exists beyond the realm of temporality, precluding it from the dialectics of infinite and finite, impermanent and eternal. This is not to say that the text defines time as temporally relative; rather, time exists on a multi-dimensional plane in which the oneness of things becomes the ground for temporal experience. The goal is thus not to flee time in light of a supposed nihilism that is our death but to relinquish our need for temporal duration so as to return to the domain of Dao. What we will come to realize, however, is that this domain does not lie with the presence of being but the restfulness of nothingness.

Chapter 4 shifts our attention away from temporal *ekstasis* toward the embracement of a non-temporal praxis of uselessness. Resting in uselessness is more than just idleness or being non-accountable—it points to self-preservation through life prolongation. Seeing the time of our lives as but an extensional protrusion of the infinite non-time of Dao, to toil away with worry and concern over its beginning and end is to force this protrusion to break free from the substrate of nothingness. To ignore the role of nothingness is to abandon Dao's nourishment and when this happens, our inborn nature becomes corrupt and artificial, leading to injury or premature death. This chapter thus employs Laozi's analogy of the clay vessel and its useless inner-void, together with Zhuangzi's old tree, to demonstrate the inherent use of that which is perceived to be useless. It further argues that such useful uselessness was used by Zhuangzi as a means to criticize humanity's cherishment of calculative thinking. The best way to experience the genuineness of life is hence to follow the natural spontaneity of Dao.

Chapter 5 elucidates how one can emulate the characteristics of Dao (still, empty, quietude) by mastering the art of forgetfulness. All told, three stages of forgetting are present in the *Zhuangzi*: epistemological, phenomenological, and cosmological. For Zhuangzi, forgetting is not so much about the recollection of memories lost and in need of re-finding, but learning how to let things be themselves. Through forgetting the trace of things, one can forget their names and images. By letting-go of things via sitting in forgetfulness and composing the mind, one brings coherency to the world. Thus true forgetting is to let go of heaven and earth such that one enters the realm where even non-being and being cease to exist. In this non-temporal, non-spatial realm, there is only the mystery of Dao and it is here where spiritual freedom abounds. At the time when such transmogrification is complete, all that remains is a spontaneous kernel, one not very different from Dao. Herein we are free in an onto-cosmological sense, a freedom whose similitude with the things of the world results in the most genuinely natural form of existence possible.

Chapter 6 offers a discourse not only on the Daoist idea of freedom but argues that for the *Zhuangzi*, freedom is none other than the meontological harmony of things. There is no such thing as individual freedom because Zhuangzi states that we need to awaken to the fact that within the ultimate reality of Dao, we are but one being amongst a multitude. In order to better convey this reasoning, the text speaks of three capacities of heaven: differentiation, measure, and harmony. These three capacities constitute the perfect virtue of Dao, one sheltered by the mysteriousness of nothingness. Given that the sage takes as his abode the tranquil silence of nothingness, he knows of neither life nor death, right nor wrong. His freedom is not dependent on any one thing and so it is the freedom of non-freedom. To be free in nothingness is thus to let go of the world and in letting go, the sage attains his returning to the One. Returning to the One is hence to unite with Dao thereby marking the completion of Zhuangzi's cosmological circle.

1

Nothingness and Dao

A Time before Being

One of the clearest pronouncements of Daoist cosmogony can be found in chapter 12 of the *Zhuangzi*, which reads: "In the great beginning there was nothingness, having neither being nor name; from it arose the One, a oneness that was without form."[1] Reading this passage, several observations can be made: first, before humans became aware of the universe around them, they simply called it nothingness; second, the universe *qua* nothingness lacked presence of being or a name designating it thereof; third, the first thing to evolve from this primal nothingness was the One; fourth, the One refers not to the oneness of a divine being but the undifferentiated potential of Dao; fifth, given Dao takes nothingness as its root and not being, it is unnamable and formless as such; and sixth, only after the universe was already filled with the creations of Dao did humanity start applying names and divisions.

One might object that the above assumptions purport a false-premise on the grounds that as primal nothingness and Dao create an onto-cosmological holism that is unknowable through conventional epistemological norms, descriptions of the latter are equally applicable to the former. If, following this logic, Dao is equivalent to nothingness and nothingness is equivalent to Dao, Dao cannot be the creative source of the universe in that it is literally no-thing. There is a theological exception to this rule (i.e., *creatio ex-nihilo*) but in philosophy, resistance to being having an antecedent nothingness runs strong. Indeed, one of the challenges Daoism presents to the Western reader is overcoming the impossibility of knowing what is directly unknowable. The task of this chapter is thus to not only clarify the *Zhuangzi*'s position regarding nothingness and Dao, but to uncover the meontological reality of Dao and the myriad things of the world which owe it their existence.

The Nature of Nothingness

Of the many issues pushing human thinking to its limits, one of the oldest pertains to the following question: Can humans formulate an understanding of our place in the universe independent of a divine order? During the Shang 商 and early Zhou 周 dynasties of ancient China, such sentiments were inexorably tied to human ritual sacrifice and other social practices in order to appease the will of *di* 帝, the High Lord. By the time of the middle Zhou, however, trust in the Shang ancestor *di* had fallen out of favor, replaced by the universal concept of heaven (*tian* 天). This would plant the seeds for the cosmology and social ethics typifying the Warring States period in which Zhuangzi lived.

Like Laozi's *Daodejing* 道德經, the *Zhuangzi* also employs the concept of Dao instead of *di* to represent the source of all natural phenomena and serve as the key to advancing human virtue. The questions that beg to be asked are: What is Dao? How does Dao define reality such that its formlessness is inherent in all that has form but not the other way around? This leads to yet another question. When Daoism speaks of Dao as the ultimate reality of the cosmos but we humans are tied to the workings of heaven and earth, how are we to know of it? Given Zhuangzi's argument that Dao operates alongside nothingness, only persons who embody the characteristics of the latter can benefit from the former. What is more, given the formlessness of Dao and that humans are of fixed form, any inkling of Dao in our midst will prove elusive.

There are thus two apparent planes of reality—that of Dao and that of humanity. The former creates and is ever-present in the latter while the latter continuously, albeit unconsciously, distances and isolates itself from the former. The issue, it would seem, is not whether Dao *qua* ultimate reality is transcendent or immanent, but how humanity can overcome the limits of understanding to entertain the idea that Dao is not in any way limited by its own onto-cosmological standing. Before we can begin to entertain such a possibility, we need to first quash our dependency on a transcendental Ultimate. This can be done by turning to the meontological side of reality, which will better equip us to conceive of Dao not as a singularly static source of creation, but as pure dynamic potentiality.

The following passage illustrates the significance of nothingness for the *Zhuangzi*:

> Brilliance queried nothingness, saying: "Are you, sir, being or are you nothing?" Brilliance, unable to get a response, carefully regarded the other's appearance—a far-reaching vacuity. He gazed the entire day and saw nothing, listened but heard no sound, reached out but was unable to grasp anything. Brilliance said: "How perfect! Who can be as perfect as this! I can grant the fact of nothingness but not the non-being of nothingness. As for nothingness, how can one realize such perfection!"[2]

> 光曜問乎無有曰: 夫子有乎, 其無有乎? 光曜不得問, 而孰視其狀貌, 窅然空然, 終日視之而不見, 聽之而不聞, 搏之而不得也。光曜曰: 至矣! 其孰能至此乎! 予能有無矣, 而未能無無也, 及為無有矣, 何從至此哉!

The above example was chosen for several reasons: first and foremost, it is the only time in the entire text where the term *wuwu* 無無 appears; second, it reinforces what we said earlier, that within the conceptual framework of Daoism, nothingness is *prima facie* the root of being. This root, however, is different from that mentioned in the *Daodejing*.[3]

Although it appears to be a relatively straightforward passage, what should we make of its penultimate sentence? If we turn, for example, to the commentary of Guo Xiang for clues, we are left empty-handed:

> This is what unique learning means. From the uniqueness of Dao, only those who study it from within can arrive at its fundamentals. Thus for those who study it well, it is not known as studying![4]

> 此皆絕學之意。於道絕之, 則夫學者乃在根本中來。故學之善者, 其唯不學乎!

That the original text should contain this term while its most recognized early commentary makes no mention of it in its glosses is no cause for alarm; it simply tells us that Guo Xiang took the term at face value and nothing more. In other words, the *Zhuangzi* was arguing for the distinction between two levels of *wu*—ontic non-being and ontological nothingness—and that to combine them in a deconstructive manner as 'the non-being of nothingness' (*wuwu* 無無) would be nonsensical. However, some modern *Zhuangzi* scholars such as Shang Geling argue exactly this. According to Shang, the doubling-up of *wu* points to the text's intent to deny *wu* any metaphysical value, thus distinguishing Zhuangzi's theory of Dao from that of Laozi, thereby deconstructing it so as to prevent any inclination of it being a transcendental other.[5]

Influenced by the work of Fu Weixun some thirty years earlier,[6] Shang takes this singular instance of *wuwu* as signifying the *Zhuangzi*'s rejection of the principle of Dao-as-Origin, saying the text "no longer treats Dao or non-being as a metaphysical category or cosmological originator but as One (*yi* 一) that throughs (*tong* 通) all different beings by their own natures."[7] Putting aside Zhuangzi's notion of oneness for the time being, Shang posited several misconceptions that need to be addressed. Although he notes that Zhuangzi's explanation of *wuwu* is unclear, Shang nevertheless goes on to say its implications are quite easy to comprehend. Surely if the concept of *wuwu* were of such importance, it would have appeared in more passages than the one quoted, and yet it does not. Furthermore, it would also have appeared within the first seven chapters of the text, those reputed to be of Zhuangzi's own hand but, again, it does not. What, then, are we to make of Shang's claim that Zhuangzi "radicalized" *wu* into its self-negating opposite? On what grounds is he justified in stating that *wuwu* "deconstructs the entire metaphysical account" of Dao?

First, Shang saw *wuwu* as the total repudiation of all metaphysical deliberations on Dao resulting in the denial of its transcendent character. Second, he depended on abstractionism to transform the ontological quality of nothingness into an imperceptible, empty process that was somehow able to preserve an original force of coming-into-being and transformation. Third, since *wuwu* was able to surmount its own immanent dualism, Shang claims it assumed monistic qualities that reaffirmed its presence of being through the act of its own negation. Finally, in being monistic, *wuwu* equalized all possibilities into One and this oneness was in turn translated as Nature. Shang thus reaches the following conclusion: "Dao is for Zhuangzi simply nothing, not nothing-ness as something primary or substantial, not no-being as being, but straight *is-not*."[8]

Much of Shang's argument, indeed his claim that Dao *is-not*, was derived from Guo Xiang's commentary to the following analogy found in chapter 2 of the *Zhuangzi*:

> There is a beginning, a not begun to be a beginning, and a not begun to be no-beginning's beginning. There is being, there is

non-being, there is a not begun to be non-being, and there is a not begun to be non-being's beginning. Suddenly there is nothingness and yet when it comes to nothingness, I do not know if it is actually being or non-being.[9]

有始也者，有未始有始也者，有未始有夫未始有始也者。有有也者，有無也者，有未始有無也者，有未始有夫未始有無也者。俄而有無矣，而未知有無之果孰有孰無也。

Given that Zhuangzi's intent here was to unmask the presumed authority of linguistic conventions and epistemological norms by demonstrating their inherent relativity,[10] to argue as Shang does that the above passage was instead describing a form of self-induced nihilism resulting in the monadic entity of Nature is to misread the *Zhuangzi* through the eyes of Guo Xiang. Indeed, just a few lines later Zhuangzi writes: "Dao has no defining boundary and speech cannot be constant. It is due to human discourse that demarcations arise." We can thus argue that the *Zhuangzi*'s differentiation between *wu* as non-being and *wu* as nothingness was part of its overall strategy to display how the ultimate reality of Dao unfurls beyond the non-being/being dyad to the realm of ontological nothingness in which it resides. Having said as much, since Shang Geling and Fu Weixun refer to Guo Xiang's use of *wuwu* in the above passage instead of in chapter 22 where it appears in the original text, it behooves us to see what Guo Xiang wrote and why Shang takes it to be one of the keys to characterizing the *Zhuangzi* as a whole. Guo's commentary reads thusly:

> When there is a beginning, there is an ending. This is known as no-ending and no-beginning, which is to unify death and life. In unifying them, it is better not to unify them but allow them to do so themselves, which is to forget their oneness. With being there are then categories of beauty and ugly, right and wrong. If one knows of nothingness but not the non-being of nothingness, then right and wrong, good and evil, cannot leave one's breast. If one knows the non-being of nothingness, then one will not yet be without any form of knowledge. When all of these forms of knowledge are forgotten, one can suddenly begin to understand nothingness. Once one understands nothingness, then heaven and earth, the myriad things, you and I, right and wrong, shall suddenly be authentically so.[11]

有始則有終。謂無終始而一死生。夫一之者，未若不一而自齊，斯又忘其一也。有有則美惡是非具也。有無而未知無無也，則是非好惡猶未離懷。知無無矣，而猶未能知。此都忘其知也，爾乃俄然始了無耳。了無，則天地萬物，彼我是非，豁然確斯也。

In reading Guo Xiang's commentary, indeed in reading any commentary to this passage, how one understands and translates the term *wu* becomes vitally important. If we recall in the original dialogue between brilliance and nothingness how the latter was held to be a state of perfection—a metaphor for Dao—to read the second *wu* as a reduplicate non-being is problematic insofar as it can no longer serve as the grounding horizon of the first *wu*. If Zhuangzi is to be successful in relativizing humanity's onto-temporal construction of reality, which is what he appears to be doing, he cannot do so if the cosmological horizon is defined in terms of a static, simple negation. Denying one non-being by way of another only leads to an infinite loop of non-beings; there needs to be something more substantial to supplant non-being while also enveloping it.

This action of mutually supplanting and enveloping falls to Dao; thus if non-being is to abandon its circular dance with being and join the holistic unity of Dao, it should assume a higher, more cosmologically oriented role. This role is found in the guise of *wu* as nothingness. In this way, rendering *wuwu* as the non-being of nothingness is not to say that non-being succumbs to a nihilistic void but that nothingness, as the onto-cosmical fabric of Dao's creative potential, enfolds non-being as part of its own self-transformation. Thus when Guo Xiang writes that to know the non-being of nothingness is to not yet be without any form of knowledge, one can argue he was not denying Dao's existence per se; rather, he was giving voice to Zhuangzi's argument that there exists no epistemological difference between the two. Once we accept the idea that non-being is just as mysterious as nothingness in that both are linked to Dao, we can forgo the dialectic of non-being and being altogether and return to a state of authentic naturalness.

Guo Xiang's commentary is indubitably an important hermeneutic tool for scholars wishing to get through the *Zhuangzi*'s cryptic language, and being the oldest complete exegesis of the text, it has earned a reputation for being a philosophical work in its own right. However, Guo Xiang was not the only commentator to provide provocative annotations: if we count the number of Chinese commentaries from the Han through the late Qing (pre-Republic era), there are approximately two hundred. Returning to our discussion of *wuwu* as it appears in the dialogue between brilliance and nothingness, a perusal of other commentaries will help put Guo Xiang's silence into context. Let us begin with Cheng Xuanying 成玄英 whose commentary is traditionally paired with Guo's:

> The knowledge of luminous brilliance is superficial in that he can only reach non-being at the loss of being. Unable to cast away being and non-being, he thus praises nothingness as most profound. Who can be so abstruse! He furthermore speaks of a non-being that is not genuinely non-being but is rather the non-being of nothingness and yet, all of the pairings and denials of being and non-being belong to the distinction between being and nothingness. As for the character *wu*, there is nowhere it cannot be applied, but given that words have their broad principle, we thus designate it nothingness. Furthermore, how can words reach perfection without doing so in the realm of non-being, in the limit of its principle or exhaustion of its nature, for they themselves do not have the mysterious virtue of the superior scholar. Who can embody it! This is superficial learning and small knowledge, and so he cannot reach perfection.[12]

> 光明照曜，其智尚淺，唯能得無喪有，未能雙遣有無，故歎無有至深，誰能如此玄妙！而言無有者，非直無有，亦乃無無，四句百非，悉皆無有。 以無之一字，無所不無，言約理廣，故稱無也。而言何從至此者，但無有之境，窮理盡性，自非玄德上士，孰能體之！是以淺學小智，無從而至也。

Lü Huiqing 呂惠卿 alternatively notes:

> In being brilliant, the great universe gives off light and so illuminates things; non-being is thus the non-illumination of things. Such brilliance, therefore, does not act according to being or non-being; wanting to ask about them, no questions issued forth. Far-reaching and vacuous, his gazing, listening, and reaching all failed to attain it; this is to act according to non-being. Only with nothingness can things be made brilliant; they cannot be so by the non-being of nothingness. This is because there cannot be non-being. When one realizes this about non-being then nothingness can be perfected, but how can such perfection be realized![13]

光曜者，泰宇發光而能照，無有則無照矣。此光曜所以不知其
為有為無，問之而不得問也。窈然空然，視聽搏之所不及，此
所以為無有也。唯其有無，所以為光曜，不能無無，是以未能
無有也。及其無有，則無所至，何從至此哉！

Chu Boxiu 褚伯秀 compiled a magisterial compendium of important commentaries dating from the Song and earlier, one of which belongs to Chen Jingyuan 陳景元, who says:

> Brilliance reflects inner luminosity; non-being reflects the root of wonderment. When inner luminosity embodies the root of wonderment, this is called treasuring the vacuity of being. When it is called non-being, there is then nothingness, for there cannot be the non-being of nothingness. To even discuss non-being and being is doubly redundant and without end. Exhausting being and cutting off non-being, how is one to understand wonderment? How utterly profound! Brilliance's question thus captures the gist of "*zhibeiyou*."[14]

光曜，喻內照。無有，喻妙本。內照體乎妙本者也，謂其有邪，
則實然空然；謂其無邪，則有無焉，而未能無無也。且論無議
有，雙衍無窮；絕有斷無，妙從何悟。微乎哉！光曜之問，知
北遊之大旨也。

From the above selections, we can see that in each of them *wuwu* is taken onto-epistemologically while at the same time confirming our theory that *wu*, in its singular sense, can also be understood as ontological nothingness. As the most fundamental capacity of Dao, meontological potential passively fulfills its possibilities in a manner that maintains harmonious equanimity between things. This goes some ways to explaining why the authentic person (*zhenren* 真人), or sage, strives to mirror Dao by making himself empty, still, and quiet. We shall say more about the relation between Dao and oneness shortly, during which time it will be argued that Dao as oneness is not congruent with Guo Xiang's thesis that Dao is self-so nature (*ziran* 自然).[15]

To return to *wuwu*, if we say it is the psychological perfection of *wu* as non-being within the mind, it would be easy to transpose such a definition onto *wu* as nothingness. To make such a claim, however, would be counter-intuitive if not erroneous. To postulate that *wuwu* is equivalent to the *wu* used by Dao would imply that Dao too is a state of mind thereby negating its role as the creative potentiality of the universe. *Wuwu* is a self-negating solipsism whose purpose is to release us from the chains that bind our traditional conceptualization of what is meant by existence. It frees our imagination to ponder all the possibilities entailed in a nondiscriminatory reality. What is needed is an alternative definition of *wu*; one whose fluid dynamism is released from our epistemological or phenomenological grasping while symbolically entailing its living presence.

By "living presence" I am, of course, being allegorical but to some degree this does contain a hint of what is meant when we speak of *wu* as ontological nothingness. I do not hold nothingness to be diametrically opposed to being, nor is it of the same stature as Buddhist emptiness; rather, for Zhuangzi, nothingness is the milieu within which Dao moves and to which it turns in order to realize its onto-cosmological creativity. Since Daoism takes Dao to be all-encompassing, it cannot be pitted against nothingness in an equation restricted to negative and positive components. The reason is that these are ostensibly human constructs imposed upon the natural world, a world which when viewed from the holism of Dao is one of continuous change and transformation amongst mutually dependent counter-elements (e.g., non-being and being, rest and motion, dark and light, etc.) that are equalized and harmonized into a collectivity by way of Dao's virtue. In this way, *wu* as nothingness distinguishes itself from *wu* as non-being in that the latter is a counter-element to ontic being while the former is the meontological material used by Dao to fulfill its own self-so nature. In other words, what changes and transforms is the presence-of-being aspect of Dao, leaving nothingness to act as its backdrop. Dao can hence remain aloof and atemporal while at the same time giving birth to the myriad things. Nothingness thus represents the facilitative capacity of Dao while being is its actual embodiment.

The Language of Nothingness

Having looked at the twofold meaning of *wu*, we can now turn our attention to the specifics of *wu* as nothingness and its symbiotic relationship with Dao. An easy way to visualize nothingness is to think of another Chinese word: *qi* 氣.[16] *Qi* is a type of living ether saturating the universe and is also the animating heart of all living things, be they sentient or otherwise. Nothingness is similarly the meontological ether through which Dao instantiates itself in things while acting as a protective cloak of mystery from the probing, calculative minds of men. Since the minds of men are easily satisfied, ontic non-being appeases their desire to explain the cessation of existence even though, onto-cosmologically, it marks the return of things to primal nothingness. We can thus refer to the temporal presence of things as being and their non-presence as non-being. The non-presence of non-being is not, however, equal to nothingnesss. Although nothingness envelops non-being, the latter lacks ontological status and is simply a placeholder for a thing's lack of presence. There is, therefore, no such thing as absolute non-being or nothingness in Daoism; both are constantly being put to use by Dao as ultimate reality.

Zhuangzi illustrates the inseparableness of Dao and nothingness as such:

> If not for these states of mind, I would not be; if I am not to be, there will be no one to experience them. This principle comes close to being true but from whence they appear, no one knows. Although there seems to be a true self, any hint of its presence remains unseen. Its manifestation may be trusted, though we cannot see its form; its reality though real, is no indication of its form.[17]

非彼無我，非我無所取。是亦近矣，而不知其所為使。若有真宰，而特不得其眹。可行己信，而不見其形，有情而無形。

It is interesting that Guo Xiang's commentary to this passage takes the self-negation of the opening sentence to be a result of what is self-so: "As for that, it is self-so. What is self-so gives birth to me and I am naturally born. Thus what is self-so is also natural to me. How utterly profound!" From this we can see why Guo's tendency to equate Dao with self-so nature is mistaken. The only course of action open to Guo as a commentator would be to differentiate himself from earlier interpreters of the *Zhuangzi* while somehow matching the brilliance of his contemporary Wang Bi 王弼 (226–249 CE) who wrote commentaries to the *Book of Changes* and *Daodejing*. We can thus postulate that in order to counter Wang Bi's metaphor of root-branch (*benmo* 本末), Guo devised his own metaphysical doctrine of naturalness. To paraphrase Zhuangzi, what governs the myriad things is hidden and unknowable, yet we implicitly trust it. How can such a thing be anything but natural? Indeed, naturalness cannot supplant or supersede Dao in that the former is but a small corner of the latter's reality. We tend to regard self-so-ness as symbolizing the manner by which things are brought to life, nurtured thereafter, and fall into death, overlooking the fact that the root of said journey lies with Dao.

We can strengthen our argument with another textual example:

> As to Dao, it exists as reality with trustful manifestations, yet is without action or form. It can be passed-on but not privately owned. Although it can be obtained, it cannot be seen. It is its own root thus its existence was secure before the time of heaven and earth.[18]
>
> 夫道，有情有信，無為無形；可傳而不可受，可得而不可見；自本自根，未有天地，自古以固存。

Dao is not predicated on existence nor is it independent of the self-determinacy of things as Guo Xiang argues with his idea of "lone transformation" (*duhua* 獨化). Dao is defined by its propensity to self-generate and as it is the root of its own being, Dao cannot be a physically realized source, which would insert it into the non-being/being dialectic; rather, Dao is a meontological non-source. Furthermore, due to Dao's self-rootedness, there is nothing it lacks; as it fulfills its nature without resorting to external forces, there is nothing beyond it. In light of these conditions, the full extent of Dao's possibilities is hidden from view and so the world likens it to a great mystery. In being mysterious, Dao can be intuited but not transmitted; its methods can be observed even though it leaves no trace. None of this would be possible if not for nothingness. Thus the root of Dao, being already present therein, exists before heaven and earth (i.e., the natural world) in that the terms heaven and earth are designators of existence while the root of Dao is traceable to nothingness. The *Zhuangzi*'s onto-cosmology presents itself unlike any other ancient Chinese text, including the *Daodejing*.

The *Zhuangzi* often referred to the historical Laozi by name (i.e., Lao Dan 老聃), having him more often than not act as a pseudo teacher to Confucius. In the *Daodejing*, Dao is famously described in the opening lines of its first chapter. What is often overlooked is the third sentence of that chapter, one that declares Dao's onto-cosmological propensity: "Being without name, it is the beginning of heaven and earth; being named, it is the mother of the myriad things."[19] Wang Bi's commentary to this statement reads: "That which exists begins in nothingness; before it is formed or named it [Dao] serves as the beginning of the myriad things." This idea is similar to Zhuangzi's, however, the difference in terms of language between them stems from Laozi's tendency toward ontological matriarchalization whereas Zhuangzi adopted the notion of unity through oneness. Indeed, many of the concepts appearing in the *Daodejing* to describe Dao also occur in the *Zhuangzi*.[20] What is more, when examining other early texts such as the *Wenzi* 文子, *Huainanzi* 淮南子, and *Liezi* 列子, similar linguistic patterns are readily apparent.[21]

For example, the *Wenzi* expressed the relationship between nothingness and Dao as follows:

> The formless is great while the formed is small. The formless are many while the formed are few . . . The formed has sound while the formless is silent. The formed is born from the formless hence the formless is the beginning of the formed . . . the named is born from the nameless hence the nameless is the mother of the named. For Dao, being and non-being produce one another, and the difficult and easy complete one another.[22]

> 夫無形大,有形細。無形多,有形少……有形則有聲,無形則無聲。有形產於無形,故無形者有形之始也……有名產於無名,無名者有名之母也。夫道有無相生也,難易相成也。

In the *Liezi*, on the other hand, the ontological connection between Dao and nothingness is much more phenomenologically situated:

> There are things born and the begetter of such things; there are forms and the giver of such forms; there are sounds and the sounder of such sounds; there are colors and the giver of such colors; there are flavors and the giver of such flavors. However, all that is born of the begetter will die, yet that which does the begetting is perpetual; all that shaping shapes is indeed actual, yet the giver of shapes is not actually existent; all that sounding sounds may be heard, yet the giver of sound does not issue them forth; all that coloring colors is visible, yet the giver of color is not apparent; all that flavors flavor may be tasted, yet the giver of flavor is not assumed. These are the duties of non-deliberate doing.[23]

故有生者，有生生者；有形者，有形形者；有聲者，有聲聲者；有色者，有色色者；有味者，有味味者。生之所生者死矣，而生生者皆未嘗終；形之所形者實矣，而形形者未嘗有；聲之所聲者聞矣，而聲聲者未嘗發；色之所色者彰矣，而色色者未嘗顯；味之所味者嘗矣，而味味者未嘗呈；皆無為之職也。

This passage reveals that Liezi employs nothingness no differently from Laozi, Zhuangzi, or Wenzi. There is, we can say, a conceptual coherency at play in Daoism motivated by the belief that humanity must overcome its incessant denial of nothingness in the face of being. This denial is not easy to shake-off however. As a response, Daoism argues that nothingness is immune to the question of the preexistence of the universe, for to say it existed before the world of being would imply that it is no longer present in the world, resulting in its own annihilation. Nothingness is absorbed by the myriad things of the world in the form of the ever-present virtue of Dao, which is why the *Zhuangzi* declares:

> That which renders things as things is not limited by things. Things have their limits, the so-called limit of things. That which is unlimited moves to the limited and that which is limited moves to the unlimited . . . that for which Dao acts as root and branch are not root and branch for it; that for which Dao acts as accumulation and loss are not accumulation and loss for it.[24]

物物者與物無際，而物有際者，所謂物際者也；不際之際，際之不際者也……彼為本末非本末，彼為積散非積散也。

The reality of Dao distinguishes itself from what we regard to be the natural world (Nature) in that only the latter may be regarded as an actual process. For Zhuangzi, Nature is associated with heaven, earth, and the cyclical processes therein. The various transformations that occur throughout the universe, on both cosmic and human levels, whether the rotation of the seasons or the alternation of life and death, all occur within the realm of Nature. However, one must be careful not to ascribe such movement to Nature at the exclusion of Dao, as this would give rise to the conclusion that they are semi-autonomous, whereby the former falls under the governance of humanity while the latter helplessly stands by. Humanity might vainly attempt to control or manipulate natural processes but such processes are themselves derived from and dependent on Dao.

The only way one can nakedly comprehend the mysterious workings of Dao is to unite with it and this is done via Zhuangzi's concept of oneness.

Although we will examine the One shortly, here we can lay the onto-cosmological groundwork for the coexistence of nothingness and the One, beginning with the *Wenzi*'s metaphor of ocean and cloud:

> As for the principle of the One, it covers the four seas. As for the greatness of the One, it is seen throughout heaven and earth. In its completeness, its solidity resembles an uncarved block. In its scattering, its diffusion resembles muddiness. In its muddiness, it gradually clears. In being flushed away, it will slowly become full again. Its undulations resemble a great ocean while its vastness resembles floating clouds. It appears to be nothing yet it exists, seemingly lost yet still present.[25]

> 故一之理，施於四海。一之椵，察於天地。其全也、敦兮其若樸。其散也、渾兮其若濁，濁而徐清，冲而徐盈，澹然若大海，氾兮若浮云，若無而有，若亡而存。

The *Liezi* analogized the connection between oneness and nothingness in the form of *qi* 氣:

> At the time of the Great One, *qi* had yet to appear. During the Great Beginning, *qi* arose. With the Great Beginning, things were formed. With the Great Elements, matter emerged. When *qi*, form, and matter existed but were unseparated, this was called undifferentiated wholeness. Undifferentiated wholeness is to speak of the myriad things as indistinguishable and not yet separated.[26]

> 太易者，未見氣也；太初者，氣之始也；太始者，形之始也；太素者，質之始也。氣形質具而未相離，故曰渾淪。渾淪者，言萬物相渾淪而未相離也。

However, the most lucid examples are to be found in the *Zhuangzi*, as the following passage shows:

> In the Great Beginning, there was nothingness, non-being, and namelessness. From it arose the One, a oneness that was without form. When things obtained it, they were born and this was

called Virtue. Before there were forms and divisions, things were innumerable and not yet separated and this was called Fate. From this flowing and moving things were born, their completion giving rise to principle and this was called Form.[27]

泰初有無，無有無名；一之所起，有一而未形。物得以生，謂之德；未形者有分，且然無閒，謂之命；留動而生物，物成生理，謂之形。

A second example is:

Emerging from what has no root, it [Dao] enters what has no aperture. It has reality but there is nowhere it dwells; it has duration but is without beginning or end. As that which emerges does so from that which has no aperture, this refers to its reality. As it has reality but nowhere to dwell, this refers to its spatiality. Having duration but no beginning or end, this refers to its temporality. There is life and there is death, there is emerging and there is entering; it may enter and emerge but one cannot see its form. This is called the Gate of Heaven.[28]

出無本，入無竅。有實而無乎處，有長而無乎本剽，有所出而無竅者有實。有實而無乎處者，宇也。有長而無本剽者，宙也。有乎生，有乎死，有乎出，有乎入，入出而無見其形，是謂天門。

Although the word return (*fan* 反) is not explicitly used here, it is nevertheless implied. For Zhuangzi, to return is to harmonize with Dao but what one physically conjoins with is the undifferentiated wholeness of nothingness.[29] The act of return takes place at the Gate of Heaven (*tianmen* 天門),[30] and being a gateway between nothingness and being, it cannot be a thing as such. The great Song dynasty commentator Lin Xiyi 林希逸 explains the matter as such:

Being cannot be born of being but is born of non-being. Thus it is said, being cannot take being to create being, it must emerge from non-being. Furthermore, this non-being is itself nothingness hence we say it is the non-being of nothingness. The *Qiwu* [chapter] says: "As for nothingness, it is the nothingness of not yet beginning to be being," which is precisely what we mean. To hide oneself is to withdraw oneself in concealment.

The sage thus conceals his heart-mind in nothingness and is said to reside there.[31]

有不生於有而生於無，故曰有不能以有為有，必出於無有。而此無有者，又一無有也，故曰無有一無有。齊物曰，有無也者，有未始有無也者，即是此意。藏者，退藏於密也。聖人之心藏於無有，故曰藏乎是。

Guo Xiang, in commenting on the sentence "being cannot take being to create being, it must emerge from non-being" argues that "this elucidation of the idea that being cannot take being to create itself is not to say that non-being can act as being, for if non-being can act as being, how can we call it non-being!"[32] We are able to call non-being an affiliate of being insofar as we are proposing a meontological deconstruction of the dialectic between non-being and being. What we are proposing is that ontological nothingness is an inward inversion such that we fulfill our claim to a phenomenological meontology by locating it within the framework of cosmic oneness. This oneness imbues the myriad things with ontological nothingness thereby allowing them to partake in the marvelous possibilities of Dao. However, Dao's possibilities are simultaneously complete and incomplete in the sense that such epistemological quantifiers fail to describe its mysteriously multifarious nature. Seen from the other side, nothingness negates any pretense of an absolutist interpretation of Dao while rendering mute any inkling of a supra-sensory mystical experience. Such is the reason why Zhuangzi writes: "Thus the one who knows to stop at what he does not know is perfect. Who knows of the argument without words, of the Dao that that cannot be spoken? If one is able to know this much, he shall be the Repository of Heaven."[33] It is also why the *Daodejing* states: "When it arises there is no brightness, when it declines there is no darkness. It is continuously so, nameless, always returning to that which is no-thing. This is called the form of the formless, the image of that which is no-thing."[34]

The significance of these varied expressions lies not in their description of a transcendent entity but that it is pointing us toward self-discovery. For Zhuangzi, what is in need of being transcended is neither being nor nothingness but the names we so readily attach to said concepts. In other words, we require a means to overcome our empiricist tendencies to view the world as filled with being and replace it with a framework that is more world-centric. The *Zhuangzi* provided us with a most vivid account as to how this could be achieved:

Let go of your body, spit out your intelligence, and forget you are beholden to others. Join the great harmony of the deep and boundless, dispel the mind and let go of the spirit, then you will be still and soulless.[35]

墮爾形體，吐爾聰明，倫與物忘；大同乎涬溟，解心釋神，莫然無魂。

We can once again assert our conviction that nothingness belongs to the fabric of reality and that its reality cannot be explained by identifying one's consciousness with it. While being is ensconced in human reality and can only partake in the cycle of birth and death, nothingness is immune to such conditions. Indeed, nothingness as the onto-phenomenological fabric of the universe exists on a plane that is beyond human manipulation or the threat of nihilism, a fate that befalls non-being. Nothingness is hence a living hiddenness whose symbiotic ties to Dao enable it to serve as the reserved, non-manifest skeleton of things, as the cosmogonist root of Dao, and as the beckoning fold of return. Nothingness does not translate into Dao but is the catalyst from which the latter germinates, assimilates, and harmonizes things. Finally, to be aware of the oneness of nothingness with Dao is to enjoy an awareness unlike any other, as the *Zhuangzi* so forcefully describes:

> Dao permeates everything. Being divided, things are complete, but such completion is also what is harmful. What is vile about such division is that things seek out its completion; what is vile about seeking such completion is that it is a completion to what is already complete [in them]. Thus they emerge but do not return, as if seeing a ghost. Emerging and obtaining it, this is called obtaining death. Exterminated and empty, they are but ghosts. Only when the formed resembles the formless shall there be stability.[36]

道通，其分也，其成也毀也。所惡乎分者，其分也以備；所以惡乎備者，其有以備。故出而不反，見其鬼；出而得，是謂得死。滅而有實，鬼之一也。以有形者象無形者而定矣。

What is already complete is Dao and Dao attains completion by holding fast to its meontological root. To the things of the world that refuse to acknowledge this, their life is but a ghostly emptiness. It is empty in that said beings are forever united in their indebtedness to Dao without ever realizing it. Should they decide to do so, they will discover this association is built upon Dao's propensity to misalign human conceptions of similarity and difference, resulting in cosmic oneness. Smashing the associative divisions between life and death, right and wrong, form and formless, allows the *Zhuangzi* to overcome any epistemological barrier on its way to uncovering the ultimate reality of Dao, a reality that is embodied in a vibrant oneness that neither delimits beings nor disavows their implicit selfness. How Dao *qua* the One avoids becoming monistic is, therefore, a question in need of answering and we shall attempt to do so now.

The Oneness of Dao

Our discussion has thus far been focused on defining the term *wu* and establishing its connection to Dao. We have come to characterize *wu* as symbiotic and meontological, as lacking dependency, determinacy, or transcendence. On the level of things, ontic non-being forces a measure of the aforementioned qualities onto ontic being, thereby ensuring its presence in the world. We need to remember, however, that for the *Zhuangzi*, *wu*, regardless of which plane of existence we choose to examine it from, is indubitably non-nihilistic in nature. As we begin to work outward so as to uncover the broader uses and implications of this meontology, we come across a critical concept not just for the *Zhuangzi*, but for a great many ancient Chinese texts—oneness. Take the opening lines of the bamboo-slip text *Hengxian* 恒先 for example:

> *Heng* precedes being and non-being; it is simple, quiescent, and empty. Being simple, it is Great Simplicity; being quiescent, it is Great Quiescence; being empty, it is Great Emptiness. Not liking to stay contained within itself, it thus gave rise to space. Given the presence of this realm of space there was *qi*, with *qi* things came into being, with the birth of things there was beginning, and with beginning there came to be passing away.[37]

> 恒先無有；樸，靜，虛。樸，大樸；靜，大靜；虛，大虛。自厭不自忍，或作。有或焉有氣，有氣焉有有，有有焉有始，有始焉有往。

While we are not concerned with the *Hengxian* per se, it offers us a new perspective on Warring States ideology, especially when it comes to the evolution of Daoist cosmogony. Like other recently unearthed texts, such as *Four Classics of the Yellow Emperor* (*Huangdi Sijing* 黃帝四經), the *Hengxian* espouses cosmogonist ideas similar to those seen in texts such as the *Zhuangzi*. Perhaps the most obvious correlation is to the Guodian 郭店 silk-text version of the *Daodejing* which uses the terms *hengdao* 恆道 and *hengming* 恆名 to describe the *changdao* 常道 and the *changming* 常名 seen in the received edition. This substitution was employed so as to avoid using the surname of the ruling Han emperor, King Wen, which was Heng. We shall not doubt the veracity of this assumption as concrete support for interpreting *heng* as the oneness of Dao abounds.

If the *Hengxian* depicts the universe as arising in nothingness before proceeding to space and *qi*, whereupon the appearance of things marks the delimitation of temporal division, wherein does the *Zhuangzi* differ? Besides the progression from nothingness to the One, the *Zhuangzi*'s cosmogonist account seems to be lacking one thing—Dao—or does it? Lü Huiqing had this to say:

> Without nothingness, the One cannot be attained and so it arose namelessly. In this way, the formless marks the beginning of heaven and earth. Since it was already called the One, how could it be nameless? In obtaining it, things were born and this was called virtue, the mother of the myriad things. What is incomplete is divided, and this situation was called fate. Fate is thus an unseparated, formless beginning. From its movement things were born, giving birth to principle, which was thereafter called form. Having gained substance, form protected the spirit, never losing it. Since each thing appears in this way, they are not taken to be unreal. What is called inborn nature is that which is not lost once a thing has form. All are like this and the myriad things are no exception, for in obtaining the One they are born. Fate has its divisions but is not separated while inborn nature preserves the spirit and is not lost, for the spirit of the myriad things is wonderful and bursting amidst heaven and earth. Cultivating the inborn nature is to return to virtue and unite with the formlessness of the One. Having perfect virtue is to be one with the great beginning but without nothingness, this cannot be attained.

Thus to be one with the great beginning is to be empty, and so emptiness exists before the emergence of things. As emptiness is to be great, greatness thus exists in different unities.[38]

無無則一亦不可得，無名則一之所起，而未形天地之始是也。既已謂之一，且得無名乎？此物得以生而謂之德，是為萬物之母也。未成者有分，且然而已，而謂之命，命則無間乎未形之初也。至留動而生物，物成生理，而後謂之形；形體保神，而未嘗失；各有儀則，而未嘗妄；謂之性，性則不失乎已形之後者也。凡此無他，萬物均之，得一以生。命則有分而無間，性則保神而不失，神則妙萬物而充塞乎天地之間者也。故性脩反德，則合乎一之未形，德至同於初，則無亦不可得矣。同乃虛，其虛至於未始有物；虛乃大，其大至於不同同之。

Oneness in its quiescent simplicity is regarded as emptiness in that it represents the amorphous nature of Dao. Since the One is affiliated with Dao and dwells in the realm of nothingness, the One for Zhuangzi is neither a numeric singularity nor a monistic absolute; rather, it serves as a holistic representation of the unfathomable mystery of Dao. To take the One as pertaining to Dao alone is to stop viewing it as one; to take the One as pertaining to humanity alone is also to stop viewing it as one. Hence the *Zhuangzi* argues:

In this way, [the sage's] likes and dislikes are reduced to one. That which is one is one; that which is not one is also one. Knowing that one is one, he is a follower of heaven; not knowing that one is one, he is a follower of man.[39]

故其好之也一，其弗好之也一。其一也一，其不一也一。其一與天為徒，其不一與人為徒。天與人不相勝也，是之謂真人。

Indeed, the *Zhuangzi*'s discussion of the One has received little attention from contemporary scholars, for much of the debate has centered on rectifying the cosmology of the *Daodejing*'s forty-second chapter—which states that Dao gives birth to the One—with that of the bamboo-slip text *Taiyi Shengshui* 太一生水 (The Great One gives Birth to Water).[40] Given that Dao is able to give birth to anything at all, be it the One, non-being, or being, the question as to its temporal disposition arises. Furthermore, if Dao generates the conditions for the becoming of things and as it is both atemporal and aspatial, the One we are speaking of also remains untouched by such movement. We shall have more to say on this in chapter 3, but for now we can agree with the assessment of Robert Neville that the movement between nothingness and being is cosmological and not exclusively ontological.[41]

Returning to the *Hengxian*, we see various conditional states—primal simplicity, quiescence, and emptiness—which, when taken together, are indicative of the original condition of the universe. Dao, as an embodiment of the primal universe, cannot itself be a thing; should it be taken as such, how could it enfold the myriad things while remaining unaffected by their trials and tribulations? It may, one can argue, be thought of as a universe-wide becoming, as a state emblematic of the beginning and end of all beings, but a beginning that is beyond time and space. Only when Dao is taken as primal simplicity, quiescence, and emptiness can it be known as the mother of the myriad things or the gate of heaven. This would explain why the *Zhuangzi* says:

> The gate of heaven is non-being hence the myriad things emerge from non-being. Being cannot be born from being hence it must emerge from non-being. However, non-being is itself nothingness. This is where the sage hides himself."[42]

> 天門者，無有也，萬物出乎無有。有不能以有為有，必出乎無有，而無有一無有。聖人藏乎是。

For Han-era Daoists interested in distinguishing their own principles of origin from that of the *Zhuangzi*, the challenge would be a daunting one. The *Liezi*, for example, turned to *qi* as the intermediary step between Dao and manifested being:

> The sages of old took *yin* and *yang* as regulating heaven and earth. If that which has form is born from the formless, whence do heaven and earth come? Thus it is said, there is the Great One, Great Beginning, Great Foundation, and Great Simplicity. The time of the Great One was when *qi* had yet to be encountered; the time of the Great Beginning was when *qi* emerged; the time of the Great Foundation was when forms were developed; and the time of Great Simplicity marked the commencement of substance. With *qi*, form and substance are complete but not yet divided, this was called undifferentiated wholeness.

Undifferentiated wholeness hence describes the undifferentiated wholeness and inseparability of the myriad things.[43]

列子曰：昔者聖人因 陰陽以統天地。夫有形者生於無形，則天地安從生？故曰：有太易，有太初，有太始，有太素。太易者，未見氣也；太初者，氣之始也；太始者，形之始也；太素者，質之始也。氣形質具而未相離，故曰渾淪。渾淪者，言萬物相渾淪而未相離也。

In the *Zhuangzi*, we witness a second type of oneness, one of epistemological import: "Heaven and earth came into being together and the myriad things and I are One 天地與我並生，而萬物與我為一."[44] One might say this is a perfect example of Zhuangzian monism but upon closer inspection, we see it is not. We are already aware that Dao is an undifferentiated wholeness that lacks form or substance. Heaven and earth, in owing their existence to Dao, partake in the purity of its ultimacy. Since Dao gives us life and heaven and earth sustain our form, our spontaneous emergence from nothingness is not traceable to a transcendent void but to the One. As we only become aware of the oneness of things after we are born, once the realization dawns on us that the reality of heaven and earth is no different from that of Dao, we can proclaim their reality as being inseparable from our own.

However, is such a position sufficient to counter the argument by those who insist that the *is not* is incongruous with the One? Zhuangzi's reply is this:

> When the form is whole and the spirit has returned, one may join in unison with heaven. Heaven and earth are the parents of the myriad things and together they form a complete body; when apart, they mark the beginning [of things].[45]

夫形全精復，與天為一。天地者，萬物之父母也，合則成體，散則成始。

Are we thus to surmise that the Great Beginning is referring to the One? Does not ascribing the name one to the One preclude it from having any of the connotations assigned to Dao? If that is the case, are we not limiting our conceptualization of oneness to the realm of being, which would run contrary to our understanding of ontological nothingness? We can thus regard the *Zhuangzi*'s cosmology of oneness as functioning on two parallel planes: on the one hand, the non-specificity of Dao as an undifferentiated wholeness dictates that whatever is derived from it necessarily carries with it an aspect of this primal creation. This we call ontological nothingness. All things are created by Dao from this living nothingness and at the time of the Great Beginning, before the emergence of discrete forms, all was united in their potentiality. Such oneness prior to creation is onto-cosmogonic. In picturing the pre-corporeal stage of things as the One, we can forgo the need to name things while sidestepping the issue of the unrepresentable as *other*. Oneness is not simply an epistemological simplification of the world in order to qualify such statements as "the myriad things and I are One;" rather, it is to enter into a state of harmonious coexistence with things such that one joins with them in mindless freedom. The *Wenzi* can be seen as taking after the *Zhuangzi* (and the *Daodejing*) when it says:

> Pure tranquility is the perfection of virtue, effeminacy and weakness are the function of Dao, and calm empty-nothingness is the ancestor of the myriad things. Using these three, one falls into formlessness, and formlessness is what we call the One. With the One, one mindlessly merges with all under heaven.[46]

> 清靜者，德之至也，柔弱者，道之用也，虛無恬愉者，萬物之祖也，三者行，則淪於無形，無形者，一之謂也。一者，無心合於天下也。

However, what becomes of things should they be unable to maintain contact with the One? The *Zhuangzi* was not very forthcoming with a response, so we turn to the *Daodejing* for clues:

> In the beginning, there was oneness. Heaven obtained it and was pure; the earth obtained it and was peaceful; the gods obtained it and were vividly powerful; the valley obtained it and was full; the myriad things obtained it and were born . . . heaven without purity would split apart; earth without peacefulness would disintegrate; the gods without vivid power would desist; the valley without fullness would become exhausted; and the myriad things without life would be exterminated.[47]

> 昔之得一者，天得一以清，地得一以寧，神得一以靈，谷得一以盈，萬物得一以生……天無以清將恐裂，地無以寧將恐發，神無以靈將恐歇，谷無以盈將恐竭，萬物無以生將恐滅。

Dao *qua* the One is not simply a metaphorical depiction of Nature's way but serves as a model of life praxis. In the process of self-becoming and self-actualizing oneself to Dao, achieving unison with the motion of the universe becomes an objective of sublime importance. Mindlessly merging with the world, as Zhuangzi calls it, is not a meditative state of mind in which the participant enters a state of non-mind; on the contrary, merging with Dao becomes a necessary measure if one is to gain spiritual freedom. Such language exhibits an exuberance that shocks the reader as much as its message. It describes the petty person as unable to tear him- or herself away from the lure of "gifts and wrappings," such that their spirit is worn down by and wasted on the shallow and trivial, all the while believing they can "unite form and emptiness in the Great One." The result, Zhuangzi says, is that the petty person "does not know the Great Beginning." On the other hand, the authentic person (sage), "allows their spirit to return to the time of no-beginning" such that they "flow like formless water dripping from great pureness."[48] As an umbrella of Dao, the One thus designates the metaphysical situation in which the myriad things are transmutable with one another.

The question of selfhood is hence rendered redundant in light of the oneness of Dao. Oneness as the pre-emergent state of ontic being cannot permit any form of classification other than the united wholeness of itself. In its most primal state, Dao *qua* nothingness has yet to be known as Dao *qua* the One, an act that can only occur after it has been named as such. Naming Dao the One, however, is to deprive it of its meontological nature and when Dao's nature is restricted, its virtue suffers as a result. The depletion and decline of Dao's virtue occurs in progressive measures, each phase marking the further distillation of its pureness until it has been squeezed from the world of things completely.[49] The One thus differentiates itself from the oneness of nothingness in that the latter is symbolic of a yet-to-be articulated possibility while the former marks the initial realization of said possibility as the undifferentiated wholeness of primal chaos.

With the concept of the One established, non-being and being emerge from their surrogate womb, populating the universe with their myriad variations. It would appear, then, that nothingness's role ends here, at the fulfillment of being's becoming. This is not the case. Nothingness persists in the world, unbeknownst to many. Undergirding non-being, the ontological nothingness of Dao nourishes beings by providing them with a form of meontological mobility they regard as the passage of time. In this way, Dao and nothingness discretely accompany things throughout their life and are there to receive them when it comes to an end. Nothingness serves yet another purpose, which is to epitomize the life praxis of the sage. In order for the sage to become a living embodiment of Dao, he needs to perfect the characteristics typifying both Dao and nothingness. The sage, in other words, need not transcend anything but turn his mind inward, returning to the nothingness that binds everything to Dao.

Returning to Dao, Overcoming Nihilism

Having shown how the creational domain of Dao lies in the meontological milieu of nothingness, we subsequently explored its phenomenal expression as the One. It now behooves us to complete the circle by examining the concept of reversion or return. Describing cosmogonist completion as a process of return might seem like an odd choice of words and it begs the question, return to what? Returning is not a process whereby one rediscovers one's empirical-self as a being amongst beings, nor is it discovery of a transcendental other; rather, it is a transformative experience whereby one harmonizes with Dao to complete the possibility of our existence. From this we can characterize returning to Dao as a positive experience insofar as we reduce the dominance of being such that it attains equilibrium with nothingness.

This act of reversal can be described as functioning on two axes: the horizontal and the vertical. The case of horizontal return is the unremarkable of the two, representing the ontic reintegration of being into the One. Horizontal return is also what humanity regards as the end-result of our passing from this world; it is a mark of our mortality and finitude of life. Each thing, therefore, returns to Dao, rendering our corporeal transformation into an expression of natural law. Although oneness is the principle law of Nature, it is not that of cosmic procession. For that to be realized we must look beyond the returning of things to the One as a horizontal transference, and turn to the vertical assimilation of the One with Dao.

Differentiation and non-differentiation take place across the plane of existence, forming unified groups of being according to their class structure.[50] This process of transformational reversal is surpassed only when we acknowledge the greater cosmological activity of which nothingness is the pivot. On this vertical axis that pierces the plane of nothingness insofar as it extends from the depths of Dao to the territory of being, the process of returning is hence a meontological tracing of things from their present living condition back to the moment of their becoming. It is, therefore, the unmasking of being so as to arrive at its ancestral root. However, arrival at its root does not deny being its existence in a nihilistic sense but reaffirms its potentiality having been separated from Dao. Horizontal reversal is hence taken as a circular progression of completion while vertical returning is infinite in magnitude and whose completion takes on the guise of non-completion.

To express the idea of return and reversal, the *Zhuangzi* used terms such as *fan* 反, *fu* 復, and *gui* 歸.[51] In order to illustrate the dynamic nature of returning to the One, and how the One can be traced back to Dao, the following examples are instructive:

> All things have their completion and destruction, yet upon their return they become one.[52]

凡物無成與毀，復通為一。

> [They see man's form] as a borrowing of different substances, coming together as one body. They forget their liver and gall, and discard their ears and eyes. Turning and overturning they end and begin, not knowing head from tail. Absently they roam in what lies beyond the dust and dirt of the world, wandering carefree in the spirit of non-deliberate doing.[53]

假於異物，託於同體；忘其肝膽，遺其耳目；反覆終始，不知端倪；芒然彷徨乎塵垢之外，逍遙乎無為之業。

> Life has its budding, death has its returning; beginning and end follow one another without stoppage and no one knows their limit.[54]

生有所乎萌，死有所乎歸，始終相反乎無端而莫知乎其所窮。

The above passages are a clear indication that for the *Zhuangzi*, return only entails the event of one's own death. We will, however, demonstrate that there is indeed another form of return, one whose outcome is complete freedom. For now, our concern is to illustrate that Dao and *wu* do not equal nihilism. Returning to nothingness is a joyful occasion, despite its inevitability, because the process of emergence and return that all things undergo is natural and without interruption. To assign one the label "birth" and the other "death" does nothing to alter the course of their journey. Sounding slightly fatalistic, the *Zhuangzi* says we should simply accept these changes as part of the natural fate of things and nothing more. The above passages were chosen in order to contrast them with the following ones from the *Daodejing*, especially with regards to their use of language:

> Returning is the movement of Dao; softness is the employment of Dao. The myriad things of the world are born of being, and being is born of non-being.[55]

> 反者，道之動；弱者，道之用。天下萬物生於有，有生於無。

> While the myriad things prosper, each one returns to their root. Returning to the root is called quiescence, and this is known as returning to one's fate. Returning to one's fate is known as constancy.[56]

> 夫物云云，各復歸其根。歸根曰靜，是曰復命。復命曰常。

As the second *Daodejing* passage includes experiential attributes of returning to Dao, it gives us more interpretative material to work with, as Lü Huiqing illustrates in his commentary:

> [Diverging from others] I take the perfection of empty quietude; upon seeing what makes the myriad things arise and multiply, I know it from my perspective and not theirs. What makes them arise is also what causes them to return. What causes them to be numerous is the same as what causes them to return to their root. I observe their returning at the moment of their arising, knowing they will return to their root at the moment of their multiplication. Furthermore, as for what is called emptiness, it is not emptiness by way of emptying; rather, it is merely that things are not full, thus they are empty. As for what is called quietude, it is not the quietude of being quiescent; rather, in the proliferation of things, each will return to their root without knowing why; in not letting this fact disturb their peace of mind, there is quiescence. And so, returning to the root is called quietude. As for fate, it is what I have received and what gives me life. Only when my nature is quiet can I return to that from which I was born, what controls the fate of all things. Thus quietude is known as returning to one's fate.[57]

而我以虛靜之至，故見萬物之所以作與其所以云云，在我而不在彼。其所以作者，乃其所以復也。方其所以云云者，乃其所以歸根也。故以其並作而觀其復，則方其云云而各復歸其根也。然則所謂虛者，非虛之而虛也，直莫之盈，故虛也。所謂靜者，非靜之而靜也，夫物云云，各歸其根而不知，而莫足以撓心，故靜也，故歸根曰靜。命者，吾之所受以生者也。夫惟靜，則復其所以生，而能命物矣，故靜曰復命。

The One, through the movement of cosmological return, embodies the original virtue of things before they assume any particularities and begin identifying with them as such. Once things isolate themselves from Dao by identifying with and assigning authority to their own particularities, they subsequently deteriorate and perish.[58] Oneness is thus the initial phase of Dao's unfolding and subsequently serves as the root of being. The source of being's root, however, is nothingness, and so the One is forever tied to the meontological nature of Dao. In this way, the One can contain the marvelous possibilities of creation while simultaneously ensuring that the holistic freedom allotted each thing is preserved therein. The inherent principle that is the undifferentiated wholeness of nothingness is hence the constancy of Dao imbued in all things, becoming the key to ensuring Dao's neutrality as things endlessly diversify and transform of their own doing.

The ontological circle spoken of in the passages cited above is a regression from quietude to fate to constancy; put differently, the phenomenal manifestation begins in the constancy of nothingness, progresses to the fate of individual things, and finds completion in their peace of mind. Peace of mind symbolizes harmonization with Dao and is endemic of a psychological awareness of the root of things in nothingness. That things owe their existence to Dao is to say that the myriad things of the world emerge from the plenum of oneness and such is their indubitable fate. Where humans go astray from the virtue of Dao lies at the moment we pledge our allegiance to names and the false reality they convey, establishing human culture as an oppositional system to the harmony of Dao. This is why the *Zhuangzi* was critical of artificial linguistic conventions, preferring to see things as they are of themselves rather than what we take them to be. To this end, the mind that is tranquil and empty of false truths is the mind of one who is authentic, a person whose thoughts trace back to the original beginning of things and the time before human demarcations divided the world.

One may also reframe the ontological circle in light of chapter 25 of the *Daodejing*: "Man models himself after earth, earth models itself after heaven, heaven models itself after Dao, and Dao models itself after the naturally self-so."[59] This, however, begs the question: If we are to achieve harmony with Dao by way of a return, is it a multi-phase or singular process? Laozi, unfortunately, was ambiguous. The *Zhuangzi*, however, contains many deliberately shocking suggestions, one of which is:

> You have only to rest in non-deliberate doing and things will transform themselves. Let go of your body, spit out your intelligence, and forget you are beholden to others. Join the great harmony of the deep and boundless, dispel the mind and let go of the spirit, then you will be still and soulless.[60]

> 汝徒處無為，而物自化。墮爾形體，吐爾聰明，倫與物忘；大同乎涬溟，解心釋神，莫然無魂。

How one goes about doing such things is, of course, open to interpretation; however, the *Zhuangzi* seems quite adamant in the need to return to a more natural state of existence, be it literal or figurative. The *Daodejing*'s evolutionary ontology, on the other hand, is broken down into four distinct stages: from the human realm to the earthly, from the earthly to the heavenly, from the heavenly to that of Dao, and from the realm of Dao to the natural law of Nature. Insofar as Laozi's meontology involves working backwards from the myriad things to their source, we can liken his idea of return to a process of regressive intuition. Although the *Zhuangzi* does not resort to the numerology seen in the *Daodejing*, the text very clearly outlines the steps needed for such a journey. These four stages occur in a story between Confucius and his disciple Yan Hui, who is attempting to conjoin with Dao. The first stage involves forgetting benevolence and righteousness, followed by rites and music. Having unlearned all social norms and epistemological conventions, Yan Hui's mind returns to a state of quietude and emptiness. He subsequently proclaims to be able to "sit in forgetfulness," a statement that confounds Confucius. This leads Yan to describe it as the discarding of his limbs and intellect, for only in abandoning one's body and mind can one become united with Dao.[61]

Yan Hui thus begins his quest at the stage of epistemological discrimination and moral certitude, a stage in which things rule over that which is natural, harming Dao in the process. Having learned to rid himself of such contrived virtues, he moves beyond the realm of the earthly and enters that of heaven. Since heaven cultivates the harmony of Nature and all that is natural, Yan Hui has to unlearn those arts associated with it (e.g., rites and music). With his mind empty of all human conventions, he successfully returns to the stage closest to Dao: the equalization of things (*qiwu* 齊物). It is here where ontological being emerges from the undifferentiated wholeness of the One. And yet, given this was still ontological being and not the ontic being we see in stage three, there remains an element of the One attached to it. This oneness that exists beyond the One is not the true One, for its existence has been classified and named. In order to rid himself of this primordial existence, Yan Hui discards his own phenomenological embodiment so as to return to the meontological ground of Dao. Only when he has returned to the pre-ontological state of being can he claim to have attained unity with Dao. This is what it means to return to Dao and this returning, for the majority of things, occurs when our life draws to an end.

Conclusion

This chapter was devoted to establishing the *Zhuangzi*'s language of meontology so as to better equip ourselves when it comes time to explicate the use and impact of the cosmogonist trinity of nothingness, Dao, and being. The deftness with which the *Zhuangzi* understands and portrays the cosmic circle of beginning and end, the question of being and nothingness, and how the One ultimately unites them by acting as Dao's realm of becoming, show the positive gains to be had over the Western theory of *creatio ex-nihilo*. Having thus outlined the meontological mechanism of Dao, we can cast our net wider by considering aspects of it that are slightly removed from the core element of nothingness. In the next chapter, we will look into how the principle of ontological nothingness manifests itself in the world by leaving clues in our midst, and how humanity attempts to encapsulate it in our thoughts and the things we create. To this end, we will investigate the Thing as the mythically perfect example of human ingenuity, providing us with the opportunity to delve into the characteristics of human craft and learning. Moreover, as a mythical entity whose abode is the One, the Thing makes its presence felt via the concept of trace (*ji* 跡). The trace, as an element of formlessness within form, is an expression of the Thing's Dao-given nature. In other words, although the present chapter has portrayed Dao as being impossibly metaphysical and seemingly forever beyond our grasp, the next chapter will reveal that it is, in fact, constantly at hand in things and as we shall see in chapter 4, in the time and space encapsulating them.

2

Dao, the One, and the Question of Being

Having established the cosmogonist model of Dao and nothingness in the previous chapter, we can now move onto the question of being. This chapter will explore in detail what the previous chapter only intimated: the progenitor of being is non-being and both reside in a state of nameless, undifferentiated wholeness called the One. As Dao's creative potential first takes root in cosmic nothingness before unfolding as the One, moving from a state of non-differentiation to multiplicity within oneness, only to return to a state of empty, still quietude, when we delve into the specifics of this movement, we soon realize that being (*you* 有) is not moving to and from the ubiquitous presence of Dao but to an original, self-replicating model within the One.

We shall refer to this ancestral model as the Thing—a mirage-like entity whose nature is as elusive as that of the sage. It is elusive in that each Thing coalesces with other Things to form the One. The One, in turn, assumes the dark tranquility attributed to Dao. This darkness is none other than the nothingness in which Dao is situated and yet, the One is neither Dao nor nothingness but the pre-phenomenological plenum from which things enter the world. Since humanity is incapable of directly knowing the Thing, we can only learn of its presence by way of lesser, mundane things. These ontic things, however, only act as temporary lodgings for the Thing. Indeed, things can only provide a fleeting glimpse of the Thing, a glimpse that amounts to little more than a trace. It is here, in the trace of the Thing, that we can cross the divide between our everyday encounter with things and our yearning to unite with Dao. The trace, in other words, acts as a signpost on the road of return to the One. This chapter will, therefore, reveal in what ways the Thing and the One are connected, demonstrating how any connection cannot succeed without the trace, while analyzing several well-known stories in the *Zhuangzi* that demonstrate the sage's unique ability to harmonize with the trace of things via the oneness of nothingness.

Original Being *qua* the Thing

Let us recall that the previous chapter worked from the hypothesis that *wu* 無 can be interpreted as both ontic non-being and ontological nothingness, and that it contributes to the generative process of things. Let us also recall that Daoism believes the idea of pure or absolute nothingness to not only be tautological, but downright illogical in that said ideas focus on things themselves rather than on the meontological creativity of Dao. In this way, *wu* can be understood as more than a simple metaphysical tool in that it becomes the very embryonic material from which Dao weaves together the myriad things and their reality. This fashioning of things does not occur in isolation but in the collective non-differentiation of the One. If we are thus to affirm our determination that the origin of the Thing lies in the One, we must not only discover the particulars of this origin, we must also uncover the process leading to their becoming. Although we discussed the following passage in chapter 1, it is worth citing it once more so as to situate it in our discussion of the Thing:

> In the Great Beginning, there was nothingness, non-being, and namelessness. From it arose the One, a oneness that was without form. When things obtained it, they were born and this was called Virtue. Before there were forms and divisions, things were innumerable and not yet separated and this was called Fate. From this flowing and moving things were born, their completion giving rise to principle and this was called Form.[1]

> 泰初有無，無有無名；一之所起，有一而未形。物得以生，謂之德；未形者有分，且然無閒，謂之命；留動而生物，物成生理，謂之形。

From the above passage, we can see that the Thing is a sub-category of the One and its dividedness follows the wholeness of the One *qua* Dao. Hidden within the formless confines of the One, the Thing has its characteristics as such. However, if we are to become aware of the reified traits of the Thing, they must also be embodied in the myriad things. The Thing is thus the first created thing to be created by Dao out of formless, nameless nothingness.[2] As ontic things arise from the Thing, a space is introduced between the moment of their conception and that of their becoming. We can thus express the time before a thing's becoming as one of pre-signification while its existence as a thing marks its transformation into something signified. The *Zhuangzi*, and in particular, the commentary of Guo Xiang, declare that one comes to know of this transitional space through the trace of being.

Given the Thing's pre-phenomenological disposition stands in contrast to the concretized things it propagates, making it knowable only through its trace, the Thing remains an inherent part of them while at the same time maintaining its own aloofness. What enables the Thing to behave in such a manner is not that it is the Thing, but that it contains an inherent nothingness congruent to that of Dao. It is because of this particularly attuned nothingness that the Thing is qualified to dwell in the One. When we read in the *Zhuangzi* allegorical stories of persons whose skill results in objects of creation taken to embody the marvelousness of Dao, we should not interpret them as a call for the emulation of said skill; rather, it is the indescribable thingness of said skill that should be regarded with utmost esteem.[3] There is more to the Thing than its mere thingness however. We can also speak of it as the highest form of representative expression outside of the One. Doing so allows us to compare the phenomenological dyad of Thing-trace with the epistemological pair of signifier-signified. From this we will come to delineate the thingness of the Thing from the trace of the Thing and hence appreciate how the sage can abandon his empirical-self so as to render himself traceless.

The *Zhuangzi* says using one thing to signify another is not as good as allowing both things to engage in mutual interaction or play.[4] In this way, to name a thing as such, including the Thing, is actually no different from saying it is a non-thing.[5] Zhuangzi can say this because Thing and non-Thing alike lose their determinate distinction in light of the traceless nature of Dao. In the passage we quoted at the start of this section, the *Zhuangzi* uses the term *xing* 形 (form) to refer to the Thing and this would, on the surface, appear to resemble Plato's theory of forms. Such an assumption would be erroneous, however, insofar as the text was just expanding the cosmogonist model begun by Laozi.[6] Needless to say, the *Zhuangzi* holds the Thing to be an intricate part of the pre-development of things and human reality. Without the Thing, we would be unable to trace things from their present state of separation back to their original unity in the One. Indeed, the space in which the Thing resides is not an otherness distinct from itself, but the link to the nothingness from whence it originated. This is not to imply that the signifier appears *ex-nihilo*; on the contrary, it is a reflection of the in-itself *qua* the Thing. Herein is the self-turning representation of the Thing. It moves between things without isolating itself from the movement or play of Dao because it represents or isolates itself in lieu of such play, never disrupting the harmonious accord of heaven and earth. Such a feat is impossible for the signifier due to its dependency on the discriminating mind of the subject.

At this stage, however, it seems we have run into a problem: How are we supposed to conceive of that which has yet to come into being (i.e., the pre-signified)? Furthermore, what mechanism do we have at our disposal that would allow us to engage in a pre-symbolic investigation of the Thing when there is no representation of it to be found? One might answer we need to search for the Thing at the time of its origin, at the time of the absolute beginning of things. The difficulty with this approach is that the *Zhuangzi* did not perceive time as having either beginning or end, thereby precluding it from discussion on whether or not it has a past, present, or future. Given the perpetual oneness of Dao, Zhuangzi's temporality is a time-beyond-time—a non-temporal time—as he so aptly demonstrated:

> There is a beginning, a not begun to be a beginning, and a not begun to be beginning's beginning. There is being, there is non-being, there is a not begun to be non-being, and there is a not begun to be non-being's beginning.[7]
>
> 有始也者，有未始有始也者，有未始有夫未始有始也者。有有也者，有無也者，有未始有無也者，有未始有夫未始有無也者。

Zhuangzi's cosmology of mutual dependence and co-arising thus makes it virtually impossible to distinguish the temporality of one thing in relation to another and as such, relations only exist in the sphere of human knowing. It thus falls upon nothingness, the meontological root of Dao, to sustain as elusive an entity as the Thing. The collectivity of Things that coalesce to form the One do so, not because of their indeterminateness, but as a result of their rootedness in nothingness. In this way, they retain their identity as the Thing without disrupting the integrity of the One or harming Dao. To tie the Thing's existence to human knowing is, therefore, to dichotomize its nature with our epistemological awareness of it. Taken further, arguing that the inseparability of the Thing from those who perceive it is the link, which brings together the signifiers of the world, is to imply that the Thing is a singularity whose generative ability stems from its capacity to be infinitely divided into things. This imposes upon the Thing an absolute historical beginning such that it must constantly propagate itself by way of signification or face annihilation. Such reasoning is unacceptable to Daoism.

That the Thing embodies a self-originating thingness explains how the space between it and human reality can be bridged rather than driven further apart. For the *Zhuangzi*, this space is bridgeable in that the One does not foretell the nullification of the Thing's thingness but speaks of it being perpetually inherited by the myriad things of the world via the meontological nature of Dao. This effectively debunks the notion that the Thing's origin is mythical and that only human creativity can produce signifiers that will successfully locate it. As a product of human thinking, signifiers are no more intimate with the natural world than the artifacts tasked with representing them. Due to their need of a place onto which they can project themselves, signifiers become entangled in the world of artificiality, unable to establish an intimate connection with either Nature or the Thing. Such reasoning stems from the fact that human thinking precludes inclusion of the Thing vis-à-vis the One, for the One is enveloped by the dark mystery of Dao. It is here, at the source of being, where the Thing is re-found, having been lost somewhere along the path of signification. And yet, from the vantage point of Dao, there has never been a time when the trace of signification succeeded in overriding the oneness of things. The *Zhuangzi* cleverly argues this point with the following tale:

> There was a man who, frightened by his shadow and disgusted with his footprints, tried to outrun them. However, the more he raised his feet, the more footprints he left behind. He ran faster and faster but his shadow would not leave him. Believing he was too slow, he ran faster still, without pause, exhausting his strength and dying. He did not know that by staying in the shade his shadow would have vanished, and that by resting peacefully any trace of him would cease. How utterly foolish he was![8]

> 人有畏影惡迹而去之走者，舉足愈數而迹愈多，走愈疾而影不離身，自以為尚遲，疾走不休，絕力而死。不知處陰以休影，處靜以息迹，愚亦甚矣！

Based on the above, we can describe the relationship between the Thing and signifier as a muted dependency of recollection. What is recalled is the retracing of the Thing's veiling, its participation in the process of re-finding and revealing what was hitherto assumed lost. Although the Thing lies concealed within the One, said veilment does not imply it is an independently represented object. If the Thing requires representation by something other than itself, then somewhere along the path of signification its nature will become clouded, if not outright discarded. For Zhuangzi, the Thing emerges and vanishes tracelessly. As it has no substantial opposition, its movement is unimpeded. Consequently, the Thing weaves a web of being that is neither limited to nor exclusionary of being, allowing for movement of the real (object) and non-real (sign). The same cannot be said of the signifier whose existence beyond the realm of the Thing is a source of tension. Being beyond the realm of signifiers, the Thing is untouched by the opposition facing ordinary objects, for only the Thing can represent itself by way of the signified. The aloofness of the Thing is also an applicable way of regarding the mystery of Dao. In light of Dao's dark, indescribable nature, both the One and the Thing inherit its meontological gift of nothingness, transmitting it to the world of things in the guise of their own thingness, which we shall discuss shortly. In the meantime, we should turn to the question of the Thing's needing to be re-found and how this is possible if, by its very nature, it is inherently shrouded by the One.

The Thing's Unveiling

Zhuangzi argues that "each thing has what is so to itself; each thing has what is acceptable to itself. There is no thing that is not so, no thing that is not acceptable . . . [thus] Dao makes them One."[9] Despite Zhuangzi's reference to ontic things and not the Thing, the principle that Dao harmonizes all things, including the Thing, still applies. After all, it falls upon the things of the world to shed light on the Thing, just as the Things comprising the One are a mirror of the presence of Dao. The mysteriousness of Dao of which Zhuangzi speaks does not hinge on privileging human culture over Nature, separating the two realms such that transcendence of one necessitates the loss of the other; on the contrary, from a cosmological point of view they are indubitably equal. There is nothing enigmatic about them and this is why the Thing resides on an altogether different plane of reality. However, the realm in which the Thing manifests itself is not a reality at all but the meontological domain of the One. Since the Thing is a non-thing and that which we call the One is in fact undifferentiated wholeness, how can we not portray them as inscrutable? What is more, as the One takes Dao as its source, which is in turn rooted in ontological nothingness, the oneness of the universe is thus a knowability embedded in the unknowable and all-encompassing mystery of Dao.

Given the Thing for Zhuangzi is meontological and hence a non-Thing, can it actually be lost by the things signifying it? If, however, we surmise that the Thing has been forgotten, this is a wholly different situation in that forgetting allows us to return to the root of being. Indeed, the *Zhuangzi* contains many well-known tales of sages who proactively forget things so as to harmonize with the oneness of their particular Thing, the most famous examples being Nanguo Ziqi losing himself and Yan Hui sitting in forgetfulness.[10] As we will have more to say on the importance of forgetting later on, let us matter-of-factly state that forgetting nourishes the Thing while allowing it to retain its own self-so nature.

If the Thing exists because humanity has conceived of it as such, the same can also be said for its disappearance. What is lost is not the object itself but the space between it and another—their in-betweenness—such that a thing's propensity for change is hampered due to the damage inflicted upon it by human calculative thinking. Of course, if what we seek lies solely within the domain of the signified, it shall never be found. It cannot be found because it is restricted to the level of ontic awareness—an awareness ruled by the heart-mind. To return the heart-mind to open, authentic thinking, we must train it to maneuver in the beyondness of nothingness. Put this way, nothingness neither distances humanity from things, nor introduces distance between things; rather, it serves as a conjoining medium between mind and things, and between things themselves. This helps explain why Wang Bi in his "Introductory Remarks to the *Daodejing*" (*Laozi zhilue* 老子指略) wrote the following:

> If one wishes to determine the root of things, though near, one must look afar for evidence of their beginning. If one wishes to illuminate the cause of things, though obvious, one must begin with their concealment in order to discuss their root.[11]

For Laozi, the mystery of the Thing exists not because human knowledge makes it so, but because all Things *qua* the One cannot be otherwise. Our craving for things on account of some imagined need does not translate into the immediate presence of said thing but causes us to jump from one signifier to another, never completing our search for the ultimate Thing that always remains on the horizon, just out of reach. Unable to explain how the Thing can evade our pursuits to claim it, we either deny it or relegate it to the unknown. The mystery surrounding the Thing's presence of being can, however, be reconciled if we see it as a meta-phenomenon whose eluding our attempts to grasp it via *poiesis* or *episteme* arises precisely because of its intimate relationship with the nothingness of Dao.

If the Thing were not meontological, existing as a linguistic construct for example, there would be nothing exceptional about it. One would only be able to refer to the Thing as a thing—a particular instead of a multitude—from which things are given the task of signification. However, since the Thing is enfolded in the One, the relationship between itself, the myriad things, and signifiers cannot be premised upon traditional understandings of hierarchy or determinism. To free the Thing of the shackles of signification—from its psychic trap—it must not only function as the ultimate of things, it must exemplify their ontological and pre-cognitive representation. In this way, the Thing is victimized by the signified—created in retrospect by humanity as a desperate attempt to repair the rift inserted between the world of Nature and the being of man. As a consequence, the Thing is presumed to assume an otherness it must overcome in order to absolve itself of succumbing to the bonds of signification. In Daoism, however, this ordeal is absent: things evolve according to the self-so-ness of their being such that all transformations are natural and untouched by humanity. To return to the One is to harmonize with Dao, and harmonizing with Dao is a process of reverse accumulation. So what is being accumulated? One would think the more advanced one's *poiesis* the more perfect would be one's virtue, and yet the *Zhuangzi* espouses the idea that we should follow Dao so as to uncover the true nature of things. How one goes about doing this is not to paint it in the language of mystical transcendence, but treasuring the gift of nothingness.

The more one understands the participatory role of Dao's meontological side, the more profound will be one's harmonization with the universe.[12] The things that populate our world are everyday examples of the potential creative power of the Thing from which they are born. The power of the Thing, moreover, is itself but an example of the splendor and creative potential of Dao. What we take to be the everydayness of things, when seen from the perspective of Dao, is in fact a coming-togetherness whose outcome rises above them in the form of a worldly Thing. Such worldliness cannot compete with the non-worldly character of the One, however, and so the oneness of things is taken as an inversion of the unifying power of Dao via nothingness. This gift of nothingness allows things to follow in the image of the Thing without realizing they are doing so; it also allows each Thing to coalesce into the One without forfeiting its own uniqueness. In this way, the restricted being of ontic things moves toward the semi-restricted being of the Thing, and the Thing returns to the apophatic being of Dao. This cosmic hierarchy was expressed in the *Zhuangzi* thusly:

> To take things as things is to remain unlimited by them. Things have their limits—what is known as the limit of things. That which is unlimited moves to the limited, and that which is limited moves to the unlimited . . . [hence] things take Dao as their root and branch yet Dao knows not of root and branch; things take Dao as their accumulation and loss yet Dao knows not of accumulation and loss.[13]

物物者與物無際，而物有際者，所謂物際者也；不際之際，際之不際者也……彼為本末非本末，彼為積散非積散也。

The gift of nothingness that Dao bestows upon the Thing is not exclusive to the realm of ontology but finds practical application in the world of ontic things too. Chapter 11 of the *Daodejing* exemplifies this point exceptionally well:

> One kneads clay to make a vessel, but it is from nothingness that the vessel gains its use. One chisels out windows and doors to make a room, but it is due to nothingness that the room has its use. Thus existence gives things their benefit while nothingness gives things their use.[14]

Clay might be the material from which the vessel's presence of being takes shape but what imbues the vessel's being with its useful nature is nothingness. The limitation of the vessel's physicality thus impels it to seek another means by which to move closer to its particular Thing, and this measure of progress toward its eventual uniting with the One comes about thanks to its inner void. Drawing near the voidless void that is the nothingness utilized by Dao, the vessel embraces this gift as its rooting center and so transcends the limits of its physicality. In this way, the gift of nothingness provides the vessel with the capacities of accumulation and loss and yet, what is accumulated and lost is not the vessel's thingness but the names "full" and "empty." This is what the *Zhuangzi* meant when it spoke of the limit of things—an ontic limitation imposed by notions such as fullness and emptiness. By embracing the virtue of Dao, however, these notions are suddenly able to transform into the interchangeably complimentary ideal of harmony (*he* 和; *hexie* 和諧).

If Laozi's clay vessel can qualify as a Thing, and its enclosing of the void signifies its emptiness, does this not establish its connectedness to nothingness? If the Thing is a signifier, and the first one at that, it is in its signifying essence a signifier of nothing other than signification as such. Indeed, the Thing as the source of things and signifiers alike cannot be held to the immobile historical time of its dependents; rather, it continuously follows along with the movement of the One *qua* Dao by way of the trace. Zhuangzi's unwillingness to enshroud the mystery of Dao in humanistic jargon meant he could discuss the root of things from a cosmological perspective. This, in turn, laid the ground for ontological nothingness out of which the One and the Thing arose. To this end, the Thing has never been a participant in the development of human social culture; rather, it shines forth because of the creative potential of Dao. Since the Thing has traditionally been colored in absolutist terms, its thingness has forever escaped our grasp. By embracing its mysteriousness through letting-be, Zhuangzi was able to draw the Thing near without knowingly doing so. Unveiled by its own meontological root, the Thing epitomizes the mundane side of the world insofar as its dwelling in the One precludes it from being disharmonious with Dao. Neither an imaginary event nor an idealized abstraction, the Thing is the final frontier between the cosmology of the One and the ontic beings populating the world. It is, in other words, the most authentic means by which one can comprehend Dao, a comprehension only attainable when we relent in denying the generative capacity of creative negativity.

The Trace and the Traceless Sage

Just now we theorized that the transitional space lying between the becoming and manifestation of the Thing could be illuminated via the trace. Before commencing our discussion of the trace, we need to clarify in what sense the *Zhuangzi* took this term. If one reads the text on a merely superficial level, the immediate conclusion one arrives at is this: as many of the examples involving the concept of trace focus on the sage and his knowledge of Dao, it is an epistemological construct. When taken in the context of the Thing and Dao, the trace suddenly transposes itself to the level of cosmology. Here is an example:

> The bright is born of the dark, the ordered is born of the formless, and spiritual essence is born of Dao. The bodily form is born of the seminal, and the myriad things give birth to each other through their bodily form. Thus those having nine orifices are born from the womb, and those having eight orifices are born from eggs. There is no trace of their coming and no outline of their leaving. They enter through no door, dwell in no room, and so wander in the four directions.[15]

> 夫昭昭生於冥冥，有倫生於無形，精神生於道，形本生於精，而萬物以形相生，故九竅者胎生，八竅者卵生。其來無跡，其往無崖，無門無房，四達之皇皇也。

Due to the nature of the Thing being inextricably tied to the virtue (*de* 德) of Dao, the latter can thereby elucidate the former. As the Thing receives its gift of nothingness from Dao and Dao draws near the meontological ground of its reality, the territory of its grounding extends so far as to be darkly immeasurable. Such being the case, how can an inkling of the Thing's arrival and departure occur? It cannot, for doing so would mean it is no longer the Thing but a thing amongst things. What allows us to have an encounter with the Thing in lieu of its unreachability is the trace. The trace of Dao, as we shall see, cannot be taken in a strictly epistemic sense in that Dao is unknowable through regular models of knowledge. Whether we are referring to the trace of the Thing vis-à-vis things, or that of the sage vis-à-vis his words and deeds, any inclination we may feel to distinguish between the source of the trace and the trace itself ought to be held in check in that both are equal, cosmologically speaking.[16] In other words, one should not cherish the trace, or "that which leaves the trace" (*suoyi ji* 所以跡) because doing so authenticates that which is beyond authentication. The *Zhuangzi* offered such advice in a fictional conversation between Laozi and Confucius with the former proclaiming:

> How fortunate that you have not yet encountered a ruler who can govern the world! As for the six Classics, they are but the stale traces of the kings of old, much less those who leave the trace! Your words today are no different from such traces. As

for the trace, it is like the imprint made by a shoe, it is not the shoe itself![17]

幸矣，子之不遇治世之君也！夫六經，先王之陳跡也，豈其所以跡哉！今子之所言，猶跡也。夫跡，履之所出，而跡豈履哉！

Here, the *Zhuangzi*—using the voice of Laozi—makes an important hermeneutic distinction between the trace and the sage-kings of old who were responsible for creating them. Although this passage serves as the foundation upon which Guo Xiang would develop his own particular reading of the trace by differentiating it from that which leaves the trace, Guo was not the only commentator to do so. Indeed, Lü Huiqing, as early as chapter 7, used the word trace to explain an encounter between Nie Que and Wang Ni. With the latter not answering any of the former's questions, Nie Que informed his master Pu Yizi of the situation, who responded: "[Emperor Tai's] knowledge and emotions were true and his virtue was authentic. He never distinguished what was of man and what was not."[18] Lü's commentary subsequently reads:

> From Wang Ni's perspective, Emperor Youyu could not keep up with the knowledge of Emperor Tai. In not keeping up, his words advanced forth and so Emperor Tai was then that which advances for Emperor Youyu. Wishing to obtain that which leaves the trace, he sought to explain the heart and the spirit. This was only to further elucidate Wang Ni's ignorance and nothing more.[19]

自王倪觀之，則有虞氏不及泰氏可知矣。不及者，言其進，泰氏則有虞氏之所以進也；欲得其所以跡者，解心釋神，深造乎王倪之所不知而已。

It would appear that *suoyi ji* is not only a desirable state of existence, one atop the ontological ladder so to speak, it is even attainable. Yet how can this be so when the trace signifying it is just as ephemeral as its source? The answer is that there can be no differentiating the two; they are either concrete epistemological tools used to delimit the world of things, or they are taken to be metaphysical ideals epitomized by the sage. If our stance sides with the former, then the trace and that which leaves it can have no affiliation with Dao; on the other hand, if we side with the latter, then the elusory nature of the trace darkly reflects the mysterious workings of Dao. Of the two, we can argue that the *Zhuangzi* preferred the second interpretation, even admitting as such when it said: "The myriad things return to their true condition and this is known as muddied darkness."[20]

This muddied darkness is not only a metaphorical representation of Dao, it applies to the Thing *qua* the One as well. If the One participates in the mutual darkness of Dao's nothingness, then the Thing as that which leaves the trace shares in such traceless mystery too.[21] Recall for a moment the earlier dialogue between Laozi and Confucius. While the author of this chapter did not explicitly use the term traceless (*wuji* 無跡), his criticism of the six Classics was an attempt to usurp their social authority by demonstrating the cosmological supremacy of Dao envisioned by Zhuangzi. Guo Xiang picked up on this point and went one step further, denying the very possibility of an attainable trace:

> That which leaves the trace is itself traceless. Who in the world can name it! Lacking a constant name, how can it overcome existence! Thus in being traceless it rides on collective change, walking through myriads of worlds—worlds that are smooth and rough—hence the trace is unattainable.[22]

> 所以跡者，無跡也，世孰名之哉！未之嘗名，何勝負之有耶！然無跡者，乘群變，履萬世，世有夷險，故跡有不及也。

Only when the inner and outer realms of reality obscurely join together does our dependency on the trace vanish and we can return to the time when things retained their original traceless nature. When Zhuangzi mocked the other schools of his day for revering past traditions and knowledge as holding the key to unlocking the true reality of things, he was not calling for the outright abandonment of said institutions, just our faith in their ability to hold sway over the ultimate, everlasting reality of Dao. Given the bond between Dao, nothingness, the trace, and that which leaves the trace, we can surmise that the trace points to the pseudo-ontological being of the Thing, while the Thing as that which leaves the trace points to the meontological being of Dao. In this way, these four elements have an inherent framework that resides in the atemporal, aspatial realm of ontological nothingness. What is more, for the sagely person, as one whose being has merged with the oneness of Dao, he too is traceless insofar as he wanders beyond the actuality of the world's mundaneness. This ability to transcend the everydayness of the world grants the sage an opportunity to experience what precedes the becoming of the Thing, a state of dark tranquility whose sole resident is Dao:

> The essence of perfect Dao is profoundly obscure and mysteriously dark; the extremity of perfect Dao is dimly muddled and enshrouded in silence.[23]

> 至道之精，窈窈冥冥；至道之極，昏昏默默。

Since darkness (*ming* 冥) makes things naturally so, it is the first characteristic of things; as such, it surpasses that which leaves the trace. Epistemologically, this surpassing can only occur through a direct knowing of the darkness of things, which hints at an implicit knowledge of the trace of things. That which knows the self-so nature of things, together with their trace, must be that which has transcended the earthly realm of being to become one with its darkness. Such convergence of the darkness of the Thing with the darkness of the trace equalizes the production of things by having their inborn natures arise from a single source. Zhuangzi also noted that the brightness (*zhaozhao* 昭昭) born from darkness and the formed born from the formless, are traces of that which is Ultimate. Thus that which leaves the trace, together with the darkness of things, cannot be derived from knowledge alone: "The form of the formless is the formlessness of the formed, and this is known by all, even though pursuing it one cannot reach it."[24]

As a consequence, the relationship between the dark and the trace is analogous to the dichotomy of inner and outer. Such dichotomy, however, does not result in the creation of the trace's agency as this would be wholly impractical given we are always one step behind it. In order to overcome our inability to grasp the perceptual gap existing between the trace and the Thing, the *Zhuangzi* turned to the darkness of the sage. Whenever the text refers to the sages of old such as the Yellow Emperor, Yao, and Shun, it was only pointing to the traces of such men and not to the traces of the works attributed to them. To do so would imply that they can be made known through a kind of epistemological trace (*ming ji* 名跡), which is unlikely in light of their traceless nature:

> [The sages] did what was upright without knowing that to do so was to be righteous. They loved each other without knowing that to do so was to be humane. They were dependable and

honest without knowing that to do so was to be faithful. They were proper without knowing that to do so was to be trustful. They moved around clumsily in service of one another without regard for the bestowal of gifts. This is to move yet remain traceless, to act yet leave no record of one's deeds.[25]

端正而不知以為義，相愛而不知以為仁，實而不知以為忠，當而不知以為信，蠢動而相使，不以為賜。是故行而無迹，事而無傳。

Thus the progression from recognizing trace to valuing it as a means by which to harmonize with Dao is not to be thought of as a separate process; rather, they are co-dependent and hence indistinguishable. The sages of old and their traces—those vestiges known as the six Classics—do not share the same relationship we saw earlier with the signifier and the Thing. Whether we refer to him as authentic (*zhenren* 真人) or marvelous (*shenren* 神人), the sage acts as a type of transcendent go-between such that his trace becomes masked, uniting with the darkness of his being (*minghe zhi ji* 冥合之跡). In this way, the sage is known by his trace while simultaneously remaining hidden and dark. The name given to him is, therefore, nothing but a trace of his darkened relational-self, leaving his actions unknowable except through their traces. This explains why we see Guo Xiang proclaim: "Although the kings of old were known as Yao and Shun, these were but their traces. The self may reside in these traces but the traces are not the self, hence the world astonishes itself."[26]

Indeed, the *Zhuangzi* contains a few passages that attempt to show the destructibility of the trace, particularly that pertaining to Confucius. It would seem these passages were meant to attack Confucius personally, as well as to mock his unwavering belief that the knowledge of the former kings was still relevant in his own time.[27] That Zhuangzi, in one fell swoop, simultaneously undermined the epistemological validity of the ancient kings and Confucius testifies to the deftness of his argumentation and makes for some rather amusing reading:

> Now here are you, master, picking up the straw dogs presented by the kings of old, calling together your disciples to wander, dwell, and sleep under them. Thus the tree under which you studied was cut down in Song, your trace destroyed in Wei, and the way of Shang and Zhou has been exhausted. Was that

not unlike a dream? Being stuck between Chen and Cai and going for seven days without cooked food, lying on the cusp between life and death, was that not unlike a nightmare?[28]

今而夫子，亦取先王已陳芻狗，取弟子遊居寢臥其下。故伐樹於宋，削跡於衞，窮於商周，是非其夢邪？圍於陳蔡之間，七日不火食，死生相與鄰，是非其眯邪？

From the above, we can see how knowledge is a kind of stale trace. As the trace is an inherent quality of the Thing, it must function on a level that is congruent with the ontological nothingness of Dao. Additionally, since the trace exists beyond the realm of being, it overrides the fundamental nature of being, bringing about its erasure. In other words, the trace becomes a victim of its own erasure and in so doing, erases the presence of being of the Thing from the world of ontic things. Thus that which leaves the trace is not the six Classics themselves but the sages who penned them. Indeed, the Classics are just the dusty embodiment of said men and the knowledge that died with them. The knowledge they contain cannot convey or capture the originating spirit of their creators, hence one must look beyond the text—to transcend the language captured and contained on their pages—if one is to discover the reality of Dao. Names, being signs, become empty shells of the persona to which they are attached insofar as they point to the presence of otherness—the dark nothingness of Yao and Shun through which the operation of Dao occurs. The trace thus comes to represent the non-representable presence that exists beyond the reach of words and signifiers. Said differently, the trace of that which transcends the truth of things is a trace of that which can never present itself, or be presented, as Guo Xiang demonstrates:

> In imitating the sages, we are imitating just their traces. These traces are a thing already passed on and are not an implement for responding to change; how could they be worthy of holding onto![29]

> 法聖人者，法其跡耳。夫跡者，已去之物，非應變之具也，奚足尚而執之哉！

Despite the fact that the sage hides himself in the darkness of Dao, making his authentic-self unknowable, Guo Xiang argued that the common people of the world could still know of him by way of his trace. For

Zhuangzi, however, this would be seen as a violation of the sagely way, for once traces become accepted into our normative system they are no longer dark, pure trace. Thus the act of naming the trace as such can be said to relegate it to the realm of a manifest and ultimately inferior trace (i.e., the trace of Guo Xiang).

The concept of trace is thus incommensurate with that of retention, which is the becoming-past of what had been present. This would seem to conflict with what Brook Ziporyn understands of Guo Xiang's reading of the *Zhuangzi*'s use of darkness to represent that which leaves the trace as signifying the self-forgetting and darkening of cognition intrinsic to self-rightness.[30] Ziporyn goes on to say that what are cognized are the traces, those objectified forms of original chaos which are the dark, self-right, self-forgetting fitness by which things come to be.[31] And yet, Zhuangzi was quite clear on the origin of traces when he said that which leaves the trace is traceless. From this we may conclude that the dimness or unknowability of the true nature of things does not stem from their wanting to be so, but because all things, including the Thing, exist in an obscurity whose presence makes itself felt in the form of trace. As the Thing is unnamable, it is said to be dark; because the trace is the non-presence of the Thing, it too is dark. Thus to trace the path of the trace will only lead to further darkness insofar as its obscurity has already dislodged itself from its creator. In knowing the trace, one cannot know of that which leaves the trace, for while the Thing that gave rise to the trace was not a thing of this realm, as all that remains of it in this realm is its trace, it signifies that it has returned to the collectivity of the One.[32] Thus that which is without trace is purely dark, the sagely-way, or the movement of Dao itself. Guo Xiang explains thusly:

> Yao, in his reality, is dark; it is his trace that is Yao. From the perspective of the trace looking at the dark, it is not really strange that the outer and inner should become foreign [to one another]. The world sees Yao only as Yao, how can they see the darkness of his reality![33]

What the trace reveals is a unique insight into the process of reversal we spoke of in chapter 1. The trace, in other words, becomes a critical link in the chain of evolutionary progression and retreat in that it is the closest we can come to palpably touching the being of the Thing. As Zhuangzi observed, "to stand without moving is easy; to walk without touching the ground is difficult."[34] The myriad things of the world surround us but they are shadowy imprints left in the dust of the earth. They are mere vestiges of the marvelous possibilities lying within the darkness of Dao. The trace is hence the empty husk of the Thing.

We can even go so far as to say that for the *Zhuangzi*, the trace as a derivative of the Thing is an imaginary event that allows for the opening of a space between the Thing and its signifier, breaking the link of dependency between them. This meontological space comes to be through the vanishing of things by way of their trace and yet, the space opened up by the introduction of the trace upon a thing's return to the One is not a realized space, but the rejoining of ontological nothingness and Dao. The weakness of Guo Xiang's interpretation of Zhuangzi's trace lies in his dislocating Dao from the cycle of transformation, resulting in things experiencing a return not to the oneness of Dao, but to their own inductive nihilism. There is, therefore, no self-becoming or self-returning to a cosmogonist root for Guo Xiang because there is no longer a Dao to which things can return. Without Dao, there cannot be the One, and without the One, there can no longer be a myriad of beings whose existence stems from it. Thus we should not lose sight of the fact that the trace for Zhuangzi acts as a link between the phenomenological world of humanity and the cosmological realm of Dao. In other words, the trace lights the way toward that which is inwardly dark and mysterious, toward the ontological nothingness imbued in things, resulting in a harmony so profound there is nowhere it does not penetrate.

Wandering in the Harmony of Dao

With the Thing and its trace now at our disposal, we can engage in a more tangible discussion of how ontological nothingness presents itself to the world and why such presence is indicative of Dao. In order to do this, several anecdotal stories from the *Zhuangzi* will be analyzed: those of cook Ding, woodcarver Qing, the catcher of cicadas, and the maker of belt-buckles.[35] Each of these tales vividly illustrates how one may utilize Dao so as to attain harmony with the myriad things of the world, but also how such harmony can be re-translated into life praxis. It goes without saying, however, that grounding one's life praxis in Dao is no simple task; it involves not only a partial loss of self—a returning of one's self so as to glimpse inside the One—but also comprehending the role played by nothingness in its guise as the meontological fabric of Dao. If we were to choose one word that describes the experiences of these characters, it would not be mystical but sublime.[36]

The first anecdote to be examined bears a disproportionate amount of scholarly attention compared to the others. The exchange between cook Ding (*paoding* 庖丁) and king Wenhui 文惠君 occurs in chapter 3 of the text. Given that this chapter deals with the principle of caring for life, it should come as no surprise that many interpretations take it to be descriptive of a spiritual encounter, although other theories abound.[37] What is more, of those who touch upon Ding's activities, none save for Wu Guangming, sufficiently account for its import in relation to the inner chapters as a coherent group. While the description of cook Ding is not the lone example of the perfectibility of life praxis, it is the longest and most sophisticated and shall therefore garner most of our attention.

Reveling in the task at hand, be it cutting up oxen, catching cicadas, or making wheels and belt-buckles, each of the men in these stories has learnt how to harmonize the humanly realm with the heavenly and, in so doing, attain perfection of life through experiencing Dao and its accompanying nothingness. For Zhuangzi, life praxis is neither esoteric nor mystical; it is a holistic state of being in which the mind and body fuse into one, and the individual comes to possess a form of meta-consciousness through which the internalization of all outward forms of awareness become one ineffable state of existence. This should not, however, be equated with transient bouts of spiritual possession or shamanic flights of fancy, as these are only capable of unidirectional modes of consciousness; rather, the life praxis of cook Ding is all about achieving a higher state of familiarity with the world, much like Zhuangzi himself experienced with his butterfly dream at the end of his second chapter.

Since the aforementioned stories involve the perceived perfection of a physical activity, we can interpret them in several ways: aesthetically, in order to point out their harmony of movement and physical beauty; metaphysically, given that each character is endowed with a talent that defies explanation; and finally, in terms of textual relevance and coherence. We can thus demonstrate how these tales are neither mystically oriented nor a commentary on the application of knowledge, but are structurally coherent examples of how the lowliest of activities can be transformed into a thing of wonderment and beauty when seen through the eyes of Dao.[38] Here is the cook Ding story, quoted in its entirety:

> Cook Ding was cutting up an ox for king Wenhui. Every touch of his hand, leaning with his shoulders, placing of his foot, support with his knee, whoosh of his blade cutting flesh, was in such harmony that it resembled the *Mulberry Tree* dance, or the notes from the *Jing Shou*. King Wenhui said, "Splendid! How

did your skill get to such a level?" Cook Ding put down his blade and replied: "What I cherish most is Dao, which exceeds any skill. At the time when I first began cutting up oxen, I only saw the complete ox. After three years, I no longer saw the complete ox. Today, I let my spirit guide me, not my eyes. My physical functions cease, giving way to my spirit. Following the great veins, my blade is guided through the great gaps and crevices, making use of what is originally there. I do not touch any of the veins or joints, much less the main bones. A good cook changes his blade every year, for he cuts with it. A common cook changes his blade every month, for he hacks with it. Today, my blade has been in use for nineteen years, has cut up thousands of oxen, and its edge remains as sharp as when it first left the grindstone. Where joints between bones exist, empty spaces also exist, and a blade's edge is without thickness. Using what is without thickness to enter what is empty, there is a vast amount of space to freely maneuver. This is how I have used my blade for nineteen years and kept it as sharp as when it first left the grindstone. Although I may encounter a knotty section, I see its difficulty and guarding against weariness, I regard it and move with caution. With careful movements of my blade, the flesh separates from the bones like earth falling to the ground. I stand holding my blade, looking all around with a sense of satisfaction, wipe my blade and put it away." Wenhui replied, "Excellent! I have heard cook Ding's words and learned of the cultivation of life."[39]

One of the first things we notice is the idea of harmony. This harmony is not the result of spiritual induction but the careful coordination of body and mind to the task at hand. A touch of the hand, leaning of the shoulders, bending of the knee, and placement of the feet are all suggestive of a rhythmic flowing of the body as if one were dancing unaware of the external world. To some interpreters, such movement is indicative of the trance during a shamanic invocation, but nothing in the story supports this conclusion. In ancient China, if there is to be dancing then there must also be musical accompaniment, and Zhuangzi provides us with a cacophony of sounds. The sound of the knife blade swishing through the air is a perfect counter to the sounds of cook Ding bending here and there, huffing and puffing as he works his way through the dismemberment of the ox. It is interesting that Zhuangzi should associate this harmonic dance with two pieces of music normally associated with sacrificial ritual: the *Mulberry Forest* and the *Jing Shou*.[40] This is to say, cook Ding's movements are carried forth with such relaxed ease that the undoing of the ox takes on the qualities of a carefree dance; figuratively in the form of a Shang-era dance whereby the cook prepares the sacrificial meal unseen and unheard, and literally as a shamanic rain dance invoked exclusively for the audience of the king.[41]

The dance of death that is the way of the cook *qua* butcher is a dance played out countless times in Nature. This is not a ruthless butchering dance but one of utmost finesse and understanding. It is so because Dao allows the ox to unfold of its own accord—an unfolding that is heavenly and natural. Through such undoing there is nourishment—the nourishing of spirit, mind, and body. These three levels of nourishment operate in unison to continuously nurture one's being until such time as it reaches its climax and we are called back to the One. The balletic gestures of the knife, Ding's arms and legs—his entire being—is thus a rhythmic coordination with Dao to the extent that he loses himself within himself, seeing what is before him as it naturally exists, yet seeing beyond its surface to unlock the very essence of its existence. In this way, he is able to dance as the spirits do inside the crevices and hollows of the ox, slipping his knife into the nothingness therein, yet preserving its sharpness as if it had just left the grindstone.

Another way we can describe cook Ding's encounter with the ox is by drawing an analogy to the process of return we spoke of at the end of chapter 1. While seeing things from the perspective of earthly conventions, cook Ding's understanding remained ontologically obstructed; the only thing before him was the complete ox. After three years of practice he had advanced to the second stage of reversal, the equalization of things. Here, he encountered the beyondness of the ox's entirety, outwardly observing its head, legs, body, and its internal division into organs, bones, muscles, and ligaments. Each element has its own internal function and natural ordering that cannot be disturbed. Having discarded his own phenomenological embodiment so as to spiritually unite with Dao, cook Ding was able to visualize the ox as a conglomerate of individual components, each of which could be known through the mind's eye. When his sensory organs failed to guide his knife, he allowed his spirit to take over, for his spirit can do nothing but follow the movement of Dao.

Cook Ding has now retreated from seeing the ox as a large lumbering figure, the intricacies of which are lost on the untrained eye, to being able to distinguish the various complexities inherent to the ox's disposition.

Having learnt to recognize the division of muscle and bone, artery and joint, however, he still runs into difficulties. Previously, he viewed the ox in its entire three-dimensional existence and so could not see beyond what was formally before him. In time, however, he internalized his knowledge by forgetting it and observed the ox in four dimensions, but even this proved inadequate, for his vision was still grounded in his being. To overcome such an imposing obstacle, to see the ox as it exists from within the ox itself, cook Ding had to learn to experience the composition of the ox in the dimension of nothingness—a modeling of reality which melds together the experiential realities of subject and object much like the Thing. This is also known as the harmonization of heaven and earth—the spiritual vision of Dao—of which more will be said in chapter 6. Thus cook Ding sees things as Dao sees them, lets them unfold as Dao unfolds them, and so uses the thick-less knife blade to enter the nothingness of the ox's hollows and crevices. In this way, his life praxis is grounded in the preservation of that which lies within things, for he uses what lies beyond them and so is able to dance with Dao.

Despite his marvelous transformation, cook Ding was still dependent upon his livelihood and thus was bound to his dependency of butchering oxen. His existence is in the world of butchery and he is thus a harbinger of death while also nourishing life. To dance with a double-edged sword is no easy task and many have failed trying. The common cook hacks while the good cook cuts. Hacking and cutting are not emblematic of dancing with Dao however; they are the deliberate acts of a singularly dimensional mind out of step with it. To change one's knife every month is to be ignorant of the harmony of Nature, thus the common man wields his knife as if it were a tool of power while the skilled man wields it as a tool of butchery. Wielding, however, is still a resistant form of yielding.

Yielding is to follow along with the harmony of things, to let things be as they are naturally meant, to dance in step with the rhythm of Dao. Thus the skilled man must still change his knife every year because he is unable to go beyond the reality of his skill. To be skilled at something is not equal to having a knack for it. Mediocrity of talent is still mediocrity and for the common man there can be nothing but mundaneness and stagnation. He is happy to switch his knife every month for he views this as a sign of his skill at butchery. In fact, butchery might be too kind a designation for one who hacks and chops his way through life. Cutting, however, is far superior to hacking. Thus the skilled man is able to get a year's use out of his blade. But even this is far short of what cook Ding can achieve. Cutting is not undoing insofar as it involves concentration of mind and body; a coordination between the earthly and the heavenly. A simple cut and an ox can be undone, but such cutting does not imply that it is a naturally so—a cleaving of natural seams and joints. Only one such as cook Ding can adhere to the natural pathways and intersections invisible to the common man. Only one such as cook Ding can use the illumination of Dao to light his way as he flows through the spaces of emptiness that are the key to undoing the ox. His is a skill of undoing—of using that which is without (i.e., the edge of the knife's blade) to enter the nothingness of the ox. Indeed, making use of nothingness is not the same as *doing* nothing, for using that which *is not* to effect that which *is*, is precisely to dance with Dao in the hall of nothingness.

Such a sublime experience allows cook Ding to use the nothingness within the ox to guide him past the great veins, joints, and bones, for these are the carriers of life: "it is the vital artery, that vital emptiness, which lets through the energy of life."[42] Recognizing these pillars of life is what distinguishes Ding from all other cooks. The ability to dance around the Dao-bearing elements of the ox, preserving its inborn nature while cutting it asunder, is the quality of the marvelous person, the sage. It is, in a manner of speaking, an anatomical co-habitation. Bone to bone, vein to vein, joint to joint, Ding knows the ox as well as he knows himself. Knowing the ox thusly, he enters its interstices and voids, allowing his knife to pass through untouched. And so, the art of butchery is more than mere chipping and breaking, it is walking without touching the ground; it is a carefree wandering through the great hollows and cavities that define and make the ox unique. By preserving those life-giving elements within the ox, Ding can thereby nurture his own life—his own internalization of Dao.

Should he encounter a place of difficulty, however, he spontaneously adjusts his disposition. Here, there is nothing magical occurring. The transient state of awareness has not passed nor is there any sign of divine intervention. It is as if the continuum of time somehow slows down, as if the flow of Dao coursing through Ding intensifies, exposing him to all possible outcomes instantaneously. But these outcomes are all natural; they are all means by which the ox can naturally undo itself. It, therefore, becomes a choice of the path of least resistance, one not based on physical reality, for remember, the knife is a nothingness entering the emptiness of the ox, but a resistance against the unity of cook, knife, and ox. When the task is carried out in accordance with the natural disposition of the ox, it simply lets go of itself as if it were earth falling to the ground. Quite an interesting metaphor—*earth falling to the ground*—for the ground *is* the earth; the earth thus returns to itself in self-completion.

Everything returns to the ground, to the earth. The Great Clod, as Zhuangzi called it, indeed has a purpose. The *qi* of the earth is what gives us life and, in return, death gives life back to it. There is a circular motion between the earth and us. As Dao sets things into motion, a circular motion, it allows for the spontaneous rise and fall of things. The cycle of coming and going, living and dying, is the essence of Dao. And so, all existence is a menagerie of nourishment, one thing feeding upon another. Cook Ding releases the ox of its being so that it may be devoured by king Wenhui. The earth will in turn devour him and this revelation teaches us about the nourishment of life praxis. In essence, we all fall to the ground as if little more than clumps of dirt. For cook Ding and others like him, however, the ox is not simply a thing to be done with as deemed fit. There is a Way to be followed—a dance. The Way of butchering oxen is not a skill to be taught and studied—that is the butchery of common men. It is an intuitive, spontaneous knack for things that is beyond words or knowledge. It is not a mechanical behavior either—a kind of memorized skillset—for then Ding would merely be on par with the skilled butchers of the world. It is indeed much more.

While butchering his ox, Ding becomes one with it, one with the oneness that is inherent to the ontological nothingness informing Dao. Such oneness allows him to internalize all aspects of the ox's being such that the knife, as an extension of his arm, comes to physically manifest the Dao in him. It is interesting that Zhuangzi should have Ding exhibit his skill in this manner. Concentration of spirit becomes enhancement of Dao; enhancement of Dao leads to further purity of spirit;[43] purity of spirit in turn leads to a great awakening, which in turn results in returning to the One. The dance of the cook is hence a self-fulfilling realization of the degree to which Dao exists inside him. There is no one-to-one relationship of man and heaven as we see in Western religious traditions, no personalization of the true Dao, for to personalize Dao is to deny it its ubiquity. For Zhuangzi, Dao cannot be personalized; it is ineffable and because of its ineffability, it both *is* and *is not*. It is the potentiality of undoing what already exists within the ox; the potential for someone like cook Ding to allow the ox to undo itself. The cook alone cannot undo the ox; the ox must permit him such an undoing. This is the natural way of things. Hacking and chopping are most unnatural and so encounter resistance over the course of said hacking and chopping. If one approaches life by hacking and chopping, one will certainly not realize the completion of one's naturally allotted years. This is why Zhuangzi applauds those who live a life of undoing—a life of non-doing—for only by living in a way that follows the path of Nature can one nourish oneself. Through nourishing oneself, one also nourishes others. This is the reciprocity of perfect virtue, the virtue of Dao.

The dance of cook Ding is also the dance of the ox. The releasing of its flesh and innards becomes a sublime representation of what is meant by harmony. It is a peeling away of outer layers to reveal its true inner-self.[44] Without Dao, however, everything becomes stagnant, rotting. Dao is what animates things, both in life and in death; things spontaneously come and take their leave because Dao enables their doing so without predetermination or resistance. The dance of death is thus a cosmic dance of life. They are both required in order to maintain unity and harmony throughout the universe, for without such harmony there will only be chaos and the disingenuous virtue of petty men. And so, king Wenhui is able to learn of the cosmic rhythm of the world and the nourishment of life praxis through cook Ding's un-letting of oxen.

Having wandered within the ox, Ding can now rest, his whirlwind of activity finished. Such carefree wandering was neither aimless nor purposive but the spontaneous wandering of universal harmony. Gathering himself up, sheathing his knife, he is now able to regain his formal, empirical-self. This is not to say he had somehow 'lost his self,'[45] for this would imply he had forgotten the world and himself, making him nothing more than a spiritual essence. To experience nothingness is to enhance one's sensory abilities; it is not a honing and refinement but, rather, an expansion and increased clarity of one's role in the cosmic dance already underway. To rest is to rejuvenate one's spirit, absorb Dao's nourishment, and protect one's allotted years. Endless effort—stressing of body and mind—can only lead to early death, thus Zhuangzi advises against such artificial life praxis. Without rest, cook Ding cannot close the dance, cannot complete the circle of being and nothingness. One must know at what speed and when to emerge or risk exhausting one's life energy; this is known as the balancing of life-forces, or the equality of things.

Yet the dance goes on despite cook Ding's need to rest. He who is in touch with Dao is always at rest, for what worries could possibly touch his heart? Rest is a figurative condition. Do we rest differently when awake than asleep? Zhuangzi is quick to criticize the goings-on of the Confucians and Mohists, their obsession with laying claim to the Way of things. Knowing one's true place in the universe, one can rest with such knowledge. To labor one's body and mind is to exhaust one's given breath of life. Knowing when to stop and let things be is a trait we see expressed in all of the characters esteemed by Zhuangzi. To let things be is to know the heavenly principle of things. Resting, therefore, should not be regarded as a period of non-doing; on the contrary, to rest is to spontaneously stop doing—a purposeful undoing. Everything in the universe needs rest, needs a moment to rejuvenate and self-compose. Without rest, Ding's butchery would be never-ending—never complete—and his art of undoing oxen would be nothing more than mere butchery, unconnected to Dao and unworthy of the king's appraisal.[46]

Cook Ding maintains the sharpness of his knife by utilizing the thinness of the blade to enter the gaps and spaces between the ox's joints and bones, but do such pockets of nothingness exist within wood? They certainly do. What is ingenious about the stories of Ding and woodcarver Qing, our next example, is that they both make use of knives as their tool of choice. The edge of Ding's knife is a thicklessness entering nothingness and the edge of Qing's chisel is no different. Both are tools of opposite dependency: one on hardness, the other softness. Qing's chisel edge is a nothingness that penetrates the emptiness of the air pockets within the wood, thereby releasing the wood of its own dependency. Like the ox, wood is bound together by the voids within; pockets of nothingness that define the physicality of its substance. Should the amount of applied pressure be equal to the force of resistance, the wood will shear off. If not, it will either hold or split into fragments. It becomes a matter of balancing what is known with what is unknown—the achievement of natural harmony—the cultivation of which nourishes one's life. This is known as matching the heavenly with the heavenly and is the core point of the woodcarver Qing story:

> Woodcarver Qing was carving a bell stand and when it was complete, those who saw it were shocked, thinking it the work of the supernatural. The marquis of Lu saw it and queried, "By what technique did you carve this?" to which Qing answered, "I am just a laborer, what technique could I possibly have! There is one thing though. When I am preparing to make a bell stand, I do not let it wear out my energy. I compose myself[47] in order to still my mind. After composing myself for three days, I no longer yearn for praise or rewards, for titles or stipends. After composing myself for five days, I no longer yearn for praise or blame, for cunning or awkwardness. Having composed myself for seven days, I forget I have four limbs and a body. At that moment, the ruler and court cease to exist and with my technique focused, all outward distractions

disappear. Afterwards, I enter the mountain forest, observing the heavenly nature of the tress. If I discover one of supreme form and can envision a bell stand within, I add my hand to the task, otherwise I let it be. This is to join the heavenly with the heavenly and is perhaps the reason why people say my talent is nothing short of marvelous."[48]

Reading about Qing's talent, we notice that although the material and craft has changed from that of cook Ding, the means of attaining life praxis is the same. The secret to self-cultivation and life-preservation lies in overcoming the desire for fame and wealth, logical distinctions, and viewing oneself as separated from Dao. It is because of this intuitive perspectivalism that we can dismiss the mysticism of encountering nothingness. What can easily be interpreted as a meditative, spiritual exercising of the mind is actually not so. Although in later texts such as the *Huainanzi* and the Daoist chapters of the *Guanzi* we see clear examples of spiritually meditative techniques, in the *Zhuangzi* there is little evidence for such speculation. Being receptive to the meontological character of Dao entails a *composing* rather than a *fasting* of the mind. This composing is a sorting out, an attempt to quiet the mind by way of emotional uniformity. It must be said that such uniformity of emotion should not be regarded as disinterest, nor should we look upon it as a form of mental sterility. Zhuangzi is not implying that the people of the world should become automatons; rather, what is needed is harmony.

One composes (*qi* 齊) oneself so that one's mind may become quiescent (*jingxin* 静心) and one's *qi* will not be consumed (*haoqi* 耗氣); this is nourishment of life praxis. After three days, woodcarver Qing had reached the level of cook Ding's common man, still seeing the entire object through which he hacks and pounds. It takes another two days for Qing to reach the level of a skilled man, seeing things in their component parts but slicing and cutting nonetheless. It takes a full seven days, equivalent to Ding's three years, to be able to dance with Dao and reach the level of Nanguo Ziqi sitting in a stupor of self-abandonment. Indeed, the ideal state of living described throughout the *Zhuangzi* is succinctly summed in the stories being discussed here. Self-importance is the destroyer of self-cultivation just as wealth and titles are an unwelcomed guest that will inevitably cut short one's years. The idea is to go beyond such petty measures, to look past the artificiality of society and return to living in harmony with the heavenly principle of things, or Dao. Forgetting one's outwardness, the preferential treatment we accord our limbs and body falls by the wayside to the extent that one becomes a being of non-mind. Only when one learns to see with the eyes of Dao can one proceed with one's craft of perfectibility.

Entering the forest, woodcarver Qing uses what is of heaven to seek out the heavenly. He then begins a dance of his own, using the vision of heaven to spy-out the material of heaven. What is of interest to the woodcarver is not the beauty of the tree itself, or even the utility of its wood; the central question becomes whether or not a particular tree has within its inborn nature the means to actualize a bell stand. By allowing the tree to realize what is inherently its own potentiality, woodcarver Qing makes use of it without deliberately doing so. This is one of the central themes we see repeated throughout the *Zhuangzi*, and in the case of trees, stories of master carpenters abound.[49] Indeed, the cultivation of life praxis is all about deliberate non-action, of letting things undo themselves in a manner best suited to their constitution. Knowing when to stop—when to let things be—serves the same purpose as getting use out of something through its apparent non-use. The idea of useful uselessness is not unique to the woodcarver though. For the common carpenter, the only thing useful about a tree is its wood. For a good carpenter, the quality of the wood in terms of both its aesthetic and structural properties is critical. The master carpenter, however, sees in the useless tree a full spectrum of potentiality: the shade it provides, the sound it makes in the blowing wind, the variety of creatures making it their place of abode, the safety offered by its branches, the strength and depth of its roots, and so on. In other words, they are aware of the entire ecosystem encircling each and every tree.

Certain trees are best used for certain applications, just as certain knives are designed for particular types of cutting. As a manifestation of Dao, trees serve no other purpose than to be themselves. Those deemed useful by man are cut down while the useless are left untouched. Which of these does carpenter Qing prefer? Trees that flower and produce fruit are treasured for their beauty while trees whose wood is strong and sturdy are treasured for their utility. Being a follower of Dao, Qing chooses neither the beautiful nor the utilitarian, preferring a tree whose existence adheres to its self-so nature rather than human standards. To seek out the heavenly in a forest of trees, Qing must himself be in possession of the heavenly and we see the steps he takes to obtain it. These steps are repeated in different guises throughout the *Zhuangzi* but what is common to them all is the idea of cultivating one's life praxis based on the guidance of Dao. It is an attuning of oneself, not to the concerns of humanity, but to the cosmos in such a way that the empirical-self loses any sway over how one engages the things of the world. This is what is known as unlearning knowledge—of adhering to simplicity—and such cultivation is what lends a sense of humbleness to Zhuangzi's worldview.

In the remaining two stories, we are further enlightened as to the means of self-cultivation in order to bring oneself into harmony with the universe. The first tale involves an encounter between Confucius and a catcher of cicadas:

> On his way to the state of Chu, Confucius was passing through a forest when he saw a hunchback catching cicadas with a pole as easily as if he were catching them by hand.[50] Confucius said, "What talent! Is there a special technique you use?" The hunchback replied, "There is. For the first five or six months, I practice with two small balls (on the end of a stick) until they ceased to fall off but even then, I still lost some cicadas. I then tried with three balls and I only lost one cicada in ten. Having succeeded with five balls, I caught them as if I were grabbing them with my hand. My body is like a broken tree trunk and my arms like withered tree branches. No matter how great are heaven and earth, how numerous the myriad things, I am only aware of cicada wings. Not rocking, not inclining, I do not allow any of the myriad things to take the place of my cicada wings—how can I not succeed?" Confucius turned to his disciples saying, "If you concentrate all of your will you, too, can attain the level of spirit—this is how we should refer to our gentleman the hunchback."[51]

The second story is another example of a master craftsman, this time a maker of belt-buckles:

> The Ministry of War's ironsmith[52] was eighty years old and had not lost the slightest edge in his ability. The chancellor said, "What skill you have! Is there a technique to it?" "There is. Since I was twenty years old, I have loved forging belt-buckles; I look at nothing else. If it is not a belt-buckle, I take no notice of it." To use something without formally using it, one will over time obtain some use from it; how much more so will he who uses nothing! What things will not come to depend on him![53]

Analyzing the two tales, we can declare our hunchback to be a magical character who dances an acrobatic ballet. It is surprising to see how easily one whose body is so contorted can become a contortionist! He contorts himself to appear as a dead, withered tree; a tree that is dead yet attracts life. Cicadas die only to be reborn. They molt, shedding their former selves in exchange for new ones. Thus the cicada exemplifies the usefulness of the useless; how obtaining use from something can be obtained without deliberately using it. Their skin has a purpose yet at a certain moment in time, that purpose expires. With their skin now rendered useless, the cicada is forced to shed it in exchange for one that is useful. It undergoes a transformation from usefulness to uselessness to being useful once again. By not deliberately exerting the useful quality of its skin, the cicada is able to nurture its life. Knowing when cicadas emerge from the ground, the hunchback anticipates their arrival and so the uselessness of time also finds a use.

The dance of the hunchback is a solitary, unmoving dance; it is a dance of life imitating death in order to lure life! In order to lure cicadas to his position, he adjusts his constitution to compliment that of the cicadas. Using the method of no-method, letting the cicadas come to him rather than chasing them, he is able to preserve his inborn nature while fulfilling those of the cicadas. The hunchback's stick is the chisel of the woodcarver, the knife of the cook. They are apparatuses for the manifestation of Dao—useless in and of themselves yet of great use in the hands of a master. Concentrating his mind such that nothing but cicada wings exist, it would be hard indeed not to catch them! In this regard, our hunchback does not use the heavenly to seek out the heavenly, as woodcarver Qing does; rather, we can place him in cook Ding's frame of mind by letting his spirit replace his dependency on physical sensation. This replacement of sensory dependency is not a numbing of the senses however. With a body like a broken tree trunk and arms like withered branches, the hunchback disguises his vitality by concentrating and allowing it to consume him.

We should be careful not to confuse concentration of spirit for spiritualized spirit; the former is a spirit of natural harmony, a state of freedom exclusive to one who wanders in the nothingness of Dao. Such a multi-variant outlook is central to Zhuangzi's understanding of how the natural world ought to be perceived and explains how the ironsmith is able to use things without actually using them, benefiting from the experience in the process. What the sage does is precisely this; he allows others to come to him and benefits from their doing so. For the man who makes belt-buckles his entire life, there is no visible gain to be had, only a knowledge of how to make belt-buckles. In fact, he has obtained much more than that. Be it making belt-buckles or swords, the ironsmith must still reach a level of knowing that is similar to cook Ding's. Knowing is not knowledge, for knowledge is what blocks us from following Dao. Knowing is a knack, an intuition, a veritable awakening of all bodily senses through interaction with nothingness, allowing the spirit to concentrate and harmonize with heavenly principle. This is where some scholars of the *Zhuangzi* mistake holistic sensory awakening for mysticism. The catcher of cicadas and the maker of belt-buckles preserve their vitality during the manufacture of real-world objects. That these objects are useless in and of themselves is beside the point; what Zhuangzi is emphasizing is the journey, not the outcome.

The hunchback catches cicadas as if he were grabbing them out of the air with his hands because he understands their Way. He commits himself to learning the art of disengaging the human side of his mind so that he may free the Dao-mind locked within. Making his body appear as dead wood and withered branches, his mind becomes still and quiet. Such quietude is vital if one wishes to enter into oneness with things, for only a mind in said condition is receptive to Dao. With the mind quiet and one's spiritual vitality focused, all possibilities of knowing are made available. This is what Zhuangzi means by cosmic harmony.

We began this discussion with the violent dissection of oxen and rounded it out with talk of bell stands and cicadas. We progressed from the taking of life to its reception; from the nourishment of others through death to the joy received in witnessing the transformation of birth. Discarding our vices and judgmental tendencies, we can look upon the beings of the world as they exist of themselves. To dance to the cosmic harmony of Dao is to experience the nothingness that transcends all forms of language and perception. In the act of letting-be we are able to effect change, one that elevates our presence of being to the level of cosmic oneness and perfectibility. Nourishing life in such a manner is to live out one's natural lifespan by wandering carefree in the world without imposing or depending upon anything other than following the way of Dao.

The tale of cook Ding is a fuller development and elaboration of the opening passage on the danger in using what is limited to pursue the limitless. Knowing that our life is finite, one should stay the middle course and not endlessly chase after the infinite. Being infinite, it is unknowable; being unknowable, one cannot possibly grasp it using what is known. Said differently, one should use the unknown to comprehend the known and not use the known to pursue the unknown. This is the heavenly nature of things and forms the basis of Zhuangzi's discussion on life praxis.

Every ox, bell stand, and belt-buckle is a metaphor for the inner potentiality of human virtue. Every time we carve one of them, we carve our ethical selves in such a way that our fate unfolds along the axis of heavenly principle. This points to the methodless method of Daoism. Such praxis, however, is also a mutual echoing of others. King Wenhui learned from his cook just as the cook learned from undoing oxen. The king interpreted the words of his cook along the patterning of heaven, undoing them as Ding undid the ox. In other words, the uselessness of the words spoken by cook Ding became useful for king Wenhui in that they nourishingly steered him toward the middle path, illuminating the adjustments required to respond to and prolong life by way of his own self-encountering with Dao. And so, the lesson Zhuangzi teaches us is that we are all at one time or another a cook Ding or a king Wenhui; here a master, there a disciple. Only in the oneness of Dao can we blur the distinction between the two and enter the vibrant, magical world that Zhuangzi took such pains to bring to our attention.

Conclusion

As we begin to delve ever deeper into the thought of the *Zhuangzi*, we are slowly unraveling the mystery that has enshrouded it for many readers. Being able to differentiate Dao from the One not only proved to be a productive exercise, it set forth the theory that Dao generates the Thing which, in turn, lends itself to the myriad things we know and interact with on a daily basis. Dao, in other words, imbues the Thing with the potential to replicate itself as other things and when at such time this potential has run its course, things return not to Dao, but to the Thing. In their togetherness, they are one and the One is not only a collectivity of Things, it symbolizes the oneness of all things. What unites things in their oneness is the potentiality of Dao coursing through them. Of course, this potential for life and death is but a trace, a trace of the traceless nothingness that is the root of the universe itself.

The stories we examined of men whose harmonization with Dao was so complete it enabled them to engage the things of the world in such a comprehensively holistic manner that they no longer saw the world from a human standpoint but through the eyes of Dao. When everything around him is in constant flux, how is the sage able to return to the constancy of Dao? Indeed, is it even appropriate to think of Dao in temporal terms when doing so would bring it into the world of human norms? These are some of the issues awaiting our attention in the next chapter.

3

Dao and the Time of Nothingness

This chapter continues with our investigation into the *Zhuangzi*'s meontological language of Dao by turning to its temporal nature, disputing the idea that time is bound to ontological being. This stems from the fact that the *Zhuangzi* did not subscribe to the impermanence of time in light of the death of the subject, nor did it hold to the belief that time's movement is linear and whose fulcrum is the lived-time of the here-and-now. This is not to say that the text views time in absolutist terms; rather, the non-temporality of Dao manifests itself through the corporeal signification of the myriad things. Not only does this eliminate the subjectivist nature of time, it releases it from the bonds of human consciousness and world formation. The goal, then, is not to flee time in light of the reputed nihilism that is a thing's impending death, but to relinquish the need for temporal duration altogether so as to return to the undifferentiated oneness of Dao.

We shall, therefore, not only explicate the *Zhuangzi*'s conception of time but also address how the human perception of it can be incorporated into the cosmological milieu without any form of dialectic. We will soon realize, however, that the pivot of time lies not in the present-now but in the resting of nothingness. The restful nature of nothingness thus becomes a critical vantage point from which to perceive the passage of time, for only from the perspective of the unmoving hub can we see the rotation of a wheel's spokes, from the vantage point of perpetual Dao can we notice the flow of finite beings. Because of this, the present chapter will put forth a reformulation of the traditional notion of time so as to reflect the meontological undercurrent of Dao and from this new theoretical envisioning, authentic time (i.e., the non-time of Dao) will come to pass as the norm of creation *qua* rest. By engaging time via creation *qua* rest, we can thus uncover the *Zhuangzi*'s definition of time while grasping its cosmological and static (i.e., human) orders too.

Dao and Cosmological Time

Before entering into a discussion of what time means for the *Zhuangzi*, it seems pertinent to first lay forth the connection between cosmogenesis and temporality. This step is necessary because the two states of existence are not mutually inclusive. Cosmogenesis differs from temporality insofar as it is a mark of a non-temporal universe populated by ontological nothingness and Dao. A time of undifferentiated wholeness, or chaos, it bore witness to the birth of the One and the eventual formation of the Thing. It was during this time—a time before time—when each Thing was unseparated from its derivatives. Dao's virtue had yet to be despoiled and everything was in a state of harmonious unity. Only after the classifications "non-being" and "being" had arisen did we then witness the commencement of temporality. And yet, to brand the temporality of being as also applicable to nothingness would be to take what is inclusive to time and apply it to that which is exclusive. Things exist in the world and the world is a temporal body, however, the temporality of the world cannot reach either the One or Dao for they dwell in the dark mystery of ontological nothingness. The *Zhuangzi*, as we saw earlier, described the formation of the universe along these lines:

> It may enter and emerge but one cannot see its form. This is called the Gate of Heaven. The Gate of Heaven is nothingness and it is from here that the myriad things emerge. Being cannot use being to create being, it must arise from non-being; however, non-being is itself nothingness.[1]
>
> 入出而無見其形，是謂天門。天門者，無有也，萬物出乎無有。
> 有不能以有為有，必出乎無有，而無有一無有。

When we look at two other examples, the first written before the *Zhuangzi*, the second after, we are presented with more vivid descriptions. The first example takes us to the *Hengxian*:

> *Heng* precedes being and non-being; it is simple, quiescent, and empty. Being simple, it is Great Simplicity; being quiescent, it

is Great Quiescence; being empty, it is Great Emptiness. Not liking to stay contained within itself, it thus gave rise to space. Given the presence of this realm of space there was *qi*, with *qi* things came into being, with the birth of things there was beginning, and with beginning there came to be passing away.²

恒先無有，樸，靜，虛。樸，太樸；靜，太靜；虛，太虛。自厭不自忍，或作。有或焉有氣，有氣焉有有，有有焉有始，有始焉有往者。

The second example is from the *Four Classics of the Yellow Emperor*:

At the beginning of constant nothingness, there was only Great Emptiness. Since emptiness is equal to oneness, the constant stopped at the One. Misty and indistinct, it was neither bright nor dark. Its spirit was subtle yet pervasive, its *qi* quiescent yet dim. Thus things cannot come to be without it; formless, it reaches everywhere while remaining nameless.³

恒無之初，迵同大虛。虛同為一，恒一而止。濕濕夢夢，未有明晦。神微周盈，精靜不熙。古未有以，萬物莫以。古無有刑，大迵無名。

What is intriguing about these passages is the variation with which they describe the progenitor of things, and the condition of the universe in which it dwells. We see three names ascribed to the progenitor (Dao, the constant, constant nothingness) and two related to the state of the universe (great emptiness, that which precedes non-being and being). Each series of names within their particular grouping are synonymous with one another. What is more, it would be quite easy to misconstrue the second pairing of names as describing the object of the first triad. Needless to say, they are in agreement that cosmic time did not start with a thing-in-itself but with Dao's emergence amidst a field of nothingness whose unspoiled, unperturbed nature proved fertile ground for the primal chaos that ensued thereafter. Nothingness as empty equanimity thus gave rise to the realization of that which is Ultimate and beyond knowing—Dao as Great Simplicity, Emptiness, and Quiescence. These are the qualities of Dao at the time of its awakening while characterizing a universe bereft of being, and explains why the *Zhuangzi* argued that Dao itself is not to be thought of in terms of thing and no-thing.⁴

We face a theoretical dilemma however. In agreeing that the universe was originally non-temporal and indiscriminate—a nothingness whose silent emptiness was unperturbed by anything other than its own self-reckoning—there appears a divergence of opinion on how to explain the transition from non-temporal nothingness to pre-temporal chaos. At the end of chapter 1, we discussed this transition in terms of a thing's return to its Thing within the One, while the beginning of chapter 2 examined it from the perspective of the Thing's becoming. The issue that now comes to light has to do with the order in which things, including space and time, emerge from the primal chaos of the One. For the *Hengxian*, Dao created space and this space was filled with the *qi* of Dao. The filling of space with the *qi* of Dao led to the birth of things and the start of temporality. And yet, *qi* does not belong to time but changes according to the spontaneous tendencies of Dao.[5] Space, therefore, is simply the milieu in which the essence of Dao proclaims itself to itself. We may thus characterize space as the spreading forth of Dao's nature and is what we have been referring to throughout this work as the empty, still quiescence of ontological nothingness. The *Zhuangzi* supports this idea, as we saw at the start of chapter 2, by associating nothingness with the pre-temporal universe. Rather than quote that passage for a third time, we can turn to the "*tianwen* 天文" chapter of the *Huainanzi* for additional insight:

When heaven and earth were without form, all was colliding vigorously, mingling imperceptibly, and was thus known as the Great Illumination. Dao began in an empty void, the empty void gave birth to the universe, and the universe gave birth to *qi*.[6]

天墜未形，馮馮翼翼，洞洞灟灟，故曰太昭。道始于虛廓，虛廓生宇宙，宇宙生氣。

When it comes to describing Dao, the most common terms include: Great Illumination (*taizhao* 太昭), Great Simplicity (*taipu* 太樸), Great Quiescence (*taijing* 太靜), and Great Emptiness (*taixu* 太虛). Cosmic time entails the embodiment of these virtuous qualities and nothing more; it is a time in which Dao self-completes itself by going forth without ever retaining anything. Although the *Zhuangzi* does not speak of the *qi* of Dao in the context of cosmological time, texts such as the *Hengxian*, *Four Classics of the Yellow Emperor*, and *Huainanzi* did. This proves to be an inconsequential omission because these texts all supported the notion that nothingness props up Dao while Dao equalizes the myriad things via its own oneness. What is more, these texts were also of the opinion that time could only take hold once the universe lost its empty, indiscriminate nature. Indeed, the *Liezi* can be said to offer the most explicit account:

> If the formed is born of the formless, then where do heaven and earth come from? Therefore it is said: There are [the states of] Great Change, Great Origin, Great Beginning, and Great Simplicity. Great Change is the state before *qi*'s formation while Great Origin marks its beginning. Great Beginning is the demarcation of forms while Great Simplicity is the start of their particular characteristics.[7]
>
> 夫有形者生於無形,則天地安從生? 故曰: 有太易, 有太初, 有太始, 有太素。太易者, 未見氣也; 太初者, 氣之始也; 太始者, 形之始也; 太素者, 質之始也。

What is interesting to note about the above is the temporal order ascribed to the cosmos as it slowly unfolds from primal nothingness toward ontic being. We also cannot but notice the *Liezi*'s call for *qi* to partake in a series of transformational states (origin, beginning, simplicity) whereby each serves as a means to an end while furthering its own onto-cosmological evolution. The comingling of these states can, therefore, be seen as a variation of the *Zhuangzi*'s idea of primal chaos.[8] The Great Change is thus equivalent to *heng* 恆, which, as we have said, is itself an alternative name for Dao. Given the procession of pre-phenomenological activity that comes to define the recognizable universe, and that time is thought of as the penultimate stage before the appearance of ontic beings, we should be careful to avoid describing said time as empty.

For Zhuangzi, the question is not so much how we ought to characterize the presence of time in relation to human experience, but that we perceive its true nature as an absolute operating within the infinite spatiality of nothingness. What this means is that cosmological time is rendered inferior and incomplete when compared to the non-time of Dao in that for every moment of measurable human time, there has already elapsed an infinite amount of Dao time. The universe thus lies within a temporal framework whose boundary is not created by humanity but is enshrouded in the perpetuity of nothingness.[9] This is why the nature of Dao lies beyond the realm of time, for to imply otherwise would mean that the non-time in which it is situated is bound to something other than itself, rendering impossible the idea that things are born from nothingness and their becoming and returning are subject to yet a higher source, resulting in a repetitive loop of infinite magnitude.

While the *Zhuangzi* does not deny the existence of the human experience of time, any authentic encounter would have to be traced back to that which existed prior to humanity's empirical measurement of time. We can thus argue that the authentic, non-temporal nature of Dao is a kind of *heng*-time, albeit one that elapses at a pace so uniform as to be unfathomable. Additionally, the *Zhuangzi* espoused the belief that time is without an absolute beginning or end, and since it takes such endless unfolding to comprise the authentic time of Dao, so Dao time is a by-product of its own arising. Cosmological time is thus neither transcendental nor idealistic but meontological. It can neither flow towards the future nor come to comprise a series of points whose collectivity results in the present-now. Time, simply put, is the potential of Dao within the negative creativity of nothingness:

> Things cannot avoid being born before they are born and cannot resist dying when they are already dead. Death and life are close to one another, yet their principle cannot be seen ... I look for its root but it extends back without end. I search for its end but it stretches on without stopping. Without ending or stopping, having no room for words, this is the shared principle of things ... Dao cannot be taken as having being, for if it did, it could not be taken as also having nothingness. To call it Dao is hence but a temporary measure.[10]

> 未生不可忌，已死不可阻。死生非遠也，理不可覩……吾觀之本，其往無窮; 吾求之末，其來無止。無窮無止，言之無也，與物同理……道不可有，有不可無，道之為名，所假而行。

The shared principle of things is thus traceable to the boundless possibilities of Dao. Fundamental events such as death and life arise within the ever-present milieu of cosmological time and yet, the *Zhuangzi* does not regard it as being *a priori* or purely intuitive, for doing so would imply that time is empty. Wherein the *Zhuangzi* was able to counter the assertion that any conception of time preceding the presence of a cognitive mind must be fallacious stems from the ever-present state of Dao. Cosmological time is perpetual, not because the very notion of it possesses eternal properties, but that the ever-lasting nature of Dao envelops time in the darkness of its own mysteriousness. The time that marks the presence of Dao thus acts as the backdrop for the ontological time of the Thing and is the root from which the branches of human causal time arise. The latter is, therefore, static insofar as it is but a pinned marker of our existence against the ever-dynamic constancy of Dao. If we wish to compare the time of our being to that of Dao, it is better, the *Zhuangzi* argues, to use something of a higher order; this is accomplished by holding it against the meontological fertility of nothingness.

Although Dao is perpetual and persists beyond the realm of time, it is nevertheless a spontaneous, self-enacting existence. It would, therefore, be easy to criticize Zhuangzi's argument that one can go further and further back in time *ad infinitum* as an example of empty time and yet, what undercuts the standing of such an argument is the fact that Dao is inseparable from the meontological nature of the universe. Though the universe continues to exist after Dao first created it, it is not a self-propagating body; it falls to Dao to continuously inject life into it. Thus the circular movement of springing forth and retreating makes it impossible to claim that Dao exists either within or beyond time; for Dao, there is only nothingness.

To speak of cosmological time as intuited becoming—a self-negating of that which is already past due to its becoming a futural other—is to think of time as a static, abstract entity whose potential pales in comparison to the creative possibilities of nothingness. Cosmological time hence involves a predicated intuiting of a single potential becoming amongst a myriad potential becomings. In order to exist unbounded by human intentionality, cosmological time must be left to its own devices so as to engage the things of the world in a non-temporal, empty manner. Knowing that things emerge from the non-differentiated darkness of Dao, they are at their most natural level when left temporally indistinct. However, those beings whose existence assumes an air of temporality due to their emerging from the One must overcome said temporality if they are to have any hope of returning to the oneness of Dao. Zhuangzi illustrates:

Nanbo Zikui said, "Can Dao be learned?"

Nuyu replied: ". . . only when one perceives one's solitude can one abolish the distinctions of past and present; only when one has abolished the distinctions of past and present can one enter the realm where there is neither death nor life. That which destroys life does not die; that which gives birth to life does not live. Given this, there is nothing it does not support, nothing it does not welcome. There is nothing it does not destroy, nothing it does not complete. Its name is known as disturbance within tranquility. In disturbance within tranquility, there must first be disturbance before there can be completion."[11]

南伯子葵曰: 道可得學邪? 女偊曰: ⋯⋯見獨, 而後能無古今; 無古今, 而後能入於不死不生。殺生者不死, 生生者不生。其為物, 無不將也, 無不迎也; 無不毀也, 無不成也。其名為攖寧。攖寧也者, 攖而後成者也。

In the above passage, Nuyu's response to Zikui not only expounds the process by which one returns to Dao, she also explicates Zhuangzi's theory of cosmological temporality. The Western tradition tends to base many of its normative values on the alternation of life and death, regardless of how we classify them ethically. We associate being with life and non-being with death, and for obvious reasons; however, for someone who has attained clarity of mind and takes shelter in the ultimacy of Dao, all divisions blend into a collective wholeness while oppositional distinctions merge to become complimentary pairings. The sage sees his place in the world as clearly as he sees the morning sun—his self has morphed into a non-self whose reflection spreads throughout all other selves. As he recognizes the benefit to be had in the non-presence of being, the sage returns to the manifold of cosmological oneness.

United with Dao and all non-manifest beings, time for the sage is a misnomer—a contrivance of the human mind—as are the categories of non-being and being. Thus forgetting the distinctions of past and present, the sage wanders in the realm where life and death are equalized and rendered moot. The Heavenly Gate was for Zhuangzi what the wheel hub was for Laozi: a place where all things come together in tranquil harmony. Though things enter and leave the world through it, the gate itself remains unchanged; though the spokes are what give a wheel its motion, the hub is unperturbed. Things are as such due to their inborn nature and this inborn nature bestowed upon them by Dao is timeless. The traditional argument that things move from not-yet-being to coming-to-pass is hence problematic, if not invalid, for what remains constant is the meontological nature of Dao while that which undergoes change in time is the ontic form of things.

Cosmological time is thus a measuring of the plenum of Dao's possibilities whose principle is ultimately unknowable. The course of transformation experienced by things is not due to the action of time but their inborn nature reflecting the way of Dao. To anthropomorphize time is to imbue it with qualities that are alien to it. Thus as things transmogrify from the darkness of primal chaos to the brightness of their being as the Thing, such transformation should not be taken as evidence of a process of continual self-negation so as to conform to the sequence of past, present, and future; on the contrary, it symbolizes the invariable and holistic breadth of Dao.

When the *Zhuangzi* speaks of a thing in the past it does not cease to be in the present-now, and when the text speaks of a thing in the future, said thing's former self in the here-and-now likewise does not fall by the wayside. To speak of time as the principle of motion such that it becomes inseparable from motion, thereby implying that on a higher plane, it is in fact an eternal absolute, is to deny it any meontological merit. Zhuangzi's cosmology forbids such a closed reading of time, as does the *Daodejing*, which says: "One can know of the earliest of beginnings and this is called the thread of Dao."[12] The universe did not begin with time but empty stillness, a nebula of dark nothingness comprising a timelessness unbeknownst to any but Dao. Given that Dao existed before the concept of time, if we wish to know the true origin of things we must follow Dao to trace their root back to primal nothingness. Tracing a thing's root from its now time to its yet-to-be time of undifferentiated chaos is, in effect, using the mystery of Dao to harmonize with the oneness of things. Wang Bi explained the thread analogy of the *Daodejing* stated above in this way:

> What is without form or name is the ancestor of the myriad things. Although present and past are different, and customs change with the times, there are none who succeeded in bringing about order except for it. Thus one can grasp the Dao of old so as to administer that which exists today. While high antiquity seems remotely distant, its Dao still exists today. Although one is here now, it is thus possible to know of the earliest of beginnings.[13]

> 無形無名者，萬物之宗也。雖今古不同，時移俗易，故莫不由乎此，以成其治者也。故可執古之道，以御今之有，上古雖遠，其道存焉，故雖在，今可以知古始也。

Based on the above, we can surmise that the Dao of old and the Dao of today are engaged in a relationship unlike any other in the universe. It would be easy to say they are one and the same, which would make them absolute, forever unchanging and incapable of uniquely affecting things.

The Dao of today is not a replica of that of old in the sense that Western thinkers have in mind when they view time as a series of now-points strung together for the duration of a being's lived experience. Instead, the Dao of old persists for eternity as that original Dao. There can be no before or after in an ontologically temporal sense since before and after have no bearing on the cohesiveness of primal oneness. This is why the *Zhuangzi* declared:

> Dao has neither end nor beginning but things have their death and birth, hence they cannot be relied on for completion. Now empty, now full, they do not adhere to one form. Years past cannot be repeated, and time cannot be stopped. Decay and growth, fullness and emptiness, each one ends and then begins anew. It is from this that we discuss the method of Great Meaning and debate the principle of the myriad things. As for the life of things, it is similar to a galloping horse: with each movement, there is change; with each moment of time, things alter. What should you do? What should you not do? One should simply allow for self-transformation.[14]

> 道無終始，物有死生，不恃其成；一虛一滿，不位乎其形。年不可舉，時不可止；消息盈虛，終則有始。是所以語大義之方，論萬物之理也。物之生也，若驟若馳，無動而不變，無時而不移。何為乎，何不為乎？夫固將自化。

Humanity has its allotted lifespan but compared to a thousand-year-old tree, of what significance is a hundred years, the measure of human longevity? We constantly wish to transcend the limits of our finitude but to what end? Time cannot be transcended because its impermanence lies in a realm wholly beyond our capacity to comprehend; such is why the sage stands outside of human time but within the non-temporality of Dao. What this means is that all things emanating from the One have a self-sameness that is pervasive without being exclusionary. The act of becoming, therefore, becomes a node of quiescence through which creation is achieved. In this regard, becoming in the form of creation *qua* rest can avoid being labeled a process insofar as it preserves the spontaneous potential of Dao on the one hand, while remaining non-temporal on the other. The by-product of becoming is of course temporally tinged; however, until the Thing begets its ontic things, its envelopment by the One keeps it in a quasi-temporal state of being. When the *Zhuangzi* says we ought to discuss the method of Great Meaning and the principle of the myriad things, it was pointing to the circularity between the indistinct time of the One and the atemporality of Dao.

In this way, all things in the universe come together as multiple threads of the oneness of Dao. Oneness is thus an undifferentiated harmony, a blending together of collective Things whose things have yet to break through the realm of non-being and enter their ontic reality of time and form. Being nondescript in appearance and indiscriminate in action, the mixing of the myriad things so as to comprise primal oneness is spontaneously natural in its ordering. Things are derived from the Thing, the Thing traces itself back to the One, the One arises due to the working of Dao, and Dao finds its home in the ontological nothingness of the universe. In this way, the *Zhuangzi*'s cosmology is not temporally grounded but rooted in the quiet stillness of meontological non-time. It is a cosmology whose unfolding is best described as anti-processional and nonlinear. In other words, the connectedness of things is not due to their presence in a particular series of now-moments but to the perpetually productive receptivity of Dao.

To limit any cosmology of time to the corporeally real would be to damage the holistic nature of the universe. Although Dao is constant, time is not. The possibility to arrest moments of time and designate them as we temporally see fit comes about thanks to the presence of nothingness. Past, present, and future are merely placeholders for the human ordering of the natural world. Within the realm of Dao *qua* ultimate reality, such designations become absurd. The causal time that is the lived-time of humanity is in fact but the spontaneous fulfillment of a particular possibility of human time come to light. Non-being and being, not-yet-beginning and beginning, are but two variations of the same happenstance. Knowing that Dao's perpetuity roots itself in the empty quietude of nothingness, whether or not one proceeds backwards or forwards in time, the outcome remains unaffected. The infinite regresses that we often encounter throughout the *Zhuangzi* are but metaphorical fishhooks intended to grab our attention and show us the error of holding onto time as a linear, being-centric movement.

If we wish to attain the holistic freedom Zhuangzi postulates through successfully harmonizing with Dao, we must accept the idea that the time of our lived-presence is beyond our control; we can no more relive the past than we can advance to the future. The time bestowed upon us, indeed, that given to all things, owes itself to its self-so nature. This self-so nature of things is but a sprout from Dao's root—it bursts forth and dies off without anyone knowing why it is so. The alternation of the seasons occurs not because they will it upon themselves, but because Dao instills in them the temporal acuity to do so. The myriad things of the world are the spokes that tie into the unmoving hub of the One, and the oneness of the hub is constituted of the dark stillness of nothingness. Motion reverts to non-motion and the propagation of becoming is countered by a returning to the naught. Through its non-deliberateness, Dao allows things to be created of their own doing—a feat only possible because of the centrality bestowed upon rest.

Dao's becoming can be regarded as creation *qua* rest because only when things are at ease do they forget their relational-self and revert to a condition of authenticity. Having coalesced around their authentic selves, things complete their naturally allotted years unburdened by the artificial passing of time. Their coming and going and endless cycles of transformation cannot hide the fact that beneath it all, there is the meontological constancy of Dao. To this end, we can conclude that the *Zhuangzi*'s notion of cosmic time is a theory that, when set against the unknowable nature of Dao, dispels the illusion of an *a priori* temporality in order to reveal its dependence on the non-temporal, non-spatial character of nothingness. If we are to accept the idea that cosmic time is a reflection of the restful silence of ontological nothingness, then we can also accept the definition of time as the symbolic representation of the creational moment of our coming-to-be. Such becoming is a durational moment whose temporality is not bound to the presentness of our being, but to the thread of oneness that binds all things together. In this regard, time is a timeless duration; its meontological structure can only follow that of Dao. We can no more personalize time than we can attach to it a label of intention. In the section that follows, we will see how this can pose difficulties for anyone hoping to identify with a particular moment of time and yet, our definition of time is a means by which to overcome the inherent dilemma facing human causal time by abandoning designations of past, present, and future so as to uncover a phenomenology of time contained in the physical being of things.

Human Measured Time

Now that we have come to terms with time in a cosmological sense, we can shift our focus to the everydayness of its presence in the guise of human measured time. As any discussion of this measurable causal time indubitably centers on the role of consciousness and how use of the mind guides our conception of world, our examination of temporal *ekstasis* commences from the Daoist assumption that the three successive states of temporality (past, present, future) are but imaginary happenstances of someone whose harmony with the non-worldliness of Dao has been interrupted. This stands in opposition to the common belief that the past is a retreating of the present while the present progresses toward and fills the future. To demonstrate the *Zhuangzi*'s unique construction of human time, the following anecdote is offered:

> Mr. Ran Xiang grasped the principle around which all things revolve and followed them to their completion. His joining with them was without ending or beginning, attainment or time. Changing with them on a daily basis, he himself remained unchanged . . . The sage has yet to begin thinking of heaven, has yet to begin thinking of man, has yet to begin thinking of a beginning, and has yet to begin thinking of things.[15]

冉相氏得其環中以隨成，與物無終無始，無幾無時。日與物化者，一不化者也，闔嘗舍之……夫聖人未始有天，未始有人，未始有始，未始有物。

That which has not yet begun (i.e., the past) has yet to surpass that which has already begun (i.e., the present). Given it has not yet come into being, that which has yet to be also has yet to enter the realm of human time. To be within causal time, that is, time measured by variables deduced by humanity, is to possess both a starting and ending point. The variables that pronounce when these two moments take place are also what determine the staticity of our lifetime. To be static is thus to be caught in the durational moment of our existence such that we are said *to be*. The being that is our condition, therefore, renders us visible to the world, and such visibility is what constitutes our temporality.

Given that Dao has neither a measurable beginning nor ending, and that it lacks attainment of being or time, Dao can only be characterized as having a spontaneity which lies beyond the realm of the knowable. The same cannot be said of the myriad things of the world however. We can, therefore, only refer to the source of all things as that whose root infiltrates temporal *ekstases* without being entrapped by it. This is why the *Zhuangzi* declared the sage joins with things in Dao and that such joining occurs beyond the reach of time. Since the sage changes along with things without being changed by them, he darkens himself with Dao's mystery. His form is a forgotten trace whose nature is infused with nothingness. The sage is mysterious in that he does not make distinctions between substance and non-substance, between concepts of this and that, so and not-so, choosing instead to live in accordance with the naturalness of Dao. Being purely empty and dark, the sage's harmony with the oneness of things is unspoiled. By preserving his place in the hub of still quietude, the sage dwells where there is no temporality whatsoever; all is existent and nonexistent, finite and infinite. It is here, in the meontological abode of Dao, where creation abounds and the true nature of things is freed of the seductive language of time, that artificial durations become little more than the rationalizations of the petty person's ego.

The sage, therefore, does not follow the linearity of *ekstasis* but the circularity of heaven and earth. Heaven, by way of its affiliation with Dao, is an embodiment of the circularity of the cosmos while symbolizing the cyclical rotation of natural patterns such as growth and decay, spring and winter, and so forth. By choosing not to resist the natural outcome of such patterning, the sage is able to see things through to their completion. In seeing the true nature of things as stemming from the undifferentiated wholeness of Dao, the sage encounters no futility in his endeavors and so rests in the creative possibilities of nothingness. Since he changes with things as they themselves change, the sage thus shares in their experiences at the time of their experiencing.

Herein is yet another key finding to unlocking the *Zhuangzi*'s cosmology: the sage forgets the distinctions between things so as to grasp their true beginning in Dao, and having grasped the begininglessness of Dao, he leaves behind what is humanly in order to conjoin with that which is of heaven. Only when he sees things as heaven does can the sage be said to move together with things, yet remain unaffected by them. For the common person, who only sees things at the level of ontic existence, measured time is both real and inescapable. The world moves in a tandem of befores and afters immune to the changes of the present-now. That the common person puts their faith in the veracity of temporal *ekstasis* is proof of their refusal to learn from heaven, blindly following the heart of man instead. Each day for the common person is the arrival of the future in the present, while the present is pushed backward into the past. All of their hopes are put into this yet-to-be future such that the present becomes little more than the awaiting of the possibility of selfish hope. It is hope because we are constantly looking to transcend the present in anticipation of a better and brighter future. This, however, is not the way Zhuangzi wished us to live.

The toil of things weaving their way through the presence of lived experience owes its authority not to the fate bestowed on man by heaven, but to the critical bearing of his empirical-self:

> Standing beside the sun and moon, embracing the whole universe, the sage takes everything and blends them into one; he ignores the confusion of distinction and treats those of different rank equally. The common man labors and toils; the sage appears ignorant and unknowing. He blends ten thousand years into one. The myriad things are what they are, pursuing their course in the same manner as the sage.[16]

> 奚旁日月，挾宇宙？為其脗合，置其滑涽，以隸相尊。衆人役役，聖人愚芚，參萬歲 而一成純。萬物盡然，而以是相蘊。

The sage succeeds where others fail because he adheres to the principle of successively modeling oneself after Dao, which the *Daodejing* phrased along these lines: "Man models himself after earth, earth models itself after heaven, heaven models itself after Dao, and Dao models itself after that which is self-so."[17] Bearing this principle in mind, we can return once more to the tale of Ran Xiang so as to examine the commentary of Lin Yidu 林疑獨:

> Mr. Ran Xiang was a sage prior to the three Sovereigns who grasped the principle of true emptiness; in its limitless movement, it complied with [the principle] of the myriad things, becoming their Dao. Without ending or beginning, it knows not of attainment or time. In changing together with things, it remains unchanged and being unchanged, it can change spontaneously. As his age had such means, [Ran Xiang] used it to return to what is naturally self-so, attaining his true character. Furthermore, using one's heart-mind to seek a heavenly teacher will surely fail. What can be done to reverse such blind following? The sage has yet to think of heaven and man, but heaven and man exist of themselves. The sage has yet to think of a beginning or things, but the beginning of things lies in selfhood. The movement of the ages bends and stretches but does not stop. Complete in motion, it remains vigilant without being excessive, joining with the dark principle of things. How can it be any other way but this![18]

冉相氏，三黃已上聖君，得真空之理，運轉無窮，隨順萬物以成其道。無終始、幾時，與物化也。與物化者一不化，一不化者能化化也。世之有為者何不合其所為而復於自然，真性可得矣。然有心於師天，則不得，況與物殉而不反者乎？未始有天有人，而天人自存；未始有始有物，而始物自我。行世則屈伸而不替，備行則守謙而不溢，與理冥合，若之何而如此也！

Saying much of what was said before him, Lin Yidu appears to support Laozi's hierarchical model while reinforcing Zhuangzi's own understanding of time. What distinguishes his reading of the *Zhuangzi* from both Guo Xiang and Cheng Xuanying was his use of the term "selfhood" (*ziwo* 自我). Heaven and man appear simultaneously but there is no distinguishing the two ontologically. That which belongs to man also belongs to heaven, and the heavenly exists in all things. Thus while common persons may see themselves as being apart from heaven, the sage says nothing of the sort. Time and being become inextricably and existentially woven together such that the idea of a beginning to things becomes a fallacy. Things begin of themselves insofar as their self-so-ness fails to be linked to any beginning other than their own spontaneous arising from Dao. From this we may conclude that the *Zhuangzi*'s take on human measured time has a more onto-phenomenological slant than one might at first presume.

The implications of this are that the time of the for-itself can no longer be sustained as a duration contained in or moving from one temporal *ekstases* to another. This is because ontic time is brought about by the ontological nature of things, a nature that is itself meontologically grounded. The stretching and bending of time can thereby be regarded as a stretching and bending of humanity's empirical-self in order to establish cohesion to that which, in its original nature, is complete and self-fulfilling. Human time is hence a measuring of our existence as a singular momentary span, whereas for the sage, time is immeasurable using units of human experience or the events of life and death; rather, the sage sees time as an indicator of the presence of Dao. During the time before things existed, there was only primal chaos. During the time before primal chaos existed, there was only Dao. During the time before Dao existed, there was only the still quietude of nothingness, the temporal abode of the sage.

For ordinary persons, however, the age in which we find ourselves living is but a temporal bending of that which is anterior while stretching in the direction of that which is posterior. This lived time, which is a continual measuring forth of the allotted period bestowed to us by

Dao, ceaselessly sways back and forth between what we perceive as past and future. The point of equilibrium is thus the constant present and yet, the constant present that forever accompanies us to the end of our days is not a moving constancy but one at rest. All that precedes and proceeds from the constancy of the now-moment is in motion; it is only by letting-go of such notions as before and after that we can stand in the pivot of Dao, resting in the eye of nothingness that lies at the center of the storm of chaos around us. In rest things remain quiet and dark, and in their quiescent darkness they revolve and transform in accordance with heavenly change—the mirror of Dao. This, however, does not account for how we, as conscious beings, experience and engage the temporality of our lived time.

We have thus far examined the relationship between nothingness and cosmological time, but how does nothingness operate in the everydayness of human time? When one normally considers the past, we tend to use expressions such as my past, in the past, what's done is done, and so forth. There is a sense of finality brought to bear when discussing what took place before the moment of the present. But herein is the catch: everything may be thought of as having occurred at one time or another before the present moment in which it is discussed. Such being the case, the present can do little but continuously slide from moment to moment, never ceasing or resting. Indeed, the idea of time as the continual flow of now-moments lends credence to such an analogy. Add to this the layer of human consciousness and we can see why one might claim the past has been exhausted of any further possibility. But why should this be the case when we can argue that the memory of past events imprints itself onto our consciousness, ensuring its survival long after the actual event has transpired.

Instead of transcending the present in order to relive the past, Zhuangzi and Laozi argue that we should forget them both. This purposeful forgetting is a letting-go of the designation "past" while forgetting through loss of memory is a symbolic obliteration of the contents of that period rather than its designation. The past is what our life has already played out; it is a recollection of images to be savored or forgotten. Try as we might, we can never forget that which has come to be, not because it has fallen into nothingness, but because the past marks the beginning of our selfhood. Phenomenologically speaking, the presence of the past represents the presence of our physicality in the universe and the start of our existence. The past thus marks the beginning of our future while symbolizing our gradual return to the One, which is why the *Zhuangzi* observed:

My life is because it is the time for me to come; my death is because it is the time for me to leave. When one quietly obeys their time for birth and quietly obeys their time to die, neither sorrow nor joy can enter their mind. This is what the people of ancient times called freeing oneself. Those that cannot free themselves are held fast by their bonds. That the myriad things cannot overcome heaven has been known for a very long time; why should I detest my condition![19]

且夫得者，時也，失者，順也；安時而處順，哀樂不能入也。此古之所謂縣解也，而不能自解者，物有結之。且夫物不勝天久矣，吾又何惡焉！

    Whenever we encounter the past, we do so in the capacity of being present in the time of the present-now. Regardless of the terminology we choose in pursuance of what has already been or will come to be, as members of a holistic cosmology, the duration of our presence of being is not quantifiable using the measurements of past, present, or future but are held against the standards of change embodied by Dao. Thus the past does not exist in isolation from the present any more than it functions as the semantic foundation that makes any concept of the present possible. Neither is the past a form of indebtedness to which a current present imposes on a former present. Indeed, there can be no distinction between past and present for Zhuangzi's sage because the idea of past and present are annulled when he takes Dao as his authentic-self. In following the heavenly or natural, past and present become but fleeting moments to which no second thought is afforded, the outcome of which is the complete abolishment of any divide between the temporal and the ontological for all is one: "Nothing lives longer than a dead child and Pengzu died young. Heaven, the Earth, and I came into being together, and the myriad things and I are one."[20]

    The past, Zhuangzi says, is a past shared with no other insofar as it is a trace of the One. Upon the actuation of my corporeal being from the One, I have become one amongst a myriad of branches emanating from Dao's root. As a singular manifestation amongst an infinite number of possible manifestations of Dao, the fact that it has managed to fulfill itself in the form of my being is nothing if not marvelous. This marvelous possibility, which has resulted in my existence, cannot, therefore, seek another root in the form of the in-itself. The sage is hence a for-itself whose self is a non-self; he is an ungrounded, uprooted spirit whose fluid freedom traces itself to the oneness of Dao's wonderment. He does not bequeath resentment toward his coming-to-be nor display any angst at the certainty of his death. However, one who clings to the past, begrudges the present, and lives in terror at the prospect of the future, is to be condemned to the bonds of epistemic norms and petty virtues. The oneness of things thus serves to protect things from any threat of alienation from either the past or the future.

Rather than be dogmatic by declaring the past is inalienably cut-off from the present such that the for-itself must find a means by which to identify with the in-itself that is its past, we ought to relish our past, not as something lost only to be rediscovered, but as the gateway through which we may peer into the dark nothingness of our ontological root. Doing so will release us from our conception of the past as a solitary event and enlighten us to the truth that there can never be "the past," only an infinitely repetitive loop of pasts and not-yet-pasts. Thus the notion of a past is as much a fallacy as is the future. It is not a question of whether we are or are not; rather, the issue lies in our willingness to accept the cosmological reality that our ontological becoming and return is but one and the same thing. This is why the *Zhuangzi* advised us to "ride along with things and allow your heart-mind to wander. Entrust yourself to the inevitable and nourish that which lies central within—this is perfection."[21]

As for the future, although it is infinite, it may still be said to belong to me in that it is a future whose uncertainty is shared by all, even itself. We are thus forced to view the present *qua* future as a time of becoming and potentiality. It is an unknown whose ominous presence forces humanity to reconcile our ever-present consciousness of it with platitudes and hope. To say the future is not included in the reality of the present is to deny it the freedom of returning to whence it came, as is the case for Zhuangzi. What is possible about the future is not the possibility of the possible, but the becoming of the future's mystery. The future in lieu of the mysteriousness of its own nothingness is none other than the marvelous potential of returning to the undifferentiated wholeness of the One.

By describing the future as a future *qua* mystery, our goal becomes to point out the deficiency of contemporary temporal understanding which takes durational progress as a series of nihilistic steps—the present nihilates the past and the future nihilates the present. This is indeed a static way of looking at things; we can instead propose something new. Time cannot be nihilated by itself any more than each individual moment of time can be said to succeed the one preceding it. Our account of present time must be taken in its entirety as it applies to the duration of my separation from Dao. The concepts of before and after can, therefore, be used to refer to the phases of emergence and return to the One. As our appearance and disappearance from the One are in fact one and the same, we may moreover clarify our temporal presence of being as but one amongst a myriad of such presences, the ordering of which can only be described as the filling and emptying of the potential of Dao. To engage in semantic quibbles over the authenticity and priority of temporal *ekstases* is to fail to see beyond the phenomenon of the world and wander carefree in nothingness. Wang Bi in his "Introductory Remarks to the *Daodejing*" illustrated this point superbly:

> Given the past and present are interchangeable, ending and beginning become identical. By grasping the Dao of old, one can manage what occurs in the present. By investigating the present, one can know of things at the very beginning of time. This is what we refer to as constancy.[22]
>
> 故古今通，終始同；執古可以御今，證今可以知古始；此所謂常者也。

By ascribing a label of irreversibility to time in our insistence that it be a series of successive transitions, we only cause it to become further entrenched in tautological dualisms. The goal of our philosophical reflection here is thus to move beyond viewing temporality as bound to being, or to insist that the three modes of temporal *ekstasis* are intra-dependent. To this end, the *Zhuangzi* viewed time as neither a nihilistic force to be reckoned with, nor something subject to nihilism. The temporality of human measured time has no inherent bearing on the onto-phenomenological nature of reality or the world. Besides being self-serving, time is but the fetishizing of human ego over the apprehension of our own mortality. Should we accept the idea that human measured time is a fantasy of our own creation, and can in no uncertain terms equal the cosmological temporality of Dao, not only will we be able to transcend our own static experiences of time, we can discard them altogether. Zhuangzi justified such discarding during a tale in which he revealed his state of mind whilst mourning the death of his wife:

> At the time of her death, how could I not grieve like everyone else! However, at the time of her beginning there was also a time before she was born. As there was a time before she was

born, there was also a time before she had a body. As there was a time before she had a body, there was a time before she had *qi*. In the midst of this vast indistinctness, there occurred a change and there was *qi*. This *qi* changed and there was a body. Then the body changed into life. Now there has been another change and she is dead. This is no different from the movement of the four seasons—spring, fall, winter, and summer.²³

是其始死也，我獨何能無概然！察其始而本無生，非徒無生也而本無形，非徒無形也而本無氣。雜乎芒芴之間，變而有氣，氣變而有形，形變而有生，今又變而之死，是相與為春秋冬夏四時行也。

Zhuangzi's analogy serves as a warning against blindly accepting any of the various modes of temporal existence for their presumed self-evidence is never conclusive. Although the sage knows of the self-evident inauthenticity of time, it remains elusive to common persons in that they constantly distance themselves from their own temporal activity. The desire for distance between one's own actions and the measured duration it takes to complete them leads to the illogical conclusion that the past of human measured time is in fact a time that has come to pass—the past is in the past, having vanished from the realm of the present, the result being that its significance is overlooked.

What we see in the *Zhuangzi* is an explication of time and temporality expunged of references to consciousness, no matter if they are made obliquely or otherwise. As the sage and Dao are not disparate entities, the sage conceals his darkness from the world, moving in conformity to the changes of things and reflecting the universe in his mind, thereby merging past and future into a state of timelessness. What is old becomes new and what is new becomes old; so too, beginning and end are identical. In this way, temporal dualism is avoided. Through Dao's unbroken extension and interpenetration, the things of the world unfold according to their inborn nature and as this nature stems from Dao, the sage responds to them without interacting with them, moving along with them while remaining at rest.

Conclusion

Humanity's deep-seated fear of being overrun by the future is an ontological misnomer and existentially incoherent. If we have learned anything in this chapter, it is that Daoism attenuates rather than destroys the dynamic nature and continuity of things, especially when it comes to time. The heavenly movement the *Zhuangzi* speaks of is none other than the movement of Dao in the universe—a motion that penetrates the myriad things by simultaneously unifying past, present, and future. In this way, Zhuangzi avoids being labeled a nihilist or monist for his emphasis on the existential meaning of time showed it to be ontologically inseparable from the presence of Dao as ultimate reality.

Wherein the cosmological time of Dao ostensibly differs from traditional Western theories lies in the latter's tendency to deconstruct present-time via the temporal and even sociohistorical condition of being in the context of past- and future-time. The *Zhuangzi*, on the other hand, chose to emphasize the meontological import of time by forgoing the distinct categories of past, present, and future so as not to deny the spontaneous emerging and returning of the myriad things from the One. In other words, the text took each moment of our existence as a realized state of Dao whose presence could be felt in the conjoining of temporal *ekstases*. The past, present, and future thenceforth are regarded as but a shift of perspective from within the selfless hub of non-temporal emptiness in which the sage dwells.

And so, the existential and ontological reality of time lies not in a theory of recalling or projecting, of past repetition appearing as future possibilities; rather, it lies in the naked realization that time is a totality whose non-temporality enfolds and dissolves any conception of there being distinct and unique temporal moments. Abolishing our association of time—our epistemologically driven phenomenology—with the everydayness of being serves to free us from the bonds of the present-now and the quest to understand and master the finitude of human temporality. If we wish to partake in the marvelous possibilities of Dao, we must engage the things of the world as belonging to a non-transcendent whole whose unity grounds itself in the principle of non-deliberate doing, pervasive self-sameness, empty impartiality, and returning to the One. Only in these modes of being can we nurture ourselves, living out our years to their fullest. This is the inherent value of being useless and forms the topic of our next chapter.

4

Zhuangzi and the Life Praxis of Being Useless

One aspect of the *Zhuangzi*'s thought that distinguishes it from other early Chinese texts is the attention it gives to illuminating the benefits of that which we take to be useless. Indeed, we may go so far as to say that Zhuangzi is unique amongst philosophers, East and West, for his discussion of the useless and how he manages to transform it into a model of life praxis. As we work our way through the remaining chapters of this book, our attention shifts from the nothingness of the cosmos to how ontic non-being can facilitate spiritual freedom. For Zhuangzi, the use value of a thing taken to be useless extends beyond any value attached to said thing such that its uselessness becomes extended to and effects all who encounter it, including Dao and its meontological reality.

Of the many examples employed by the *Zhuangzi*, a favorite choice for illuminating the means by which the useless obtains its usefulness is unquestionably the old, withered tree. Before turning to the story of the tree in section two of this chapter, we must first discern the basis of Zhuangzi's understanding of uselessness. We will do so by entertaining the idea that life praxis rooted in uselessness is not only possible, as the text indicates, it is actually already pervasive amongst the myriad things of the world. This chapter is thus a challenge to the idea that usefulness renders the useless irrelevant, arguing against the assumption that things are assumed to be useful by proxy and that life praxis only arises out of a discourse that is proactive.

Useless by Proxy and the Proxy of Usefulness

The keenness with which the *Zhuangzi* wrote of its surroundings is nothing short of remarkable. Take the following passage as an example:

Zhuangzi said, "One must first know of the useless before one can discuss the useful. The earth is most certainly broad and vast, but a person only uses the area on which their feet are planted. However, if one digs away the soil beneath one's feet until the yellow springs are reached, would one still be able to use it?" Huizi replied: "No, it would be useless." "Then," Zhuangzi responded, "it is clear that the useless has its use."[1]

莊子曰: 知無用而始可與言用矣。天地非不廣且大也，人之所用容足耳。然則廁足而墊之致黃泉，人尚有用乎？惠子曰: 無用。莊子曰: 然則無用之為用也亦明矣。

What did Zhuangzi mean when he said that one must first possess knowledge of the useless *before* one can enter into discussion on the useful? How peculiar of him to posit such an idea. One normally does not engage the things of the world by assessing the usefulness or uselessness of their characteristics; if anything, we tend to shun that which is useless and frown upon the discarded, for in being discarded, it has lost whatever use was originally ascribed to it. Zhuangzi was thus prodding us to question the priority and proximity of the normative values assigned to the things of the world. He wished to turn our social norms upside down insofar as they are predisposed to the being of man and not that of the natural world. We view the soil surrounding our feet as little more than a clump of earth and fail to see its extended purpose, one whose non-intentionality gives way to a purposeless purpose. The soil of the earth is what defines the earth as such; it is the heart of the worldliness of the world insofar as we continue to support the axiom that we rise from and return to said soil. This gives way to the view that our being owes its existence to the earth and as such, we come to possess it in ways that other living things do not. Creation, however, is not an act whose sole purpose is to serve humanity but the world in its entirety.

Like the parable of the fish that transforms into a bird in the opening lines of the first chapter (*xiaoyao you* 逍遙游), Zhuangzi alludes to the idea that we are conditioned and limited by our environment. The fish are limited to the water in which they swim just as birds are limited by the air needed to lift their wings. In the case of that which is taken to be useless, it is left to the condition of human desire to deem it useful or not. We take for granted the usefulness of everyday things, expunging on a whim their inborn merits. To take the ground beneath our feet, which is useful on its own, as but a clump of earth is to deny the earth its self-so nature to be said earth; in calling it a clump we thereby make it *our* clump. Never for a moment do we ponder the notion that our feet are purposely designed as a result of the physicality of the earth. If we dig away the earth until there is none supporting us, this will not only redefine the relationship between our feet as an instrument for motion and the ground upon which they depend for such motion, it will also dismantle our place atop the ontological ladder. Thus while the ground appears to be without purpose, its non-purposiveness turns out to be its purpose. This is why the *Zhuangzi* said, "the area of earth upon which one's feet treads is small, and although small, they still rely on the untrodden earth around them."[2]

Taking the earth as an example of the usefulness of the useless—useless in and of itself yet useful as that which supports the feet standing upon it—does not, however, reach the heart of the matter. To do that, we must turn to the mundaneness of everyday things. In chapter 2 we saw how the Thing acts as the ontological root for ontic things, ejecting them from the milieu of undifferentiated wholeness in which they dwell. This discarding of things from the One was not the result of their being useless; on the contrary, given that they were derived from the oneness of Dao, they are imbued with useless nothingness from before the time of their inception. Their inception and subsequent cessation is hence an unfolding and refolding of the ontological nothingness lying at their core. It is owing to this inbred quality of empty stillness that things gain the freedom to grow and develop in ways that are not incongruent to their nature. We shall have more to say on this in chapter 6; however, it is important to bear this in mind as we investigate the merits of uselessness. It would seem, then, that there are two distinct types of uselessness to be accounted for: the first type is a pragmatics of the useless while the second type is the idea that life prolongation is best served through unpretentious self-reliance and harmonization with Dao. We can offer a third type of uselessness—the linguistic—but the *Zhuangzi*'s epistemological relativism is a well-worn path and so we shall leave that discussion for another time.

Returning to the pragmatics of uselessness, traditional understanding defaults to a discourse by proxy. Take for example the following anecdote: "A man from Song who sold ceremonial hats went to Yue, but the people there cut their hair short and tattooed their bodies, and so had no use for them."[3] Wherein ceremonial hats gain their use is, of course, as a head covering, but for a culture whose people do not groom their hair and shroud their bodies in fine robes, such decorative items are irrelevant. What is of use for one people is thus, by proxy, taken to be true for all others. With something as banal as a hat we can view Zhuangzi's objections to its implied use-value from several implicit perspectives: material, epistemological, and even ontological.

Materially, a hat is but a head covering and yet, its use stems not from its ability to cover, protect, or warm one's head; rather, it functions as a sign of social standing. People from the kingdom of Song were eager to flaunt their status and wealth whereas those from Yue held no such aspiration. The assumption was that the finer the material used to make the cap, the greater would be its use-value. A hat made of coarse hemp is useless because it possesses none of the required criteria from which one can assign it a nominal value. This says nothing of the emotional or symbolic value given things despite their outward plainness. None of these were behind Zhuangzi's anecdote of the usefulness of the useless however. To look at the problem in this light would be to see things merely as things. This is the perspective from which the common person sees the world—as a massive jumble of disparate entities whose chaotic interaction holds no logical sequence or meaning.

Epistemologically, Zhuangzi's criticism of the man from Song was both directed to the ritual practices and social etiquette of the Yin people of high antiquity while, at the same time, tacitly acknowledging that said institutions were of importance in regulating human civilization. The ceremonial hat represents an achievement of learning for the Ru scholar in that it was a mark of one's success in securing government office, an idea abhorrent to Zhuangzi. For Zhuangzi, the person of wisdom is an individual who has united with Dao, forgoing human knowledge altogether. Thus while the people of Yue may be said to live freely, they were most definitely not sagacious.

We see more examples of the mundane in a series of exchanges between Zhuangzi and his sophist friend, Hui Shi. In the first, Hui Shi complains about some gourd seeds of his that have produced gourds too large to be of any use; in the second, Hui Shi describes Zhuangzi's words as being as big and useless as an old, gnarled tree. In the latter case, Zhuangzi's response was nothing if not amusing:

> Now, you have this great tree and worry over it not being good for anything. Why not take it and put it in the land of nothingness, in the limitless wilds, so that you may wander in non-deliberate doing by its side, or sleep carefree beneath it.

Its life won't be cut short by an axe, nor will anything bring it harm, for it is useless for everything![4]

今子有大樹，患其無用，何不樹之於無何有之鄉，廣莫之野，彷徨乎無為其側，逍遙乎寢臥其下。不夭斤斧，物無害者，無所可用，安所困苦哉！

One might take Zhuangzi's response as being sarcastic but when we continue reading the text, it is not long before the answer appears as to why he dismissed Hui Shi's anxiety:

As a result, the sage does not walk along the path of distinctions but views things in the light of heaven. Even *this* is a way of *that* and *that* is a way of *this*. However, *that* has its right and wrong, and *this* has its right and wrong. Is there, in fact, a distinction between *that* and *this*, or is there no distinguishing between them? Where *that* and *this* cease to be in opposition, one takes Dao as the pivot. Standing in the pivot, one can deal with the infinite changes of right and wrong. Thus it is said, the best thing to use is clarity.[5]

是以聖人不由，而照之於天，亦因是也。是亦彼也，彼亦是也。彼亦一是非，此亦一是非。果且有彼是乎哉？果且無彼是乎哉？彼是莫得其偶，謂之道樞。樞始得其環中，以應無窮。是亦一無窮，非亦一無窮也。故曰莫若以明。

Humanity delegates the title *useless* by proxy whereas heaven does not. Be it a gourd seed, a crooked old tree, or what have you, heaven sees everything as both *this* and *that*; each gives rise to the other and each completes the other. Within the framework of Dao there is no designation of useful or useless—everything just is. Before we digress into semantics, let us return to the original issue at hand, that being how one can know of the useless before knowing the useful.

The wheel hub to which Laozi referred in his eleventh chapter is the same as the socket of which Zhuangzi spoke. The spokes that tie into the hub are no different from the socket fitted with a hinge; both are symbolic of the capacity of the useless to transform into something useful. Such transformation is not the result of human doing but is imminent in each of the myriad things. Whether living or inanimate, each entity emergent from the One is imbued with the qualities of non-being and being through which our manifest potentiality fulfills itself via an infinite series of onto-phenomenological changes. The catalyst for such change depends on whether or not non-being is suppressed by being or vice versa. In other words, Zhuangzi's theory of uselessness was a reflection of his meontological cosmology. The crooked tree was able to complete its heavenly allotted years because the element of nothingness has been freed from the chains of being such that it becomes ontologically quiet and harmonious with the empty stillness of Dao. Herein lies the crux of Zhuangzi's life praxis—to be inwardly quiescent while outwardly unmoving.

Praxis by way of proxy, however, is doomed to fail since it is a doctrine of the useless whose only recourse is to recount the indomitable presence of being. This, however, does not give us many examples with which to explicate the usefulness of the useless. The aforementioned tree is one, of which we shall say more shortly, the clump of earth is a second, while Laozi's example of the clay vessel is a third. Indeed, the clay vessel best illustrates the usefulness of what we perceive to be useless.

The vessel demonstrates the utility of its useless void in two manners of speaking: as a taking and as a keeping. What it takes in is nothingness; it is scooped up and collected by the wall of clay as the potter molds and shapes its form. That the vessel is made of clay is not what lends it its functionality though. Indeed, all qualitative aspects of the vessel fail to convey the true purpose of its inner void. The following passage from the *Zhuangzi* helps us understand why this is so:

> Thus what can be looked at and seen are but forms and colors; what can be listened to and heard are but names and sounds. How sad, that the people of the world take form and color, name and sound, as sufficient for expressing the truth of things! Since form and color, name and sound, are insufficient to express the truth of things, then those who know do not speak, those who speak do not know and yet, how is the world able to know this![6]

> 故視而可見者，形與色也；聽而可聞者，名與聲也。悲夫，世人以形色名聲為足以得彼之情！夫形色名聲果不足以得彼之情，則知者不言，言者不知，而世豈識之哉！

What we desire in any object is the emotive quality conveyed to us, the observer. Seldom do we ponder its inner presence of being, that unquantifiable aspect whose inclusion in its constitution results in its completion as such. The vessel's thingness is incapable of being disclosed through the medium of its being just as Dao cannot be fully articulated using words. The uselessness of the vessel's inner void thus lies not in its imperceptibility but in our ignorance of its potential in the form of ontological nothingness. Dao speaks through the nothingness lying at the center of the vessel as the vessel's giving and receiving. By constantly giving and receiving while also retaining nothing for itself, the vessel is forever self-completing and whole. We cannot speak of this process of self-completion and self-nourishment, however, in that it does not belong to humanity but Dao.

The nothingness that forms the vessel's inner void does not belong to that particular vessel, or even to all vessels as such; rather, that which is found within and beyond all things is a constant, coherent nothingness from which particular or localized instances of it assume spatial traits. The potter does not form this object in, or around, a so-called void; rather, the void that is nothingness is preexistent and alters as the vessel slowly takes shape. Herein is the key to knowing how nothingness gains its temporal presence of being. For Zhuangzi, the void that defines the shape of the vessel is seen meontologically—not as an *a priori* substance but as the dark matter underlying the fabric of reality. And so, it is because of its pliability that nothingness becomes entrapped in the everyday objects of the world, be they vessels, rooms, or our own bodies. It is a distinction of the subtlest kind for sure but it is nevertheless an important point of clarification.

We can make a similar argument regarding the hollow that is the vessel's void not being that which lends it its gift of pouring but, conversely, that which allows the act of pouring to occur in the first place. Zhuangzi demonstrated this idea with the following account:

> When the great earth breathes, its name is wind. If it does not issue forth then nothing happens, but should it do so, the myriad apertures give out a furious roar. Have you not heard the howling wind before? In the winding crevices of mountain forests, whose trees measure a hundred spans around, their apertures resembling noses, mouths, or ears, as a pillar's support, as a goblet, a mortar, or as a deep pool or shallow pond, the sounds flaring off them resemble the sounds of rapidly flowing water, arrowheads flying, harsh breaths, fine breaths, great shouts, howls of sorrow, some deep, others small, some like they are leading a chorus, others like echoes. Small wind gives birth to small responses; great wind gives birth to great

responses. When the great wind stops, the apertures become empty and quiet. Have you not seen the shaking and wavering that occurs?"[7]

子綦曰：夫大塊噫氣，其名為風。是唯無作，作則萬竅怒呺。而獨不聞之翏翏乎？山林之畏佳，大木百圍之竅穴，似鼻，似口，似耳，似枅，似圈，似臼，似洼者，似污者；激者，謞者，叱者，吸者，叫者，譹者，宎者，咬者，前者唱于而隨者唱喁。泠風則小和，飄風則大和，厲風濟則眾竅為虛。而獨不見之調調，之刁刁乎？

By themselves, the holes and hollows of the trees would appear to be useless and yet, when the wind blows through them, they alight with sound only to fall silent once said blowing comes to an end. Similarly, the empty nothingness that carves out a hole at the center of the vessel is but a quiet opening until such time as it finds use as a bearer of liquid. We may ring off a long list of mundane artifacts whose sole purpose is to remain useless for the benefit of others. In this way, the useless is able to preserve its use-value while that which was originally useful is rendered useless. Indeed, Zhuangzi extended his argument of the usefulness of the useless to the realms of epistemology and ontology too.

Our body contains orifices without which our existence would be fundamentally altered, if not outright impossible. As empty spaces, these orifices permit the presence of ontological nothingness to flow throughout our being in a manner reminiscent of cook Ding's edgeless blade entering the gaps between the ox's joints and muscles. Zhuangzi thus conveyed the usefulness of the useless—the importance of preserving that which is whole—as the key to life praxis. The following tale acts as a good illustration:

> The ruler of the southern sea is called Shu. The ruler of the northern sea is called Hu. The ruler of the center is called Chaos. Shu and Hu would frequently meet in the land of Chaos, and were always treated well by him. They consulted each other on how to repay Chaos' kindness, saying: "Men all have seven openings, for seeing, hearing, eating, and breathing, but Chaos alone has none. Let us try and give him some." Each day they bore one opening into him and on the seventh day Chaos died.[8]

南海之帝為儵，北海之帝為忽，中央之帝為渾沌。儵與忽時相
與遇於渾沌之地，渾沌待之甚善。儵與忽謀報渾沌之德，曰：
人皆有七竅以視聽食息，此獨無有，嘗試鑿之。日鑿一竅，七
日而渾沌死。

What is inherently useless to one thing turns out to be a source of sustenance for another. The message Zhuangzi is trying to get across is epistemologically pushed on the one hand while being ontologically pulled on the other. It would thus appear that his message is two-pronged: in order to achieve a life praxis that will see one live to the end of one's heavenly allotted years, one must in turn be prepared to abandon certain normative principles and logical presumptions. The one thing that we take for granted the most is nothingness and yet, our lives could not be carried out as they are without it. From the physiology of our bodies to the vast expanse of space in which our planet is positioned, nothingness is omnipresent without being omnipotent. It exists without our realizing and its presence is as obscure and mysterious as Dao. However, because of its ability to perplex us, we deny it can be good for anything and so toss it aside. This, Zhuangzi argued, is fundamentally wrong. The only way, he claimed, to preserve one's state of wholeness is to remain useless, and the only way one can keep one's wholeness intact is to return to Dao. Returning to Dao so as to uphold one's state of uselessness was Zhuangzi's notion of life praxis, and the example he took as a model was not from the world of men, nor even the sage, but the old withered tree.

Learning from the Useless Tree

Living in turbulent times as he did, it should come as no surprise that Zhuangzi sought solace in a realm as far removed from humanity as possible. The search for solace and a life praxis that was not predicated on the ethics of an empirical-self took him to the world of Nature. Neither idolizing nor succumbing to the tendency to anthropomorphize Nature, the text contemplated the things whose lives came as close to symbolizing Dao as possible, settling upon those great trees whose lifetimes are measured in centuries not decades. Zhuangzi took the old withered tree as his model not because of its size or owing to its grace and beauty; rather, he based his theory of life praxis on said oaks and pines in that they live for themselves without interfering in the lives of others. In doing so, they bestow upon others the means by which to carry out their own lived experience and this is what Zhuangzi referred to as "going both ways":[9]

> From the perspective of utility, to take something as being of use due to there being some degree of usefulness to it, then among the myriad things of the world, there will be none that are not useful. To take something as being useless due to there being some degree of uselessness to it, then among the myriad things of the world, there will be none that are not useless.[10]

以功觀之，因其所有而有之，則萬物莫不有；因其所無而無之，則萬物莫不無。

We walk down a road leading nowhere, down a useless path for which the only positive outcome is the self-realization that life cultivation can only come about once we relinquish our desire to objectify things to fit our preconceived conception of them. To say that the useless has its use is not to relativize things, but to be aware of their being on a more fundamental level. The argument for and against the myriad things being either useful or useless if only one of them is such is not to deny the possibility of differentiation amongst them, for Zhuangzi was saying something much more conceptually driven than that. Recall how we earlier revealed that the myriad things all tie themselves back to the oneness of Dao, and how the thread of Dao's nothingness weaves its way through them; we can now understand why Zhuangzi valued the idea that all things can be useful despite appearing useless.

Turning to the useless tree, Zhuangzi's thesis was that the tree preserved its life because it adhered to the thread of Dao, and this thread was in turn transmitted to those other beings for which the tree had become centrally important. Indeed, Zhuangzi devoted a considerable amount of time to the discussion of trees but what we must bear in mind is the distinction between trying to be useless and being so naturally. Uselessness that is naturally so is a uselessness endowed by heaven and is thus the outpouring of heavenly virtue as the gift of self-preservation. The sage's knowledge may be regarded as useless yet people are drawn to him; the sage does nothing yet he leaves nothing undone.[11] The fruit produced by a tree is useless to the tree but for those who would pluck it, such plucking only brings the tree harm as we cling to its limbs and pull on its branches instead of letting the fruit fall of its own accord. The same can be said for those people who feign uselessness due to injury or what not.

The *Zhuangzi* was most scornful of such disingenuous acts of uselessness in that they were carried out under the pretext of false virtue. When false virtue fills the minds of men, Dao becomes harmed and things lose their way; losing their way, things move away from their mutual dependency and cohabitation with other things of the world, turning this relationship into one of isolation and self-gain. With the false virtue of those ruling the world, Dao is subsequently discarded and forgotten. It is owing to this that the text espouses a life praxis modeled after the naturalness of Dao, and a usefulness derived from the so-called uselessness of nothingness. Zhuangzi demonstrated this principle as such:

> The mountain is weakened by the trees growing on it; the grease administered to the fire causes it to be fried. The cassia tree can be eaten and so is cut down; the varnish tree can be used and so is covered with incisions. Men know the advantage of being useful yet no one knows the advantage of being useless![12]

> 山木自寇也，膏火自煎也。桂可食，故伐之；漆可用，故割之。人皆知有用之用，而莫知無用之用也。

For Zhuangzi, life-prolongation is achieved through self-obfuscation. Since the tree cannot inwardly remain hidden in the darkness of Dao as does the sage, its only recourse is to outwardly conceal its use to the world—to hide itself from the perils of being useful:

> Thus birds and beasts do not detest great heights, and fish and turtles do not detest great depths. As for one who wants to keep whole their body and life, they must hide themself, detesting neither the depth nor remoteness of the place.[13]

> 故鳥獸不厭高，魚鱉不厭深。夫全其形生之人，藏其身也，不厭深眇而已矣。

As the gift of pouring defines the usefulness of the clay vessel, here such an attribute would have disastrous consequences. Whereas the gift of the vessel lies in its inner void, the tree, as a metaphor for the sage, lacks such recourse to nothingness as a means for ontological fulfillment. In other words, the life praxis of the tree is not due to the proxy of its being but from its withdrawal of being to the realm of nothingness. In ridding itself of all outward adornment, the tree can thus escape the axes of men. To escape the axes of men is to escape the perils of being useful and to escape the perils of usefulness is to engage in the practice of life-prolongation.

Life-prolongation, however, is not simply extending one's life as far as possible; this would achieve nothing but extend one's physical toil. The earth bequeaths our body and takes it away, which explains why Zhuangzi holds that: "The great earth provides my physical form, gives me a life of toil, provides me with leisure and comfort in old age, and is my resting place in death. Thus what is good for my life is also good for my death."[14] The interchangeability of the designations useful and useless is thus comparable to this and that, dark and light, and yet, these terms only refer to the everydayness of the useless, not constant uselessness. Only by adhering to constant uselessness can one engage in the nourishment and prolongation of life. That which is constantly useless is nothingness but what gives it its useful purpose is the marvelous creativity of Dao. From nothingness all things arise, and from uselessness all things obtain their use. We can see this idea quite clearly in the "*jingshen* 精神" chapter of the *Huainanzi*:

> When the people of Yue catch a python, it is seen as something precious for eating. When the people of the middle kingdom catch one, however, it is seen as useless and so discarded. Thus knowing a thing is useless, even someone who is greedy would decline it; not knowing a thing is useless, even someone who is incorruptible would be unable to part ways with it . . . Knowing that a fan in winter and a fur coat in summer are of no use, the transformations of the myriad things is but chaff and dust. Therefore if one uses hot water to stop a thing from boiling, the boiling will never cease; if one truly knows its root, all that needs to be done is to snuff out the fire.[15]

> 越人得髯蛇，以為上肴，中國得而棄之無所用。故知其無所用，貪者能辭之；不知其無所用，廉者不能讓也⋯⋯知冬日之簟，夏日之裘無用於己，則萬物之變為塵埃矣。故以湯止沸，沸乃不止；誠知其本，則去火而已矣。

We may thus understand the useless epistemologically, not in terms of redacting the useful to the useless, which would imply that the useless is merely a less functional form of usefulness; on the contrary, to be useless is to be altogether removed from the spectrum of human desire thereby granting it a degree of freedom utterly beyond the grasp of the useful. All men know the use of the useful but fail to know the use of the useless because such men live by proxy and not in accordance with Dao. To live by proxy is to use things in a manner unnatural to their inborn nature. It is easy to use something only later to discard it; it is an altogether different matter to not use something while still benefitting from it. By allowing others to avail themselves of the opportunity to be useful, the useless remains intact and pure. The purity of its intactness is the wholeness of Dao; thus to be useless yet remain in accordance with the wholeness of Dao is to be in harmony with the oneness of everything in the universe.

The *Zhuangzi* contains two passages that describe how the useless tree can be taken as a model of life praxis. The first occurs in chapter 2 while the second occurs in chapter 4. One passage offers a warning against the danger of being useful while the other is a critique of Confucian normative judgments pertaining to uselessness. While the first instance is actually two separate analogies, the second is an extended discussion that makes use of a common literary element in the *Zhuangzi*—the dream.

The crux of the first tale is as follows: Nanguo Ziqi came across a tree of such enormity that it could shelter a thousand oxen. Proclaiming it to be of tremendous use, he proceeded to inspect it more closely only to discover its wood was utterly unusable. He hence concluded that it could only have grown to such great size because of its uselessness and that this must be that to which the sage clings. Zhuangzi then went on to offer us a different account, albeit one whose message is the same.[16] He described a region in the state of Song that was famous for its trees, some of which were used as monkey perches, others for roof beams, while the best quality wood was taken to form the walls of coffins. In the former case, the sage took hold of the principle of being useless while in the latter, doing so would have separated him from Dao leading to his premature death. Thus Zhuangzi argued that the useless has its use while the usable is inherently useless insofar as it induces danger to one's being.

These two stories serve to reinforce the message Zhuangzi was trying to get across in a previous, lengthier example involving carpenter Shi and his encounter with and dream of an old oak tree. As we have more to say about this tale, it would be best to first quote it in its entirety:

> Carpenter Shi was on his way to the state of Qi when, having reached a bend in the road, he saw an oak tree next to the altar of the god of earth. This tree was so large that it could shade thousands of oxen, measuring a hundred spans round. It rose up like a mountain, reaching a height of 70 *chi* and more before throwing out any branches. Of these branches, there

are ten or so from which a boat could be carved. People came from all directions to see it, such that the scene resembled a marketplace, but carpenter Shi did not even glance at it, continuing on his way without pause.

His apprentice Yan looked at it with admiration, before running to catch up with carpenter Shi to ask: "Since I began following you with my axe, I have never seen such a beautiful tree. Why did you not even stop to take a look but keep on walking?"

Carpenter Shi replied: "Enough, say no more! This tree is useless. To make a boat from it, such a boat would certainly sink; to make a coffin from it, such a coffin would quickly rot; a piece of furniture would soon fall apart; a door would be covered with seeping sap; and a pillar would be infested with insects. The wood of this tree is of no use hence it has lived to such a great age."

After carpenter Shi returned, the tree appeared to him in a dream, saying: "With what other tree do you propose to compare me? Will you compare me to a tree having use? There are hawthorn trees, pear trees, orange trees, teak trees, gourds and other fruit-bearing plants. When their fruits are ripe, they are stripped-off and thrown to the ground. Their main branches are broken while their smaller ones are torn away. Because of their ability to produce fruit, they encounter suffering and are unable to complete their given lifespan. Such is the case with all things. I have sought to be useless for a very long time, such that it nearly killed me, but now I know how and it has been of great value. If, supposing I possessed some use, could I have attained the great size that I am? Furthermore, you and I are both things; how can you as one thing judge me, another thing, in such a manner? How are you, a useless man, able to know so much about me, a useless tree!"[17]

In this story, people were drawn from far and wide but their drawing-near was not due to the gracefulness of the old oak; rather, they amassed so as to gather in the clearing created by its enormous canopy. Under the umbrella of its limbs and branches nary a fruit or flower bloomed. Thus what the oak had to offer was nothing of practical use other than the uselessness of its shielding mass. In the nothingness of its shadow things took shelter and thrived. This thriving and sheltering is hence symbolic of the gathering power of Dao, a gathering that clears itself of prejudice and avarice. In other words, the gathering of nothingness that arises from the clearing of being results in a delimited zone of ontic emptiness marking the unfolding of Dao in the world of beings.

Given that Dao is demarcated by the meontological resonance of non-being, the *Zhuangzi*'s theory of life praxis is thus by extension, a phenomenology of how ontological nothingness manifests itself in human reality. Just as the uselessness of the vessel's inner void defines the outer usefulness of its walls, the useless outer boundary of the tree's canopy defines the inner usefulness of the region falling under its shadow. Furthermore, while the gift of the vessel stems from the pouring forth of its inner liquid, the gift of the tree stems from its ability to retain said inwardness. The vessel is hence useless to the world only to the extent that its self-contained void cannot be extended beyond the boundary of its physical being; its degree of usefulness, in other words, is directly proportional to its material presence of being. If one were to smash the vessel, one would no longer be able to make use of its inner uselessness. This is what makes the nothingness that is the vessel's inner-void so valuable. The old tree is no different in that what makes it useful to others is absolutely of no use to itself. Had it grown to merely medium height, it would be no different from all the other trees and would hardly garner the attention that it did. Had it flowers or fruit, the unspoken use of its shadow would surely have gone unnoticed. Thus with no discernibly useful qualities, the tree is utterly useless as an object in and of itself and yet, in being so completely lacking, it attained its greatest strength—self-preservation. And so, with this rather innocuous example, the *Zhuangzi* has carefully revealed one of the key principles of following Dao.

As a symbolic representation of Dao, the tree roots itself in the endless darkness of the earth's soil, soaring toward heaven as if trying to embrace it. With its great height, said tree offers refuge to the beings on the ground below, just as the harmonizing oneness of Dao shelters the myriad things of the world from succumbing to the petty desires of their ethical selves. Moreover, the clearing created by the tree's girth is a clearing away of being so as to uncover the nothingness lying beneath; it is a clearing away of the presence of being in favor of the non-presence of nothingness. In light of this, we can look at the story of the useless tree by employing an altogether different perspective. Take, for example, the following:

> Confucius said: I once served as an envoy and was in the state of Chu when I saw some piglets suckling on their dead mother. After a while, they all became scared and abandoned her. This is because they were no longer seen by her and regarded her as not being of their kind. The piglets loved their mother, not for her physical form, but for her spirit. When a man is killed in battle, at his funeral there are none of the customary images adorning his coffin. For a man whose feet have been cut off, he no longer has a reason to love wearing shoes. In each case, these things have lost their root.[18]

To the little pigs, the body of their dead mother has lost its utilitarian value just as the wood of the twisted old tree is useless to the carpenter wishing to make a house or boat out of it. As for one whose feet have been cut off, the shoes that he previously adorned are now discarded and looked upon as wholly irrelevant. From these examples, we can see that for Zhuangzi, the labels useful and useless are inconsistently applied and are thus relative in their designation. Regardless of the moral implications one can attach to the morbid images of a dead pig and mutilated man, we should remember that Zhuangzi holds the mother pig and crippled man as being emblematic of how things suddenly and spontaneously transform from one state of existence to another. Whether the body's animating spirit has departed, or the integrity of one's physical form has been broken, these are but minor variances in light of the oneness of things. Faced with such uncertainty, how can we not come to view the utilitarian or beautiful as useless and the mundane and grotesque as useful!

Encountering the old tree once more in a dream, carpenter Shi was accused of unfairly comparing it to trees having use. This was not an argument based on aesthetic or other quantitative factors such as the type of fruit they produce, the size of their gourds, the quality and aroma of their wood, and so forth; rather, Zhuangzi wanted us to look beyond these superficial merits when deciding what is of use or not. He told us that if a tree produced fruit, harm would befall it. In the course of such suffering, hope becomes lost and the way of Dao abandoned. Once Dao has been abandoned, things are discarded or cut down in mid-life. The dilemma, then, is how to disrupt the tendency to view trees of use as inherently more valuable and worthy of preservation than those that are deemed to be useless. Indeed, the old oak tree itself says it has sought to be useless for such a long period of time that it nearly cost it its life, but what does this mean? How does one seek to be useless? Part of the solution lies in the act of forgetting, of which we shall say more in chapter 5, but for now we can only surmise it is closely dependent on the playful interaction that takes place on a thing to thing level.

Uselessness arises out of the discriminatory behavior one thing directs toward another and is not a trait imbued in it by Dao. Indeed, in the eyes of Dao, the useless becomes useful while the useful becomes useless. Such mutually complimentary characteristics ensure that universal harmony prevails and that things may continuously engage in self-cultivation, living out their naturally allotted years. In light of this, we can understand why Daoism is seen as a philosophy of the middle way, never favoring one side over its perceived opposite, and why its cosmology is neither idealistic nor deterministic but links itself to the indescribable characteristics of Dao. To disprove a particular attribute using a similar attribute is not as good as using a non-attribute to do so. This holds true for the useless in that it can only serve as a base of comparison for the useful in that the useless manifests the qualities of Dao in such a way that the useful remains unchanged because of it. Thus in the story of the belt-buckle maker it was said: "To use something without formally using it, one will over time obtain some use from it; how much more so will he who uses nothing!" The useful, then, instigates change in others through which its purpose becomes realized; the useless, on the other hand, leaves things to their own devices and while this may sound eerily similar to the idea of non-deliberate doing, the useful is based on a conscious decision while the useless is a non-decisive recourse whose unity with the oneness of things prevents it from making conscious-driven decisions at all.

If, however, we base our judgment of what is useful on our experience of what is useless, how do we know it is useless, and naturally so at that? The useless is found in the everydayness of being and its presence of being takes the guise of nothingness. Nothingness is thus the ultimate state of uselessness and yet, it is from nothingness that the myriad things acquire their form. Born amidst nothingness rather than from being, those things closest in their state of being to the nothingness from whence they came are also said to be the most genuine in disposition. This is why the *Zhuangzi* made constant mention of the darkness of the sage, the inherent uselessness of things, and those disfigured persons and artisans whose life praxis was none other than practicing the art of Dao.

To be useless in a manner that is not artificial entails harmonizing oneself with the world. Through the process of unification, the nothingness of Dao supplants the uselessness of the Thing such that it incurs a measure of usefulness. In this way, what was formerly useless is now useful while the formerly useful reverts to a state of uselessness. Before their separation from the One, all things are useless, for to be otherwise would imply they have already assumed an ontic presence of being, which in itself, is grounds for usefulness. The challenge then is to successfully lose one's air of usefulness so as to return to one's original condition of useless oneness, a returning that is not cosmologically rooted but ontic in bearing.

Conclusion

In their quest to reacquire their inborn uselessness by reuniting with Dao, many beings fail; for the few that do succeed, they are rewarded with a lifetime uninterrupted by toil or hardship. This would explain why the old oak tree said it sought to be useless for a very long time, such that it was nearly killed, but knowing how to succeed in said endeavor proves to be of great value. By shunning its need for self-flattery in the form of fragrant wood or flowers, the old tree was able to break away from the shackles of humanity's conception of utility and beauty. Having learned how to return to a life praxis that is natural to its inborn nature, the tree was thereby able to live out its remaining years untouched by the axe of the carpenter while drawing others to it, rendering its newfound state of uselessness useful. Given the non-sagacious character of carpenter Shi and the holistic existence of the old tree, is it any wonder the latter questions the authority of the former when referring to it pejoratively as a useless thing? Thus the useless has its use while the useful becomes useless.

The question that was previously raised, and which remains to be answered, is how does one go about making oneself useless? In the case of things, it would appear losing a physical trait is sufficient, but for humanity that is not necessarily a desirable outcome. Owing to the presence of an empirical-self, however, humans have the unique capacity for psychological reversion; a reversion not in the sense of a regression of our mental capacity but the ability to shut off our conscious mind through the act of forgetting. The idea of forgetting—either as a literal forgetting of one's being or as a composing of mind—plays a central role not only in the *Zhuangzi*'s model of life praxis but also in its understanding of the steps needed to return to the nothingness of Dao. Although the present chapter has illuminated the much-overlooked framework engaging conceptions of what it means to be useless, it falls upon the next chapter to approach uselessness as representative of the ontological nothingness of Dao from the standpoint of forgetting so as to achieve a state of simplicity. Simplicity is, in turn, achieved through composing the mind, the outcome of which informs the final chapter of this book—a holistic freedom whose culmination leads to harmoniously uniting with Dao.

5

Discovering Dao through Self-Forgetting

Humanity has been blessed with a mind whose sophistication is unmatched in the natural world, or so we think. It is our greatest strength, and yet its loss is something we fear tremendously. Zhuangzi was well aware of the power of the mind to inflict harm on oneself and others. His solution, which some might deem as nothing short of epistemological relativism, was quite the opposite. To accuse Zhuangzi of relativism is to be relativistic; it is to lose sight of the centrality of nothingness and collapse the bridge being forged between it and the realm of being. This bridge, which I refer to as the plane-of-nothingness, is the pivot through which things respond to the spontaneous changes of Dao and where the process of returning to the One is initiated. In our previous chapter, we discussed how things partake in such returning by acquiring an air of uselessness, one that ultimately came to inform Zhuangzi's model of life praxis. Due to the dominating nature of our empirical-self, however, we find it extremely difficult to follow this route and so humanity requires an alternative approach, one wherein we may attain longevity while preserving our link to Dao. Such a path is offered via the act of forgetting.

Forgetfulness as perfection of human life praxis cannot be achieved in one fell swoop however; indeed, mastering the art of forgetting is carried out in a series of measured steps beginning with the ontic, working one's way through the ontological, before culminating in the cosmological. The present chapter, therefore, will discuss these three stages of forgetting, arguing their progression is not only a necessary preparation if one is to wander carefree in nothingness, the focus of chapter 6, but in doing so one harmonizes with the oneness of things in an onto-cosmological manner. To forget the division of mind and body such that one's relational-self (i.e., conscious self) rejoins the non-selfhood of Dao is to reach the highest level of awareness an individual can attain. The challenge for Zhuangzi, therefore, was methodological; rather than ascribe humanity the task of forgetting the ontic world and the things contained therein, forgetting the epistemological differences pertaining to their names and reality was instead the chosen course of action. This most mundane form of forgetfulness is, moreover, the most problematic and calls for special attention. When it comes to the mildly rarefied form of ontological forgetting, Zhuangzi coined two expressions to specifically address it: "forgetting of one's self" (*zuo wang* 坐忘; *wu sang wo* 吾喪我), which can be interpreted as a form of phenomenological self-reduction, and "composing the heart-mind" (*xin zhai* 心齋), whereby ontological coming-into-being is rarefied to the extent it is taken as a non-presencing presence. These, in turn, give way to a cosmological forgetfulness that has one no longer associating ontological presence with an empirical-self but with the meontological nature of Dao. Playing in nothingness not only allows us to forget our own existence, it is, as we shall see in chapter 6, the penultimate step toward attaining spiritual freedom.

The Mundaneness of Forgetting

In chapter 4, we looked at how the banality of the useless, when taken in concert with nothingness, offered a strong rebuke to the nihilistic inclination of the everydayness of being. Our practice of dismissing useless nothingness out of hand should, in light of the *Zhuangzi*'s counter-arguments, start to unhinge themselves. This unhinging has thus far been carried out in a manner that directly addressed the corporeal but it now behooves us to examine its more psychic elements. What needs to be questioned, therefore, is the means by which one can actually experience nothingness so that the everydayness of being is rendered conceptually useless without disrupting its harmony with Dao. Said differently, the unhinging of our being upon encountering the still quiescence of Dao results not in the loss of consciousness or free will; rather, such undoing is the unwinding of our repository of memories in the face of forgetfulness.

Unlike one common understanding of truth as a symbolic uncovering of what was previously masked by one's mind, or the minds of others, the *Zhuangzi* sees things quite differently. Instead of drawing lines of attachment between images and words in order to uncover their authenticity, Zhuangzi believes that the concealment of things, indeed the world at large, lies in our habitual tendency to associate with things through human linguistic constructs. The Daoist concept of truth is hence not to be sought via the deliberate disclosure or denial of a thing's trace, but through the process of return. In doing so, the norms of human cognition become disassociated from our memory of them as a result of their being forgotten, and purposeful self-forgetting is epitomized by composing of the mind. Zhuangzi thus argues that we need to first learn how to forget before we can be free, for only in forgetfulness are we able to recover our non-empirical, natural selves:

Forget about years and discriminating principle, hurl yourself into the infinite, making it your place of abode.[1]

忘年忘義，振於無竟，故寓諸無竟。

We may characterize the distinction between forgetting and forgetfulness as a matter of degree in that to forget things, including life itself, is an act forever tied to the conscious mind, whereas the state of having forgotten how to forget is an onto-spiritual conjoining with the oneness of the world. What is more, when Zhuangzi speaks of forgetting, he is not acknowledging the existence of a temporal past, or attempting to attenuate an ontological difference between how a thing associates the self of today with its self from yesterday; rather, forgetting is taken to be the means by which all things learn to perfect their inborn virtue so as to partake in the infinite virtue of Dao. This explains why the text contains statements such as: "Forget things, forget heaven, and be called a forgetter of self. The man who has forgotten his self may be said to have entered heaven."[2] As for forgetfulness, it is akin to the constancy of nothingness insofar as it represents the fulfillment of one's return to universal oneness and the abandonment of any inclination of self-identity other than with Dao. In other words, the perfection of forgetting takes the form of a perpetual letting-go of names and designations such that what remains is only profound mystery: "Even if you forget the former me, I will still have something which cannot be forgotten!"[3]

The *Zhuangzi* saved the bulk of its discussion on forgetting for the outer and miscellaneous chapters. Any mention of the heart-mind was done under the pretext of its nourishment or potential detriment to the well-being of our human nature but again, the text happily chooses to ignore the extent of the relationship between mind and memory. Owing to this, we cannot make the argument that forgetting the signifiers of the world is akin to rendering knowledge of things an impossibility. If this were indeed the case, any recalling memory would amount to nothing more than fetching what is already present in the mind. The problem with this is that fetching an image already embedded in the mind is to cause said image to be forgotten once its recollection is complete.

Acknowledging that one's mind belongs exclusively to oneself and is inaccessible by others, forgetting is thus an exclusive act of one's own mind and cannot be extended to others. Hence any loss of memory due to the subversion of forgetfulness cannot be attributed to an outside source but originates within the mind alone. In this way, we are only able to remember that which we have forgotten—a remembered forgetfulness. In other words, forgetting is little more than the symbolic representation of a thing's absence. With nothing before us we are prone to forget it. The act of recalling the forgotten thing's image is, therefore, a reaffirmation of the impression left in our mind. If anything, memory understood along these lines functions as the means by which things undergo a re-presencing of their being; however, it says nothing of the actual absence of being from which one can discover true insight into the truth of nothingness.

Of central importance to the *Zhuangzi* was the unification of one's authentic-self (i.e., non-self) with that of all other things on the level of Dao *qua* ultimate reality. In order to accomplish this, one must lose the empirical-self of human measured time so as to allow the relational-self to return to the cosmological temporality of the One. Of the various ways this can be achieved, progressively forgetting the world is certainly an attractive option. If we look past the surface of this statement, however, we will soon realize that ontic forgetting is little more than a first step toward fulfilling the greater objective of onto-cosmological forgetting. The *Zhuangzi*'s goal of returning to the oneness of things in Dao not only involves the forgetting of ontic beings and their ontological differentiations, but the mind and selfhood of the one doing said forgetting too:

> One forgets one's feet when the shoes are comfortable; one forgets one's waist when the belt is comfortable; and one's knowledge forgets right and wrong when the mind is comfortable. No change occurs internally and no compliance occurs externally when the assemblage of events is comfortable. If one begins with what is comfortable and never experiences the uncomfortable, one can forget the comfort of the comfortable.[4]
>
> 忘足，履之適也；忘要，帶之適也；知忘是非，心之適也；不內變，不外從，事會之適也。始乎適而未嘗不適者，忘適之適也。

When one is in an environment conducive to letting-be, it is not the physical being of things that is left alone, but the distinction between them. Hence shoes that fit as if they were a second skin are forgotten in that they do not impinge upon the self-so character of the feet wearing them. The same is true for the waist belt. The belt that is too tight restricts the movement of the wearer, just as shoes of an improper size make for difficult walking. Wherein each element succeeds is attributable to its ability to preserve its inward completion while engaging others in a way that does them no outward harm.

This says nothing of the role given to the mind however. Zhuangzi said that when the mind is comfortable, the distinctions of right and wrong are forgotten. As right and wrong are but a *this* and a *that*, each being a mutual pairing to the other, in the realm of Dao where there is only unity, they are forgotten. Oneness in Dao leads to comfort of mind while stillness of mind signifies that one has attained harmony with the world. In its comfort with Dao, the mind forgets the distinctions of right and wrong, allowing the myriad things to exist according to their naturally imbued character. In this way, things that are in harmony with Dao preserve its constancy within while endlessly responding to its changing potential through outward transformation. This is why the sage is described as inwardly dark while appearing outwardly bright. To begin with the comfortable, one shall never encounter the uncomfortable, and to forget the comfort of being comfortable is to roam in the realm of nothingness, the topic of chapter 6.

What we are most comfortable with, of course, is not the unknown nothingness of a dark universe, but the historical condition of our own existent being. This self-presencing existence of our ontological constitution within a temporal framework that comes to define it, as such, is not a historical event, which would involve binding the meontology of Dao to the mind of man; rather, freedom vis-à-vis ontological forgetting is a letting-go of the world and our temporally historical conception of it so as to return to a state of non-particularity and sublime openness. To argue for a historically authentic form of forgetting such that the mind both garners the ability to recall previous images of consciousness and actively relives them, not only contradicts the *Zhuangzi*'s interpretation of time and temporality discussed in chapter 3, had the text done so, it would have immediately dismissed such notions on the grounds that any reliving of said memories would be inauthentic and detrimental to the self-so naturalness of Dao. On a more fundamental level, such assumptions would have been wholly implausible given the meontologically atemporal nature of the universe. Although forgetfulness of mind can be seen as positivistic, the objective of Zhuangzi's deconstruction of mind and memory is to instill in us an awareness of the danger of having a one-dimensional outlook insofar as we fail to utilize our mental and sensory faculties for purposes other than selfish indulgence and personal gain, both of which detract from our self-enrichment and cultivation of heavenly virtue.

The life praxis of useful uselessness we spoke of in the previous chapter is yet again prevalent in our discussion of forgetfulness, only now it is in reference to unhinging one's dependency on mind so as to forget one's fellow man and return to the One. Of course, Zhuangzi was not insinuating that we should literally forget everything in the world; on the contrary, he was implying that our tendency to regard the outward appearance of things while forgetting their inner virtue was behind the decline of Dao witnessed in his lifetime:

> For my entire life, I have encountered you from an arm's distance yet I lost you, how sad! What you perceive of me is that which can be seen. It, however, is already exhausted yet you still seek it, believing it exists; this is like seeking out a horse when the fair is over and done with. I serve you best when I have completely forgotten you, and you serve me best when you have also completely forgotten me. Given this, what do you have to worry about! Even if you forget the former me, I will still have something that cannot be forgotten.[5]
>
> 吾終身與汝交一臂而失之，可不哀與！女殆著乎吾所以著也。彼已盡矣，而女求之以為有，是求馬於唐肆也。吾服女也甚忘，女服吾也亦甚忘。雖然，女奚患焉！雖忘乎故吾，吾有不忘者存。

We see in one another the psycho-physical constitution of our being while overlooking what is responsible for it in the first place. Looking past the image of being that meets the eye, we soon come to the realization that the properties comprising our state of existence are linked to but a few core components. The spontaneous manner in which Dao transforms and re-envisions itself can do nothing but result in its appearing anew on a daily basis. As certain as night follows day and day follows night, Dao follows itself and thus remains intact and unmoving; it does nothing for its own sake yet manages to complete others nonetheless. Given that our birth is already on the road toward death, Zhuangzi says we should not fret over what is in fact the natural course of the universe. This is why the time before my life belongs to Dao and should be forgotten, and why the time following my death also belongs to Dao and should likewise be forgotten.[6]

As we learn more about the arts of Dao, we must ask ourselves why Zhuangzi at this earliest stage of perfecting our life praxis wished us to go beyond simple ontic forgetting and engage in mutual forgetfulness on an ontological level. Take, for example, the following:

> Fish are mutually happy in water; men are mutually happy in Dao. Living in water, the fish are able to obtain their provisions by cleaving the pools; having Dao, men do nothing yet their life is sustained. Thus it is said: Fish forget each other in the rivers and lakes; men forget each other in Dao.[7]
>
> 魚相造乎水，人相造乎道。相造乎水者，穿池而養給；相造乎道者，無事而生定。故曰，魚相忘乎江湖，人相忘乎道術。

Similar notions are given several passages earlier, albeit in the context of the sage:

> The genuine person of old knew neither to love life nor loath death. At the time of his birth he showed no elation; facing his own death he offered no resistance. Unconstrained he entered and left the world. He did not forget from whence he came and did not inquire as to where he would finish. He received things in joy and he returned things in forgetfulness. Such is called not exercising one's heart-mind to abandon Dao, not wielding men to aid heaven. This is what I call the genuine person.[8]
>
> 古之真人，不知說生，不知惡死；其出不訢，其入不距；翛然而往，翛然而來而已矣。不忘其所始，不求其所終；受而喜之，忘而復之，是之謂不以心捐道，不以人助天。是之謂真人。

The above passages reveal two key arguments: first, freedom in Dao is attained not through an act of transcendence but through forgetting; second, the ethics of forgetting is as much about letting things return to their natural selves as it is about cultivating one's own authentic-self. For the sage, to wander carefree in the realm of Dao is to spontaneously engage things in a playful, traceless manner. Each encounter avoids being reduced to a historical moment insofar as the genuine person retains no aspect of said event for himself; his embrace and releasement of things is as traceless as his own darkened virtue, rendering his relationship with the world one of becoming-with rather than becoming-for. The historicity of things is thus bound to our memory of them as opposed to things themselves, yet the sage is able to preserve his atemporal, ahistorical nature through the praxis of forgetfulness. In this way, his mind *qua* memory and ontological being remain traceless and whole.

Ontic forgetting for the *Zhuangzi* was thus implicitly tied to forgetting any and all epistemological values attached to things, be they titular or descriptive. Having let go of the implicit authority attached to words, the trace of things can subsequently be forgotten. To pursue forgetfulness along these lines is to open oneself to the perpetually silent nothingness of Dao. Letting-go of words and their images—the two most common representations of truth—through forgetting not only allows Zhuangzi to offer a uniquely original take on how we perceive and utilize language, doing so became emblematic of the journey required to become a sage:

> The trap exists because of the fish. Once you have the fish, the trap can be forgotten. The snare exists because of the rabbit. Once you have the rabbit, the snare can be forgotten. Words exist because of meaning. Once you have the meaning, the words can be forgotten. In light of this, where can I find a man who has forgotten words so that I can share some words with him![9]

> 荃者所以在魚，得魚而忘荃；蹄者所以在兔，得兔而忘蹄；言者所以在意，得意而忘言。吾安得夫忘言之人而與之言哉！

Words are but temporary utterances that fail in their capacity to convey the underlying truth of things. Such being the case, what better way to express their intent than via imagery and yet, images are themselves but empty traces of the Thing. Words, being born of images, exist as words, but they are nevertheless unable to express the original meaning of the images from which they are derived. Seeing as words are derived from the minds of men and not heaven, they are merely the words of humanity and are not the authentic non-words of Dao. Wherein we must forget words so as to obtain the images underlying them, and thereupon forget the images so as to obtain their meaning, comes from the need to expose their being in a manner that is as unconcealed as possible, for words do nothing but conceal the truth of reality.[10] If Dao is unnamable and its indescribability is not due to an insufficient vocabulary on the part of humanity, but arises from the singular dimensionality of our language, then is the reality of the myriad things any different? It is indeed.

The idea that we must forgo language in order to comprehend the visual cues comprising the world was a notion shared by all early Daoist thinkers. Zhuangzi, being the second in this lineage, was pushing us to go beyond the dichotomy-driven nature of our value-laden epistemic norms toward a more nondiscriminating and intuitive means by which to engage the world. This is why the text stresses that to see the myriad things from the perspective of their names (e.g., snare and trap) was to fail to see the broader image lying beyond the horizon (e.g., rabbit and fish). Even this, however, is not good enough, for what awaits us beyond the horizon are the non-words grounding the images behind names. Such steps might succeed in getting someone to the ontological level of forgetfulness, but it would fail to advance them any further than that.

We cannot, therefore, take these three stages of forgetting (i.e., words, images, and meaning) as representing a comprehensive picture of the *Zhuangzi*'s ideal of cosmological forgetting in that they are still mind-dependent forms of forgetfulness. It would serve the sage no good to remain tied to the very thing that binds him to humanity's onto-phenomenological reality. If he is to successfully return to the One in a capacity other than through his own death, he will not only have to let go of the desire to view everything from the perspective of lived-being, but learn to see things from the vantage point of their root. Viewing things from the standpoint of Dao thus entails engaging them as cook Ding engaged the ox—from the nothingness permeating the universe while outwardly embracing the ox in the entirety of its oneness.

Forgetting the names, images, and significance of the things of the world is, of course, more than just an indiscriminate forgetting; it is a complete re-evaluation of how we perceive and distinguish them. In the course of our perceiving and distinguishing, things make an impression on the mind, the image of which is recalled in the event of our forgetting. This returning to the forgotten image becomes a projection of one's mind onto the trace of things; however, it is a forgotten projecting toward a long-vanished presence of being. The vanishing of a thing's mark of existence can thus be taken as the meontological potentiality of said thing insofar as its return is not to a state of being, but to the primal nothingness supporting Dao.

In other words, Zhuangzi holds the ultimate realm of truth lies not with ontological being but with the meontological reality of Dao. From this we can draw the conclusion that in order to attain true ontic forgetting, one must not only forget how things present themselves to the world, we must also forget their trace. Given this, forgetting in the sense Zhuangzi implies does not result in the fragmentation of reality but in its cohesion. Wherein the act of forgetfulness brings about a degree of cohesion between things is attributable not only to the fact that it is the human mind that is being forgotten but more importantly, that this forgetting absolves the tendency of the mind to delineate a thing's name from its ontological trace. In contrast to the sage, the common person clings to this supposed distinction and so unavoidably succeeds in what Zhuangzi so poignantly referred to as forgetting that which is real (*chengwang* 誠忘):

> Thus if one's virtue endures, appearances can be forgotten. When men do not forget the things they ought to forget, and forget the things they should not forget, this is a case of forgetting that which is real.[11]

> 故德有所長而形有所忘，人不忘其所忘而忘其所不忘，此謂誠忘。

To forget the genuinely real is one of the greatest errors a person can commit for Zhuangzi, insofar as it is a forgetting of one's own rootedness in Dao. To forget that the being of one's existence is intimately connected with the ontological nothingness of Dao is to overshadow the authentic virtue of Dao using the impurity of humanity. This is why Zhuangzi stated above that physical deficiencies could be overlooked so long as one's moral virtue remains equivalent to that of Dao. If, however, the virtue of Dao is forgotten, such forgetfulness may be considered a forgetting of that which is real. Examining the commentary of Guo Xiang, this theory would appear to hold:

> When one's virtue endures when following things, things forget their vileness. When enduring by preceding things, things forget their preference. With birth there is love, with death there is abandonment. Thus when it comes to virtue, there is nowhere in the world it can be forgotten; when it comes to form, there is nowhere in principle it does not exist. Thus when it comes to forgetting form, it is not forgetting; to not forget form but forget virtue is to forget what is real.[12]

其德長於順物，則物忘其醜；長於逆物，則物忘其好。生則愛之，死則棄之。故德者，世之所不忘也；形者，理之所不存也。故夫忘形者，非忘也；不忘形而忘德者，乃誠忘也。

Cheng Xuanying likewise offered a commentarial reading in line with our assessment, saying:

> Daying and Zhili both have a moral virtue that is exemplary and far-reaching, satisfying the needs of the Dukes of Qi and Wei, allowing them to forget the vileness of their bodily form. The real has its actuality. What can be forgotten is form; what cannot be forgotten is virtue. To forget form is easy but to forget virtue is difficult. Thus it is said, what is known as form is forgettable and what is known as virtue is unforgettable. To not forget form but forget virtue is the true actuality of forgetting. This is what is meant by virtue without form.
>
> 大瘦支離，道德長遠，遂使齊侯衛主，忘其形惡。誠，實也。所忘，形也；不忘，德也；忘形易而忘德難也，故謂形為所忘，德為不忘也。不忘形而忘德者，此乃真實忘。斯德不形之義也。

From the above we can see that ontic forgetting for Zhuangzi involves a letting-go of the outward trace of things and is not inexorably tied to the mental recollections of said things by the subject. Each encounter with the things of the world is hence at once stored in the mind and not in memory per se and yet, this encounter and its subsequent recalling must already be present to both the mind and memory if it is to succeed. Wherein forgetfulness poses a potential danger is in its capacity to not only eradicate our memories, and thereby undo our conceived knowledge of the world, as an unchecked aspect of the mind, it could also devastate the very existence of the subject. Zhuangzi was able to nullify said threat by treating the trace and act of forgetting as a means by which one may return to and unite with the cosmic oneness of things; it is, in other words, a form of life praxis rooted in the art of useful uselessness while embodying the self-nourishing power of Dao.

If our memory is constantly being held hostage by the effacement of its trace from forgetting, then as it is an integral part of our assumed historical condition, the loss of our ability to recall or recognize former occurrences of memory cannot but be seen as nihilistic. Forgetting, in this sense, is regarded as a threat whose progression must be slowed or halted at all cost. Such a threat, we must reiterate, did not exist for Zhuangzi in that forgetfulness was held to be a necessary measure to becoming more authentic and in touch with Dao. Additionally, the dilemma over *ekstasis* we raised in chapter 3 does not figure into Zhuangzi's doctrine of forgetting either, rendering moot the idea that forgetfulness occurs in the past while remembering is a recalling of said past in the present-now.

Indeed, Zhuangzi argues that we must go even further by unlearning the artificial value attached to our epistemological norms as a necessary first step if we are to recall and join in the oneness of things. Through forgetting we forget being, and in forgetting being, we retrieve non-being and set it free. To forget, in other words, is to recall how all things take nothingness as their root and Dao as their source. Forgetting is thus not an addressing of the temporal state of being referred to by one's mind during the act of remembrance; on the contrary, it is an opportunity for humanity to have a glimpse at the freedom awaiting us when we forgo the pursuit of fame and profit, right and wrong, and other socio-ethical coveting that takes us down a path ever-more deviating from the way of Dao. In order to rectify such deviation, we must not only learn to forget things in their ontic sense, we must also learn to forget them ontologically, and this is attained through perfecting the art of "losing oneself."

Losing Oneself in Forgetfulness

Thus far we have focused on how the *Zhuangzi* makes use of the idea of ontic forgetting in order to initiate the process of return to the One. In this section, we will continue to examine this process by delving into how ontological forgetting through loss of the relational-self can further the authentic person's quest for cosmological freedom via a spiritual union with Dao. If the first stage in the journey toward a holistic experience of forgetfulness centered on epistemological forgetting, the second can be said to revolve around a phenomenological letting-go. As for the title of this section, it contains a metaphor we will get to shortly but for now what can be said of it is best illustrated with reference to an altogether different passage, one that nevertheless contains an equally powerful expression:

> To stand without moving is easy; to walk without touching the ground is difficult . . . Look at that which is empty. The empty room gives birth to a state of pure whiteness and in

such stillness, fortune and blessing gathers. If you do not stop there, this is called sitting while the mind gallops.¹³

絕跡易，無行地難……瞻彼闋者，虛室生白，吉祥止止。夫且不止，是之謂坐馳。

Stage one forgetting (i.e., the ontic) took a course of action proactive in bearing, requiring the subject to physically engage the myriad things of the world so as to forget their images and trace. Given the relatively high frequency with which the terms for "forgetting" (*wang* 忘) and "non-mind" (*wuxin* 無心) appear in the *Zhuangzi*, we are quite justified in referring to it as a wholly mundane, even banal notion. And yet, Zhuangzi's attention on the ontic form of forgetfulness was only one in passing; indeed, his refusal to engage it in any sort of profound discourse spoke volumes of his disinterest. When it comes to the second and higher level of forgetting, however, the number of textual examples available to us shrinks considerably while Zhuangzi's interest rises noticeably. What is more, the *Zhuangzi* spent more time on this form of forgetfulness than on either of the other two forms combined, and for good reason.

What needs to be said regarding the passage quoted above is that it is a prerequisite for composing a still and quiet mind. This is where the forgetting of trace comes into play, for without the letting-go of trace and its superimposed image, the mind will continue to race even though the body may be at rest. Stillness of mind is thus first needed in order to open it to the possibilities of a genuine engagement with Dao. Should one stubbornly cling to fears and desires, events past and those yet to come, the situation will arise whereby one remains sitting while the mind gallops asunder. We ought, Zhuangzi writes, to learn to see with the non-mind and listen without the intellect, shuttering and turning inward our eyes and ears, for nothing is better than seeing and listening with Dao.

Characterizing the mind as an empty, brightly lit room is to describe it as being synchronous with the nondiscriminate, nonexistent mind of Dao. In being still and empty like the room, the sage, too, is able to receive all things; in being purely white, he reflects all things without retaining any aspect of them for himself. Although the white emptiness is in fact a metaphor for both Dao and the mind of the sage in his state of oneness with the world, its allusion here to Dao should not be misconstrued for the dark mysteriousness of its original meontological condition. We are thereby able to distinguish between whiteness and darkness in that the first points to the sagely mind that has yet to achieve an ultimate clarity of things (i.e., attained second-stage forgetting), whereas the sage regarded as dark and mysterious has not only exceeded the highest level of forgetfulness in which both body and mind cease to exist, he has reached a degree of freedom only possible by conjoining with Dao on a spiritual level.

The holistic, experiential immersion required of self-forgetting was broken down by Zhuangzi into a series of measures the text describes thusly: "Cultivating the will, one can thus forget the body. Cultivating the body, one can thus forget profit. Being devoted to Dao, one can thus forget the mind."[14] Thus Zhuangzi understood forgetfulness as a pushing forward or going beyond the limit of our own being and not as a sign of weakness or mental retreating. Following the *Zhuangzi*'s line of reasoning as seen in the passage just quoted, three modes of phenomenological forgetting may be discerned—things, self, and body—all of which precede the onto-cosmological forgetting that is embodied in the act of composing the mind. Each of these three stages occurs in some of the most well-known allegorical passages of the text though, oddly enough, Western scholars have failed to pay them their due diligence. The same, however, is not true of the Chinese commentarial tradition, wherein each example is amply supported with debate and insightful discussion. What is interesting to note is that the majority of these allegorical examples involve Confucius or one of his disciples. This technique of creatively repeating the words of elders (*chongyan* 重言) was one of the many unique traits of Zhuangzi's thought and, in collaboration with two more terms (*yuyan* 寓言 and *zhiyan* 卮言), constitute his philosophical discourse on language.[15] One cannot help but notice the irony here—the *Zhuangzi* placed the call for the forgetting of ethical norms into the mouths of Ruists, calls they themselves would have found inconceivable.

With regard to the first type of loss, that of the self, Zhuangzi employed several terms to express it: one literal (*wu sang wo* 吾喪我), another metaphorical (*xing ru gaomu, xin ru sihui* 形如槁木, 心如死灰). They take place in a story from chapter 2 of the text between Nanguo Ziqi and his disciple Yancheng Ziyou:

> Nanguo Ziqi, sitting behind his desk, exhaled and turned his head skyward, his expression stupefied, his self-seeming to have left him. Yancheng Ziyou, who stood in attendance before him said: "What is this? Can the body appear like withered wood and the mind like dead ash? How is it that your sitting behind this desk now is not the same as when you sat here before?" Ziqi said: "Yan, the question you ask is a very good one! Just now I forgot myself, do you understand?"[16]

南郭子綦隱机而坐，仰天而噓，嗒焉似喪其耦。顏成子游立侍乎前，曰: 何居乎？形固可使如槁木，而心固可使如死灰乎？今之隱机者，非昔之隱机者也。子綦曰: 偃，不亦善乎，而問之也！今者吾喪我，汝知之乎？

It is clear that Ziyou's remarkable description of his master's countenance referred to his physical form but what was Ziqi implying when he claimed to have forgotten himself? Here, we can point out that the phrase *qi ou* 其耦 has the meaning of paired-self or relational-self, and that in his commentary to this sentence, Sima Biao 司馬彪 (ca. 306 CE) wrote that such pairing was between one's relational-self and the soul (*shen yu shen wei ou* 身與神為耦). In order to supplement our understanding of what Zhuangzi meant by the expression "lose one's self," let us turn to several of the commentaries, the first of which is from Wang Pang 王雱:

> The sage embodies Dao and is thus without a relational-self. Being selfless, there is nothing in him to oppose the world, hence Nanguo Ziqi resembles one who has lost his companion. As for this companion, it is his equal. There is not a thing that is without its opposite and Dao alone in its marvelousness is unequaled. Being without equal and returning to the One, one can forget the difference between self and other. This is the equality of things. Thus the body can be said to be like withered wood and the mind can be said to be like dead ash.[17]

聖人體道而無我，無我則無對於天下，此南郭子綦似喪其耦也。夫耦，匹也。物莫不有匹，而惟道神妙而無匹，無匹則歸於一致而忘彼我。此物之所以齊也。故形可使如槁木，心可使如死灰。

Whereas the *Zhuangzi* used the expressions *sang qi ou* 喪其耦 and *wu sang wo* 吾喪我 to convey the sage's loss of his relational-self, Wang Pang adopts just the first and replaces the second with the phrase "forget the difference between self and other" (*wang bi wo* 忘彼我). In the original text, the character for loss (*sang* 喪) is reduplicated, conveying a sense of parallelism and continuity. What is lost in both cases is the empirical-self; it is lost because the sage embodies Dao and Dao itself is selfless. The implication of this state of existence is that the sage is no longer regarded by others as an ontological being, but someone who has become a transcendent companion of Dao. Wang Pang, however, believes the sage remains in the world of men and merely lets-go of his relational-self through the act of forgetfulness. Such behavior will not only prove to be more practical when the time comes to recall the self, it exempts the sage from finding himself in a situation similar to the one we spoke of in chapter 2, where the Thing is lost and needs to be re-found.

For Wang Pang, Ziqi's companion was lost not because his ascension to the spiritual level of Dao induced its destruction, but out of the need to forget the ontic distinction between empirical-self and other, as well as the pairing of the relational-self and the meontological non-self. What we see, then, in Wang's argument is that only amidst the marvelous possibilities of Dao can Ziqi find his authentic-self, one that identifies with the myriad things through their partaking in the oneness of Dao. In this way, the body and mind are rendered as but temporary placeholders which, when vacated, result in what Zhuangzi peculiarly characterized as a state whereby one's body resembles withered wood and the mind dead ash.

If we turn to the commentaries of Lü Huiqing and Lin Xiyi as further points of discussion, we immediately notice that they did not use an expression resembling Wang Pang's *wang bi wo* but retained Zhuangzi's original language of *sang qi ou* and *wu sang wo*. Lü Huiqing's commentary is as follows:

> All men have their body and their mind and because of this there is the 'I' of the self. If there is no 'I' then one would be no different from dead ash or withered wood. Ziyou does not know from whence I arise, taking his body and mind as laboring without rest, not knowing where they reside and how they can be used to reach such a state. However, at the time of his forgetting, he came to realize that his former and present leaning on the table were different and so he examined them anew. His former leaning was a time to reflect on things; his present leaning is a time to forget things. If I know from whence I arise then existence and loss neither begin nor exist in me. If we say that a flute is a thing then all men can listen to it and know that its empty void lacks being. As for what I take as being myself, such is the case too.[18]

> 人之所以有其形心者，以其有我而已。苟為無我，則如死灰槁木，不足異也。子游不知我之所自起，為形心所役而不得息，不知何居而可使至此也。 然於嗒然之間，知今昔隱几之不同，則其觀之亦察矣。益昔之隱几，應物時

也。今之隱几, 遺物時也。苟知我之所自起, 則存與喪未始不在我也。比竹之為物, 人皆聞之, 知其空虛無有也。我之所以為我者, 亦然。

Lin Xiyi's commentary reads thusly:

> Leaning against the table is to depend on it; where there is forgetting, things take on an appearance of the non-mind. Losing one's companion, men all take things to be their counterpart, hence they are forgotten. Withered wood has the meaning of no-life; dead ash is a heart-mind that has yet to arise. As for the leaning of today, it is to say that the man leaning now is not like the man who leaned here earlier. When there is an 'I' then there are things but when the 'I' is lost, the self also ceases to be; with no 'I' things no longer exist. You know this, so I say you also know its principle. The self is in fact the 'I' but one does not say I have forgotten I; rather, one says I have forgotten myself. To speak of man's ability to draw a line between a selfish mind and one that does not change is to say what lies between I and myself have a difference. The three words 'I forgot myself' achieve this idea most superbly.[19]

隱几者, 憑几也; 嗒然者, 無心之貌也; 喪其耦者, 人皆以物我對立, 此忘之也; 槁木者, 無生意也; 死灰, 心不起也。今之隱几者, 言今日先生之隱几非若前此見人之隱几也。有我則有物, 喪我, 無我也, 無我則無物矣。汝知之乎者, 言汝知此理乎。吾即我也, 不曰我喪我, 而曰吾喪我, 言人身中纔有一毫私心未化, 則吾我之間亦有分別矣。吾喪我三字下得極好。

According to Lü Huiqing, what distinguishes the sage in this story (Ziqi) from the common person (Ziyou) is the former's ability to recognize that the true suchness of selfhood does not reside within himself but is the natural self-so-ness of the myriad things. Forgetting one's self, therefore, leads to the realization that the transformation of things takes place in a non-temporal plane of reality, and being without beginning or end, it is the perpetual non-self of Dao which comes to supplant the relational-self, rendering it forgettable. Knowing that death and life are but a continuous cycle seen throughout the universe, the sage clings to his constant root, which is nothingness. He behaves in a similar manner when differentiating the ontic and ontological self. This is why Lü Huiqing employs the image of the hollow bamboo flute, for it nicely reflects the *Zhuangzi*'s idea that the human body is a shell whose vitality is none other than the *qi* of Dao.

Lin Xiyi's explanation was certainly the most colorful of the three we discussed and it stands out for its introduction of the concept of non-mind (*wuxin* 無心)—a rejection of one's reliance on things, including the idea of self. Epistemologically, Lin's argument over the separation of "I" and "self" appears to be one of semantics. Cosmologically, however, we can declare that which puts the "I" into the "self" is the vitality of Dao. In this way, the self becomes subject to the whims of our *qi* and the physical form of our being. Bequeathing our body as it does, Dao instills in us its enervating nature and it is for this reason that its cosmic spirit is taken to be the companion of our corporeal selves. The heart-mind, however we view it, is simply a tool by which to engage things in logical or emotive terms; it has no bearing whatsoever on the state of our partnership with our spirit, but influences how far one is able to progress in harmonizing with things. Given that the myriad things partake in the *qi* of Dao, we owe them no allegiance, nor are we dependent on them. Our dependency can only be traced to Dao itself, nothing else.

What we must bear in mind, moreover, is that the sense of self which we tend to assign ourselves is not the self that exists in the eyes of Dao. Recalling our earlier discussion of the One, things possess a degree of particularity about them, yet such qualities are at the same time assimilated into the oneness of all things, thereby rebuking any individualism they may experience in favor of one belonging to the collectivity of the One. In this way, the "I" that I identify with ontically is forgotten when viewed from the cosmological "I" of Dao. Indeed, to say that Dao has an "I" would be to describe it as an ontological thing, something that is infeasible; rather, the "I" of Dao is a meontological "I" that equalizes all disparate "I's" into a singular "non-I."

If the "I" of myself is not the "I" of Dao but its "non-I," it does not require too great a leap in logic to arrive at the realization that any forgetting of the egoistic "I" is in fact a remembrance of the "non-I" of Dao. The act of forgetting one's self is, therefore, an act of uniting with one's non-self in Dao insofar as it is an inward self-extension of nothingness that partakes in the oneness of the myriad things collectively. Since Dao is atemporal, the "I" that is the "non-I" of the One cannot be forgotten. This is why those who have written commentaries to this passage are in agreement when they say that the forgetting which leads to the loss of one's self is actually a reflecting on the true nature of things, while the forgetting that takes place while one is still in possession of one's self is an occasion to begin forgetting things so as to lose one's self.

The reason it is crucial to lose one's self is that the presence of the "I" diminishes the presence of Dao's spirit in one's body. It is as Zhuangzi states: "The genuine person breathes with their heels while ordinary people breathe with their throats."[20] In order to keep our bodies intact and preserve our spirit, we must not only rid ourselves of the desire for fame and profit, we must learn to view the world using the *qi* of the universe and not the heart-mind of humanity. This involves hiding our spirit rather than flaunting it, nourishing it by forgetting the things of the world, after which all that remains is the non-essence of Dao. If all that remains is Dao, how can our spirit suffer harm? If all that remains is Dao, of what need is there to forget things so as to return to simplicity? The answer lies in a life praxis grounded in nothingness:

> Those who have a head and feet but are without a heart-mind or ears are numerous. Those having form believe they can exist alongside that which is without form or shape but they end up being exhausted. Men have their movement and stoppage, their death and life, their decline and arising; of these we can do nothing. Believing our governor lies amongst us, we can forget things and heaven, and are named a forgetter of self. He who has forgotten his self is thus known as one who has entered heaven.[21]

> 凡有首有趾無心無耳者眾，有形者與無形無狀而皆存者盡無。其動，止也；其死，生也；其廢，起也。此又非其所以也。有治在人，忘乎物，忘乎天，其名為忘 己。忘己之人，是之謂入於天。

In the previous chapter, we spoke of a life praxis modeled after the usefulness of being useless, but this would not be nearly as effective as cultivating oneself in forgetfulness so as to return to the equanimity of nothingness. Zhuangzi's advice that we ought to hide our spirit so as to preserve our presence of being shows the extent to which his meontological understanding of the universe permeates his philosophy. Owing to the oneness of all things as demonstrated by the fact that everything emanates from and returns to Dao, it is the source of both our body and spirit. If body and spirit alike take Dao as their source and nothingness as their root, then the notion that humanity possesses them independently of Dao is untenable. Without the animating spirit of Dao, we cannot attain oneness with Dao, rendering our body and heart-mind to withered wood and dead ash.

Having said as much, where does this leave us with regard to the forgetting of self? The idea of a self whose existence is autonomous of Dao has now been proven inaccurate, and that which we refer to as the heart-mind only clouds the clarity of Dao's essence within us to the extent that we associate mind, spirit, and body as one amalgamated entity. Dao gives us our form and sets it alight with its *qi* but the mind of man is, at its core, a limited thing, preventing us from encountering the boundless potential of nothingness. The best way to bring equality to things is to discard the selfish concept of self and think in terms of a selfless non-self. Letting-go of the "I" in myself is to be like the small pile of ash produced by an individual incense stick which joins the main pile of ash filling the cauldron—each heart-mind disintegrates into the non-mind of the selfless-self, the outcome of which is "heaven, earth, and I came into being together" and "nothing lives longer than a child who dies young."[22] In other words, dichotomies such as death and life, old age and youth, self and other, become meaningless when considered against the backdrop of nothingness to which they all inevitably return and arise anew. Forgetting the self is thus a means by which to illuminate the error of our ways as we go about dividing and assigning names to things; it is, in other words, a non-deliberate doing that awakens us to the fact that it is the naturally self-so, not human knowing, which acts as the true standard-bearer by which things coexist with one another.

To forget the self is to forget things, and when things are forgotten, one can forget the distinction between heaven and earth. Thus a person who practices the forgetfulness of things, self, and heaven and earth, is a person who has entered the realm where neither non-being nor being exist; there is only the profoundness of Dao. It is here, in the realm of Dao, that true onto-cosmological freedom occurs. Such freedom in the oneness of things is only accessible to the nondiscriminating mind of the sage, one that forgoes its associative dichotomy with the body to root itself in the constancy of nothingness. Thus while we have seen how loss of self equalizes humanity and the myriad things of the world, if we are to transcend this realm and reach cosmological freedom of a spiritual bearing, we must learn to master what is arguably the most difficult stage, that being sitting in forgetfulness.

Sitting in Forgetfulness

In his story of cook Ding, Zhuangzi outlined three stages one must traverse in order to master the art of butchery. Our current discussion on the art of forgetting displays a similar pattern of progression. We have thus far looked at two stages of forgetting: things and self. The third stage, the art of sitting in forgetfulness, can be regarded as approximating cook Ding's ability to view the ox from within by using the nothingness of the knife blade to enter the gaps between the ox's joints and bones. Employing the analogy of the cook is valid in that sitting in forgetfulness not only obliterates the heart-mind and body, but is a sitting whose scope extends to the essence of spirit itself. If we are to truly become one with the myriad things—to join with the ox as does cook Ding—forgetfulness of this magnitude must not only touch the core of our spirit, it must nullify it along with the initial act of forgetting, for only when we have forgotten our heart-mind and body can we attain the cosmological freedom engendered by the ontological nothingness utilized by Dao.

In the *Zhuangzi*, the word forget (*wang* 忘) is seen eighty-seven times while the expression "sitting in forgetfulness" (*zuo wang* 坐忘) appears just three times,[23] all of which are in a conversation between Confucius and his disciple Yan Hui:

> Yan Hui said [to Confucius], "I have forgotten benevolence and righteousness." Confucius replied, "That is good but there is more to be done." After a few days, Yan Hui again saw Confucius and said, "I have made progress." Confucius asked, "What do you mean?" Yan Hui responded, "I have forgotten rites and music." Confucius said, "That is good but there is more to be done." After a few more days, Yan Hui again saw Confucius and proclaimed, "I have made progress." Confucius asked, "What do you mean?" Yan Hui declared, "I can sit in forgetfulness." Confucius, startled, said, "What do you mean by sit in forgetfulness?" Yan Hui answered, "I discard my limbs and lose my intellect. Leaving my body, I abandon wisdom and unite with the Great Connector. This is called sitting in forgetfulness."[24]

曰：回忘仁義矣。曰：可矣，猶未也。他日，復見，曰：回益矣。曰：何謂也？曰：回忘禮樂矣。曰：可矣，猶未

也。他日,復見,曰:回益矣。曰:何謂也?曰:回坐忘
矣。仲尼蹴然曰:何謂坐忘?顏回曰:墮肢體,黜聰明,離形去
知,同於大通,此謂坐忘。

Yan Hui's progressive development toward total forgetfulness is carried out in three stages. To begin, Yan proclaims to have forgotten benevolence (*ren* 仁) and righteousness (*yi* 義), qualities which, oddly enough, helped define the Ruist gentleman (*junzi* 君子). The irony here cannot be overlooked; Zhuangzi was not only discreetly criticizing the Ruists for clinging to what he viewed to be artificial motivators, his call for their dismissal added to his mocking by deeming them unworthy of preservation as one pursues unification with Dao. Zhuangzi thus wrote:

> The Ruist wears a round cap to show he knows the time of heaven, walks in square shoes to show he knows the form of earth, and hangs jade ornaments around his waist to resolve disputes when they take place. The gentleman has his Way but he does not need to adorn himself with its robes; wearing its robes, he may still fail to understand his Way.[25]

儒者冠圜冠者,知天時;履句屨者,知地形;緩佩玦者,事至而
斷。君子有其道者,未必為其服也;為其服者,未必知其道也。

What the Ruists took to be the most redeeming characteristics of humanity, the *Zhuangzi* in turn criticized as misguided. Indeed, the text went so far as to say that any form of self-cultivation whose principles were founded upon the centrality of the human heart-mind would do nothing but lead people astray from the path of Dao. In light of the fact that both benevolence and righteousness are morally inspired forms of engaging the world, their being forgotten can thus be regarded as equivalent to Zhuangzi's first, ontic stage of forgetfulness.

Whereas the cultivation of *ren* and *yi* were appropriated by the Ruists as ideals whose normative value is essential for a stable and harmonious society, the *Zhuangzi*'s mockery was not a sign of vindictiveness but an attempt to point out the inadequacy of cultivating such human-centric values over those found in the natural world. That which is natural is derived from Dao and so to cultivate the natural can only lead to further naturalness while bringing us closer to its source. In order to do this, we must let go of the artificial that keeps us from the One and embrace the unity of oneness that traces itself back to Dao. Thus, when Yan Hui stated he has forgotten *ren*, *yi*, and *li* 禮 (ritual), he was in fact relinquishing what inwardly defined him as a practitioner of the socio-ethical code constituting his Ruist upbringing. To forget said beliefs would not ensure his successful attainment of spiritual freedom however. To do that, he must continue with his endeavors and learn to forget his body as well.

Despite his apparent progress in forgetting things, Yan Hui had yet to forget his body. Translating the forgetting of one's body into Confucian terms, Zhuangzi wrote that Yan must abandon his use of ritual propriety and music (*yue* 樂). Ritual and music were without doubt two of the central pillars of early Chinese civilization and saw their incorporation into Ruist doctrine at the time of said school's inception. As the principle means by which one outwardly expresses oneself, ritual and music were not only internally standardized, they were also outwardly conformist in nature. Those who follow ritual etiquette or engage in musical performance were not only bound by the rules of their activity, they were at the same time bound to those acting as spectators. This type of inward fusing with outwardly rectified behavior was far from natural and was severely frowned upon by Zhuangzi. How one behaves, he argued, should not be the subject of an overarching body of rules; rather, it ought to be spontaneous and in harmony with the self-so nature of the person involved.[26] Only when this occurs will one be able to forget one's body and proceed to the next stage of forgetting.

With self and body now forgotten, Yan Hui had at last reached the culminating stage of his quest for total self-forgetting. Sitting in forgetfulness is an intriguing metaphor given Yan had already dismissed any epistemic and phenomenological awareness of his presence of being. To what, then, was Zhuangzi hinting with the phrase "sit in forgetfulness"? Yan's answer that he had simply united with Dao seems simplistic and inadequate. Is it not obvious from the previous two stages of forgetting that he had discarded his body and dismissed his heart-mind? It would thus be more than reasonable to declare that sitting in forgetfulness is but the culmination of the first two stages of forgetting and nothing else, but surely there is more to it than this?

In his commentary on the passage containing Yan Hui's final reply to Confucius, Cheng Xuanying made this observation:

> The Great Connector is like Great Dao. As Dao can penetrate and give birth to the myriad things, it is thus called Dao the Great Connector. What is external is separate from bodily form—a false emptiness—and this explains discarding one's

limbs. What is internal is discarded pursuing what the heart-mind knows—a sudden ignorance—and this explains dismissing one's intelligence. He who is like withered wood and dead ash mysteriously joins with Great Dao. Making progress in this way is called sitting in forgetfulness.[27]

大通，猶大道也。道能通生萬物，故謂道為大通也。外則離析於形體，虛假，此解墮肢體也。內則除去心識，悗然無知，此解黜聰明也。既而枯木死灰，冥同大道，如此之益，謂之坐忘也。

What we hear with our ears and see with our eyes are but traces of things. Knowing they are merely traces we can thus forget them. This is why we are able to dismiss our four limbs. If, however, we are to discard our intellect and purge ourselves of selfhood and heart-mind, we must not only forget the traces of the myriad things but also that which leaves the trace (*suoyi ji* 所以跡). The many occurrences of forgetting spread throughout the *Zhuangzi* all point to this central idea of sitting in forgetfulness. What is more, all exemplars of sagacity indicate and embody Yan Hui's feat.

What is interesting to note in all of this is that those figures which have completed their return to the One are social outcasts, or suffer from a physical ailment, while those who are in the midst of mastering this skill are disciples of Confucius, or Confucius himself. Zhuangzi's attack on the Ru was, therefore, hermeneutic and practical at the same time. Sitting in forgetfulness thus became a course of action whose directive was to facilitate people partaking in a double awakening: the first, small awakening, is to the nature of human finitude and the limits of our knowledge; the second, great awakening, sees the breakdown of humanity's struggle to view things from the point of view of the infinite vastness of Dao and its endless potential for change.

Our awakening to Dao from within the cocoon of human reality does not secure our transcendence though; on the contrary, sitting in forgetfulness succeeds in much the same way as things trace their origins back to the One. The experience of Yan Hui, while marvelous in its own right, was neither transcendental nor mystical for he engaged himself from within himself so as to forget himself. There was no union with a higher source, no sense of enlightenment or privilege because of it; rather, Yan engaged himself in a form of self-reductionism whereby with each successive stage of forgetting he lost one insistent layer of human autonomy preventing his return to the One. We may think of it in this way: each time

Yan Hui forgot himself he darkened his self, becoming ever more sage-like. As the dark is synonymous with the still quietude of nothingness from which everything emerges and returns, Yan must in turn make himself mirror those characteristics if he is to have any hope of transforming into someone who is inwardly dark while outwardly luminous. This is what separates Yan Hui as a prospective sage from the prognosticating shaman. The shaman engages in flights of spiritual fancy so as to conjoin the gods and spirits of the dead, whereas the sage exists in a realm where there is no distinguishing between the spirits of the dead and those of the living. There is no ascending to heaven for there is no leaving Dao; one can only inwardly revert to Dao so as to outwardly conjoin with it.

For Yan Hui to return to the One he must, as a final measure, sit and become dark through the act of forgetfulness. Sitting on the ground, Yan breathes with his heels and loses himself to the great clod that is planet Earth. Embracing the Earth as if it were an arm or a leg, he breathes the breath of the Earth, becoming one with it. As the great clod is already united in a state of oneness with the myriad things treading upon and within it, Yan's losing himself such that his limbs become no more important to him than the ground upon which he sits, symbolizes the totality of his physical forgetting. No part of his body holds preference over the others, just as the Earth shows no favor for one of its compositional elements over any of the others. The Earth's ecosystem hence serves as a reflection of his own physiology in a manner not dissimilar to how cook Ding inserted himself into the ox in order to undo it. All the relationships, variables, cycles, and mutations of the world's ecosystems are now clear to him, but he does not use this clarity to conquer or manipulate it, for he recognizes it as embodying the self-so-ness of Dao.

All of this informs Yan Hui as to the phenomenology of sitting in forgetfulness; it does not inform him of the onto-cosmological side of doing so. To uncover this aspect, we must analyze the process involved in such sitting, one whose entailment is not immediately apparent from either the passage quoted above describing Yan Hui or the appended commentaries. Indeed, while the phrase "sit in forgetfulness" occurs in chapter 6 of the *Zhuangzi*, the concept describing the process involved in such sitting—composing the heart-mind—appears earlier in chapter 4. Thus, while we are clear about the three stages of forgetting that culminates in composing the mind, what exactly such composing entails remains unclear. The goal of the next section of this chapter is to address this issue by solving the mystery of how one mentally composes oneself whilst engaging in sitting in forgetfulness.

A Taste of Spiritual Freedom: Composing the Heart-Mind

Abstinence from food is something normally associated with physical fasting, but what are we to make of abstinence of the heart-mind? It is a queer turn of phrase, so much so that the Chinese term for it (*xinzhai* 心齋) appears only once in the entire *Zhuangzi*.[28] While the term *xinzhai* is typically translated as "fasting of the mind," doing so can be misconstrued for the Buddhist idea of discarding or denying the mind. Here is the passage wherein this perplexing phrase occurs:

> Yan Hui asked, "What is composing the mind?" Confucius answered, "Concentrate your will and dismiss all distracting thoughts. Do not listen with your ears but with your heart-mind. Do not listen with your heart-mind but with your *qi*! Let your listening stop with the ears and let your heart-mind stop with what is appropriate. *Qi* is an emptiness that awaits the appearance of things and Dao gathers where there is emptiness. Such emptiness is composing of mind."[29]

> 顏回曰：敢問心齋。仲尼曰：若一志，無聽之以耳而聽之以心，無聽之以心而聽之以氣！聽止於耳，心止於符。氣也者，虛而待物者也。唯道集虛。虛者，心齋也。

Sitting in forgetfulness is thus to compose the mind in order to make Dao one's abode. When we speak of housing Dao we are not referring to a consciously deliberate intervention, but to use the words of the commentator Wang Pang, "concentrate the will and the heart-mind will determinately consider things clearly and with quiet emptiness in order to reach where Dao gathers itself."[30] Wang goes on to say:

> In the midst of this emptiness, Dao gathers and there is no use for external knowledge, only internal virtue. Thus it is said: "One does not listen with the ears but with the heart-mind." As the heart-mind has obtained it, so will one's *qi*. Thus it is said: "One does not listen with the heart-mind but with *qi*."[31]

> 夫中既空虛，而道集非由外知而由於内得也，故曰：無聽之耳而聽之心。心既得之，則然後以氣而得之也，故曰無聽之以心而聽之以氣。

Composing the heart-mind is just that—a reorganization—and not an ascetic attempt at enlightenment. By reprioritizing the goals of the mind and spirit, the conscious mind that we so desperately cling to for guidance in our daily life is moved from the forefront of our attention to the rear. It is thus cloistered so as to bring about quiet, still, emptiness, and a non-presumptuous outlook. In other words, if we are to allow Dao to gather within the confines of our heart-mind, the latter must mimic the conditions favored by the former in its self-gathering tendencies. Only when our mind changes into a non-mind can it act as a receptacle for Dao. Having become an empty space which Dao thereupon occupies, our mind gives itself over to *qi*. In releasing our mind, we must find a substitute by which we can continue to function as a human being and this substitute is *qi*. As we are now one with Dao, our *qi* has of its own accord transformed into the *qi* of Dao, one shared by the myriad things of the world. We are thus able to listen with this *qi* as if we are listening with the ears of Dao; we are able to see with it as if we are seeing through the eyes of Dao. Being one with Dao, we indubitably become indistinguishable from it. Dao and my former self have thus been spliced together to the extent that I am no longer myself—I have lost myself through forgetfulness.

Of all the commentaries to the *Zhuangzi*, when it comes to the passage on composing the heart-mind, none is more illuminating than Lin Yidu's, quoted here in its entirety:

> To compose is to treasure emptiness of heart-mind. If the heart-mind still contains things, to use it for the act of composing will be difficult indeed! To compose for the sake of ease is negligent and inappropriate given the sheer vastness of heaven. Listening with the ears is considered the proper way to listen; listening with the heart-mind is considered the reverse of listening; and listening with *qi* is not to listen at all. Proper listening is done with the ears which exhausts the principle of things. Reverse listening is done with *qi* which exhausts the fulfillment of one's nature. Not listening at all uses emptiness to achieve one's ultimate fate. To listen with the ears and stop there is not like doing so with the heart-mind; as the heart-mind has its differentiations, there must be division and agreement before they can be combined. When intention reaches *qi*, there is no more listening for emptiness but awaiting things and nothing more. It is because of this

that Dao gathers itself and composing the heart-mind has its marvelous uses. When the *Liezi* said: "The body combines with the heart-mind, the heart-mind combines with *qi*, and *qi* combines with the spirits [of deities]," it is essentially this meaning. Yanzi[32] already knew this and so said: "Before Hui obtained it." When Confucius let him compose his heart-mind starting from the fact that he was Hui, having obtained a use for composing the heart-mind, there was no longer any 'I.' Confucius again said, although you [Yan Hui] have already reached emptiness, it is like entering the land of action where only names are able to move the heart-mind. If the heart-mind resembles the *guan* and *yue*,[33] it emptily awaits a breath. When one enters it calls out, but when none enter it stops. How can such a thing contain the heart-mind? Allowing the myriad things to exit and enter, there is no door; they hand themselves over to the self-governance of the world and there is no harm in this. Embracing the One as one's dwelling, if one is unable to obtain it one must first stop and then arise in response to things. Residing in the principle of things and not having any of one's own is to fulfill one's destiny. To fulfill the principle of one's nature and destiny, no matter what one does, it will not be in accordance with heaven. Acting on behalf of men, it is easy to use the untrue; acting on behalf of heaven, it is hard to act untruly. That wings fly and knowledge knows, such metaphors tell us that Yanzi must reside in ultimate emptiness, a place where things transform. Looking at his previous condition and understanding empty nothingness is to know the heart-mind. Where whiteness is born Dao gathers and this is what we call the self-so. If one abandons determinate spirits then temples will come to a stop; if they cannot stop, then the body will sit while the spirit gallops. As for what can be determined, the ears and eyes do not necessarily have to be external and the will of the heart-mind does not have to be internal. Thus the difficult has its considerations and courses of action, and not fording the breath of the world, ghosts and spirits will come to dwell, yet this does not speak for human beings.[34]

齋，貴虛心，若心猶存有，則其為齋也難矣！以齋為易而忽之者，畔天不宜。聽之以耳，正聽也；聽之以心，反聽也；聽之以氣，無聽也。正聽以耳，將以窮理；反聽以神，將以

盡性；無聽以虛，將以至命也。聽止於耳，不若於心；心有
分別，符則分而有合；意至於氣，則無所復聽，虛以待物而
已。道由此而集，心齋之妙用也。列子云：體合於心，心合
於氣，氣合於神，與此義同。顏子既悟，乃曰：回未得。仲尼
使之心齋，實自有回；既得使心齋之後，未始有回，則無我
矣。夫子又語以汝雖已至虛，若入於有為之地，當不動心於名
可也。心如管籥，虛以待氣，氣入則鳴，不入則止，何嘗容心於
其間哉？任萬物之出入，無門者也；付天下之自治，無毒者也。
抱一自居，不得已而後起以應物，寓其理於物而不自有，則盡
矣。盡性命之理而有為者，其為莫非天也。為人使易以偽，為
天使則為偽也難矣，翼飛、知知以喻顏子必有至虛之宅，方能
化物。瞻彼前境，了然空虛，以喻心也。生白則道集之謂性，
舍神定則吉祥來止；不能止者，形坐而神馳矣。夫能定者，耳
目非必在外；心志非又在內。故雖有思有為，而無涉世之息，
鬼神將來舍，而況於人乎。

Dao gathers in emptiness for emptiness is the meontological medium of Dao. Lin Yidu's reference to the heart-mind as analogous to a wind instrument is both insightful and inspirational. It is certainly a comment that shows influence from Zhuangzi's own story of the wind blowing through the hollows of trees.[35] Here, however, we are discussing the mechanism of the heart-mind and not the relativity of language. Putting aside these minor differences, the idea at work is essentially the same. The heart-mind can be thought of as a flute and its purpose is inherent in its design; on the other hand, the potential that lies dormant within it cannot be realized without the proper "wind." Place a flute in the hands of a child and what follows will be anything but musical; place it in the hands of an amateur musician and things improve remarkably. It takes the skill of a master, however, for the remarkable to become extraordinary. Whereas the child and amateur know how to blow into a flute to produce sound, only the master has enough insight to know the benefit of silence. Such silence is the link that binds the master of an instrument to the nothingness of Dao.

The silence that allows sound to rise up and interact with those already in play is only possible if said silence is recognized to begin with. When Lin Yidu said the heart-mind is like a flute, he was reflecting Zhuangzi's idea that to use one's heart-mind to manage the affairs of the world only yields hollowness; it would be better to practice the arts of Dao. That which comes from Dao shines forth only in a clearing of empty tranquility; it is a clearing that shines forth with the bright illumination of mutual clarity. Such brightness is described as being pure and white because no other color can accept change without retaining part of that change itself. White noise is thus the sound of emptiness, a sound whose harmony with all other sounds is complete and unalterable; it is, in other words, the sound of oneness. The time when the flute falls silent is the time when it can be said to be in a natural state of emptiness. No longer used for the will of men, the silent flute forgets itself, returning to equanimity with Dao.

In silence, the hollows of the tree await the wind—the *qi* of the Earth. The flute likewise awaits its own form of wind—the *qi* of man. There is no presence of mind here, only still emptiness. As the flute has the inherent ability to return to emptiness, and hence the One, Lin Yidu has adopted it as a metaphor for the spiritual state of being that humanity ought to achieve. Sitting in forgetfulness is thus the clearing of one's mind to make way for the pure whiteness of Dao. It does not involve the deliberate blocking out of memories or the heart-mind as a whole; rather, it is a posture through which the mind gives way to non-mind and the body gives way to non-presence of being.

As spiritual essence points to the *qi* of Dao, listening with *qi* instead of our ears is to engage the things of the world, not through the filter of individuality that is human hearing, but the holistic ear of the One. In listening with the ears of man we hear things, but when we listen with our *qi* what is heard is the togetherness of the myriad things as they pass through their cycles of change and transformation. Thus sitting in forgetfulness is to sit in emptiness so as to make the oneness of things our dwelling. Such dwelling in the oneness of things is thus on par with the process of return, the primary difference being it is a temporary dwelling marked by our ability to return from such returning in the form of a reconstituted presence of being. It is as if we could suddenly shrug off our temporally grounded corporality—as a molting cicada can shrug off its skin—leaving our authentic selves unhindered to interact with the myriad things of the world.

The ability of the sage to enter into and return from dwelling in the nothingness of the One is a vital component of the *Zhuangzi*'s cosmology. As we are not dealing with a spiritual being but Dao, any attempt to twist Dao into being such an entity comes across as unduly naïve. Although Zhuangzi would have believed in the spirituality of the subtle, his belief would not have amounted to religiosity. How could it? Given that Dao not only creates things but also enables the possibility of said creation, it is hard to see how his philosophy can be interpreted as mystical or even hinting at mysticism, despite his frequent use of the word mystery (*xuan* 玄)! Zhuangzi was well aware of the fact that our eyes and ears root themselves in experiential knowledge, but he was also well aware of the fact that this kind of knowledge is inauthentic.

The *Zhuangzi* construed the memories that constantly badger our minds and haunt our actions as but the chaff and dregs of a time whose passage should not be relived or taken as authoritative. Embracing the oneness of things has taught us as much, as has the praxis of being useless. Sitting in forgetfulness factors into the equation in that forgetting the disparate traits of the myriad things of the world we ourselves become forgotten, and having forgotten the notion of self, we can hence forget our bodies. Out of the praxis of non-self and non-presence of being, a quiescent and empty spirit comes to bear, the culmination of which is cosmological freedom. It is for this reason that Zhuangzi reserved sitting in forgetfulness as the final measure wherein man learns to forgo his self-assumed place in the world so as to return to the root that is ontological nothingness: "Thus in nourishing the will one can forget his body, in nourishing the body one will forget profit, and in arriving at Dao one will forget his heart-mind."[36]

Conclusion

This chapter has been a continuation of our previous discussion on the praxis of uselessness. Having gained insight into the usefulness of being useless, our analysis shifted to how one can become engaged in the forgetting of things, the relational-self, and one's body and heart-mind. Despite their different approaches, these methods achieved their intended goal—an unequivocal freedom of being stemming from the embracement of ontological nothingness. Freedom in Dao is a freedom that lets things be; in letting things be as they are, Dao ensures they will live out their allotted years in a manner most attuned to their way of existence. In light of Dao's utilization of nothingness, the freedom it affords those who conjoin with it is both spiritual and cosmological. How we can escape the anxiety of our own finitude is the subject of our next chapter, one that will show us everything a living freedom has to offer, while at the same time, putting us on the path toward the highest state of freedom possible—the freedom to wander carefree with Dao in primal nothingness.

6

Wandering Carefree in Nothingness

Among the many concepts that have made their way into the development of philosophical discourse, freedom is without doubt one of the more contentious. The tendency of modern society to associate it with autonomy and individualism has only contributed to the idea that freedom must be viewed as the overcoming of a challenge whose threat endangers the subject's very existence, especially when it relates to the mind. Indeed, the contemporary world has framed the question of freedom in such a way that it has become one of the most fundamental issues of human thinking. While this may appear an insurmountable challenge, the notion that personal freedom stands in opposition to forces of restraint or constraint, be they from other people, the state, or more recently, technology, never plagued the intellectuals of ancient China—if anything, it was human desire that proved to be the major hindrance to social harmony and equality between individuals. In the case of Daoism, authentic freedom exists in only one guise—the onto-cosmological.

The challenge we face here is how to tackle the *Zhuangzi*'s concept of freedom when the term for it, at least in the modern Chinese sense of *ziyou* 自由, did not exist. One might argue that the term *zaiyou* 在宥 is equivalent to freedom, however, the word *you* (to forgive, pardon, or indulge) only appears twice in chapter 11, which contains it in its title, and once in chapter 33 (*tianxia* 天下). *Zaiyou* might thus be construed as a state of leisure or indulgence, but it cannot be extrapolated to embody the entirety of the *Zhuangzi*'s theory of freedom. What we have instead are inferences to freedom as an ideal whose basis lies not in the workings of humanity, but as heaven.

To this end, the *Zhuangzi* formulates three heavenly principles (*tianli* 天理) in order to formulate an onto-cosmological understanding of freedom, with Dao its pinnacle: heavenly differentiation (*tianni* 天倪), heavenly measure (*tianjun* 天均), and heavenly harmony (*tianhe* 天和). Defining freedom along these lines not only allowed Zhuangzi to break free of any dependency on human ontology, it enabled the possibility for a universally applicable freedom wherein the world no longer plays a role in the grounding or establishment of social and ethical norms. The result is that all things now share in a singular form of freedom, one leaving them open to spontaneously engage and transform with one another. To be free, therefore, no longer means to be free from something, but to embark on a journey of forgetfulness such that one comes to embrace and unite with Dao meontologically. Out of this situation, the world embraces harmony and when harmony pervades all corners of the world, the sage wanders carefree. This chapter thus explores Zhuangzi's unique theory of freedom by showing how the above triad of heavenly principles equalizes all things via the nondiscriminatory, non-mind of Dao. Owing to the fact that Dao is situated within nothingness, it equalizes the myriad things of the world to the extent that its perfection is epitomized by the spiritual ideal of uninhibited roaming (*xiaoyao you* 逍遙游).

Cosmological Freedom

Contemporary theories of freedom would have us believe it is an expression of one's emancipation, or that it represents a transcendental bliss bestowed on us by a higher spiritual authority. Invariably, however, such definitions fall back on the dichotomies of body and mind, mind and spirit, or otherwise resort to dualisms and moral platitudes. Use of such techniques might be justifiable in many of the world's religious traditions, but for Daoism the problem-set was wholly different.

Let us begin with the idea of the body. If freedom grounds itself in the autonomy of the body, how we delimit our bodies becomes a matter of central importance. This is quite straightforward when the body and mind are inseparable properties of being but in the case of the *Zhuangzi*, they are seen as distinctly separate aspects of human existence. To be more explicit, the terms *shen* 身 and *ti* 體 refer to the physical body while *ji* 己 represents the empirical self. To which of these should freedom point? The matter becomes even more complex when we take into consideration the *qi* 氣 sustaining one's personhood, let alone those components that can be used to further refine what exactly personhood entails—inborn nature (*xing* 性), emotional composure (*qing* 情), spirit (*shen* 神), and form (*xing* 形). It would thus seem that defining the Daoist ideal of freedom according to typical Western understandings would fail quite spectacularly given the multifarious ways in which we can frame the question: to what does freedom pertain?

Indeed, whether we frame the question of the corporeal presence of our being in terms of body and/or self, such framing more often than not comes back to the idea that being is the core essence of one's nature. Here, however, we run into a new question, one that asks what, if anything, is the crux of freedom? Given these initial musings, if we are to develop a comprehensive theory of what freedom entails for the *Zhuangzi*, we face not only questions surrounding its applicability, but the additional challenge of coming to terms with what this notion inherently signifies.

When we speak of being free, are we saying something substantive or are we in fact saying nothing at all? Zhuangzi posed such a question very early on in his text because if we wish to ask a serious question such as the nature of freedom, we must be sure of our motives:

> Speaking is not simply the blowing of wind. Words have something to say, but what they intend to say cannot be determined. Since what words have to say is uncertain, do they really say something or do they say nothing at all? Is speech any different from a young chick's call? Is there any distinguishing between them or is there none?[1]

> 夫言非吹也，言者有言，其所言者特未定也。果有言邪？其未嘗有言邪？其以為異於鷇音，亦有辯乎，其無辯乎？

To speak of freedom is to assume that the act of being free is one in response to some particular event, be it causal or otherwise. The resultant granting or denial of freedom is then studied for indications as to whether or not it was predetermined or somehow coerced. Due to these degrees of condition, we can postulate that ontological freedom is a measure of choice—a choosing whose essence can be traced back to the condition of a thing's being. To think of freedom in such terms, in options and matters pertaining to the will, is to see freedom from the perspective of man and not that of heaven. Even if we were to elevate ontological freedom to the realm of spirit by tethering the condition of a being's ontological presence of being to the successful union with ghosts and other non-corporeal entities, this promoting would still fail to relay the full import of cosmological freedom, let alone the meontological. The problem, it seems, is how to dispel the cloud of nihilism that hangs over our desire to transcend our imminent passing so that ontological liberty can be had.

For Zhuangzi, the nothingness accompanying Dao is, as we have seen, neither nihilatory nor deterministic. It is not what causes human reality to arise of its own doing because if freedom were only to emerge out of the transcendent suppression of nothingness, it would still remain a conditioned freedom as its roots lie in the ontic-ontological dichotomy of human finitude. The freedom that Dao offers us is unconditional and requires no transcendental act. It can be like this because the freedom associated with Dao, in being meontological, does not have us seek out the obliteration of our being but incites us to delegate it as merely a trait of our existence rather than its true center.

Freedom of the holistic kind seen in the *Zhuangzi* is thus one whose dependency on the reality of humanity's onto-phenomenological existence has been smashed and whose mental will has been discarded. For Zhuangzi, freedom is not limited to the being of man but applies to the cosmogony of the myriad things in their collectivity. Reality, and our ability to define it, loses any viability when we learn, as Yan Hui did, to ontically forget things. While human reality may very well be genuine and of factual value, it does not approach the ultimate reality of Dao. As it is thought of as being reality on all known levels of existence and beyond, Dao is in fact the non-reality of reality. Its non-presence makes the presence of the myriad things all the more real and yet, said authenticity lies with the creative possibilities of primal nothingness.

In order to better elucidate the relationship between freedom and nothingness, what we require is a more salient vocabulary. Any choice of words taken from outside the *Zhuangzi*, however, will prove insufficient in conveying the sublime beauty of its call to let go of our body, heart-mind, and self. While the accounts of sitting in forgetfulness and composing the mind best approximate Zhuangzi's theory of onto-cosmological freedom, they only speak to the physical steps involved without indicating what it means to be free in an onto-cosmological sense. Bodiless, the genuine person does not nullify his or her own ontic presence but envelops it in the luminosity of oneness shared by the myriad things. Mindless, the genuine person forgets the world of being and so undergoes a spiritual (i.e., great) awakening. What remains is thus no different from the state mentioned by Yan Hui when he sat in forgetfullness—a spirit whose ties to the corporeal world of humanity are no longer present, for it has relinquished itself to the constancy of ontological nothingness. To relinquish one's ontological self to the meontological realm of Dao is thus to become still and soulless; it is, in other words, a sign that one's journey back to the One has reached its completion. Freedom for the *Zhuangzi* is hence the act of letting-go and letting-be in such a way that one no longer engages in the pursuit of being but defers to its self-arising from Dao.

Zhuangzi thus understands freedom to be neither a form of causality nor a symbolic representation of the gateway from whence the truth of existence emerges. The search to uncover the truth of being, to unveil the truth of existence itself, occurs in the act of letting-be. This letting-be, however, substitutes the being of our living present with that of the towardness of death. The finitude of our being instills in us the desire to flee the confines of our corporeal form and we do this by bestowing upon our spirit a sense of infinitude. This propensity to frame freedom in terms of the everlasting will of humanity, and the spiritual omnipotence of ghosts and spirits, such that we have a means at hand to overcome and conquer the finitude of our own temporal existence, enslaves such theories of freedom to the narrow tract of man's own ontology.

All is not lost, however, and our search for a vocabulary salient enough to lift freedom out of the dust and dregs of being and into the magnanimous light of Dao might at last be at hand. In speaking of Dao, we are not pointing to anything concrete but to its unknowability; it is a mystery that frees all without revealing anything of itself. We can thus describe the freedom afforded by Dao as the illumination of a beclouded inner-virtue long lost in our pursuit of that which is artificial, including the truth of being. To speak of the revealing of Dao as an emerging from and returning to that which is free, is to be entombed in the presupposition that an onto-cosmological difference exists between the free and not-free. More fundamentally, the assumption that freedom only pertains to the human guise of being, rather than all beings, would appear irrational to Zhuangzi. If we are to speak of freedom being tied to Dao, we cannot refer to it in language of the free and not-free, for Dao is neither. To be free thus involves letting-go of freedom such that the concept of freedom vanishes completely. For Zhuangzi, freedom in Dao is hence the cosmological harmonization of things through which one partakes in a carefree wandering that is neither hindered nor tainted by concerns over what it means to be free. There is, therefore, no such thing as individual freedom; rather, freedom presents itself as a great awakening to the nothingness incipient in all things.

Three Heavenly Principles of Freedom

In light of our conclusion that freedom results from a spiritual awakening of such magnitude that it harmonizes all things on a cosmological level, the question that now needs to be asked is, how does it arise? If we recall at the start of this chapter our mentioning of the fact that the *Zhuangzi* employs three heavenly principles to symbolize cosmological freedom—differentiation, measure, and harmony—which constitute the natural laws of the universe, we can now argue that said principles ensure that all beings are permanently free in their togetherness. There is, as a result, no need for an individual to escape from this holistic oneness in order to exert his or her claim to a unique or particular individuality. This is because from the vantage point of Dao, all things are united in oneness. Furthermore, from the vantage point of Dao, all things are free in and of themselves and yet, this freedom is not a barrier placed before them, but a reflection of their rootedness in nothingness. Since Zhuangzi locates freedom in the meontology of Dao, as opposed to the being of man, freedom is not a condition one is born with, earns, and loses; rather, it is the authentic condition of reality taken as a prospective whole. If one wishes to speak in terms of the free and not-free, one must learn to speak of the degree to which a thing is harmonious with Dao. Freedom is thus a constancy whose measurement lacks any form of gradation. It cannot be otherwise, for if freedom is to be emblematic of the perpetual nothingness nourishing Dao, it too must have a degree of permanence. Having said as much, we must acknowledge the fact that harmony is not static, and so freedom cannot be realized in human measured time without it. In order to better explicate the role played by harmony in freedom, let us examine the passage containing Zhuangzi's three heavenly principles:

> What is called harmonizing things with heavenly differentiation? It is said that affirming and not affirming are the same, as are the so and not-so. If the so is really so, then as it is clearly different from the not-so, there is no need to differentiate them. If affirmation is really affirming, then as it is clearly different from not affirming, there is no need to differentiate them. The transformation of [wind] into sound is a mutual dependency that is, at the same time, not mutually dependent. Harmonize them with heavenly differentiation, allow them to mutually clarify each other, and in this way, you can complete your

allotted years. Forget about years and standards, stop and only take the infinite as your end, and in the infinite, you shall dwell.²

何謂和之以天倪？曰: 是不是，然不然。是若果是也，則是之異乎不是也亦無辯；然若果然也，則然之異乎不然也亦無辯。化聲之相待，若其不相待。和之以天倪，因之以曼衍，所以窮年也。忘年忘義，振於無竟，故寓諸無竟。

Freedom is to harmonize things with Dao and harmonizing things with Dao is to let them be. This letting-be is not taken in an ontological sense but according to heaven's distinguishing things. The term *tianni* 天倪 as understood by Guo Xiang means "natural distribution" (*ziran zhi fen ye* 自然之分也) in which affirming and not affirming, so and not-so, self and other, all become validated and indistinguishable. It is this indistinguishability of things that Zhuangzi took as symbolizing the differentiating virtue of heaven. What is more, it is carried out not in a theological capacity, but in the sense of what is natural. Cheng Xuanying reflected this in his commentary, adding that as right and wrong lack an overseer (*shifei wu zhu* 是非無主), debating them would be pointless.³ What is not pointless is the original generosity of Dao, and the idea that Dao bestows all things with life, nurturing them through old age, and welcoming their return at the time of their death. It does so without direction, influence, or any benefit to itself, and so all things reap this bounty. The natural thus becomes synonymous with heaven, and the heavenly becomes synonymous with Dao. All three can thus be said to act in concert as the differentiation of heaven, one lacking any kind of difference.

The non-differentiation of heaven can thus be taken as the means by which the sage engages the myriad things of the world in that it alone acts as the equalizing measurement of a thing's virtue. Indeed, the equality of which we speak also lends itself to heavenly measure, the second of Zhuangzi's principles of cosmological freedom. To view heavenly measuring as equivalent to an absolute measuring of things—as a form of equalizing—would imply that heaven is the one doing the equalizing when in fact things equalize themselves in harmonic accordance with Dao. In knowing the world, the incipience of Dao's measure in nature discards all notions of non-commensurability and exclusivity. Due to humans being causal creatures—we live through the doing of our actions—the way in which we come to possess an understanding of things directly conflicts with the principle of heavenly differentiation. Our tendency to dichotomize the world, to relegate things to their various classes of good and bad, right and wrong, is destructive not only to our own self-cultivation, but to the coherence of the myriad things populating the world as well. This is why Zhuangzi wrote that "due to human discourse, demarcations arise . . . the sage contains his within his breast while the common people flaunt theirs in order to show one another."[4] Thus ordinary persons engage in discourse using the differentiations of men rather than that of heaven, which is no different from using a horse to show that a horse is not a horse.[5] It would be better to use a non-horse to show wherein two horses differ, which is to say, that which is ultimately free has always been so, it just does not hold itself to standards of the free and not free.

To conduct one's life by flaunting one's knowledge through displays of this and that, is and is-not, is to distance oneself from the freedom awaiting us on the other side of forgetfulness. The way to overcome such epistemological relativism is to make way for nothingness by creating a clearing in our constitution that is free of our relational-self, enabling us to complete our return to the One. Sitting in forgetfulness while engaged in composing the heart-mind allows the clearing of nothingness that is the measure of heaven to take hold. To wander in the realm of carefree bliss is thus to encounter the spontaneous self-transformation of things emblematic of the natural world. Such transformative power of self is not to be misconstrued for human determination; rather, the myriad things change according to the self-so nature bestowed to them by Dao. The progressive profundity of our forgetfulness as we approach the realm of nothingness demarcating our reception into the One is thus a necessary measure if we are to engage the world according to the measure of heaven.

The principle of heavenly differentiation can hence be seen as a mysterious blending of the many into one; it is a oneness that is at once harmonious yet creational. Recognizing that life and death are but natural transformations, we can forget temporality. Recognizing that right and wrong are no different from the wind blowing through the hollows of a tree, we can forget discriminations. Accepting that words and images can be forgotten once we obtain their meaning, we can return to a state of silent naturalness and forget propriety. Returning to naturalness, we simultaneously become spontaneous, and through such spontaneity, we experience the ultimate reality of Dao. And yet, if the myriad things of the world avail themselves of Dao via the virtue of heavenly differentiation, as a form of distinction, it itself needs to give way to something higher, and that principle is known as heavenly measure (*tianjun* 天均):

If no goblet words come forth each day to harmonize things via heavenly differentiation, how could I have managed this long! The myriad things all have the same seed and use their different forms to alternate with one another. Their start and end form a ring of which none can grasp its principle. This is known as heavenly measure. Heavenly measure is thus heavenly differentiation.[6]

非卮言日出，和以天倪，孰得其久！萬物皆種也，以不同形相禪，始卒若環，莫得其倫，是謂天均。天均者天倪也。

Despite the above passage ending with the claim that the measure of heaven is no different from heavenly differentiation, there is in fact a modicum of difference. In order to uncover what this difference is, we need to first examine the sentences leading up to the above-quoted passage:

With these goblet words that come forth each day, things are harmonized via heavenly differentiation and I can complete my allotted years. When words are not used there is equality, however, this equality and my words are not equal, and my words and the original equality are also not equal. Thus it is said: No words. If one speaks without words, then in speaking one's entire life, one will not have said anything. If one doesn't speak one's entire life, this doesn't mean one has not spoken.[7]

卮言日出，和以天倪，因以曼衍，所以窮年。不言則齊，齊與言不齊，言與齊不齊也，故曰：無言。言無言，終身言，未嘗不言；終身不言，未嘗不言。

The character *qi* 齊 (to be equal), not to be confused with *zhai* 齋 (to compose), should be familiar to us as it appears in the title of chapter 2 of the *Zhuangzi*. Leaving aside the debate as to how one should translate this chapter title—as "on the equality of discourses" or "on equalizing discourses"—we can make a case that in the present context both *qi* 齊 and the *jun* 均 of *tianjun* 天均 are best understood in the sense of equalizing measures rather than absolute equality. When the above passage hence states that the measure and differentiation of heaven are identical, it would be erroneous of us to translate *jun* as a verb (i.e., to equalize) as this would imply that heaven actively participates in and influences the ontological condition of things. To equalize is to take upon oneself determinate measures—assessing for the purpose of demotion or promotion—actions that are not within the purview of Dao. Dao as heaven's shadow takes no-thing upon itself; it mingles and responds to things through non-deliberateness so as to reflect back onto them the spontaneous self-so-ness of their encounter. Any hierarchies deemed to exist in the natural world are thus the result of the imaginative musings of humanity. If Dao were to embark on a mission of equalization, the resultant choice of what to equalize would lead to an unnatural state of affairs. In other words, it would be introducing a nihilatory element into the world from which the being of certain beings becomes suppressed at the cost of the onto-cosmological freedom of others. This is neither heavenly measuring nor freedom in Dao.

Heavenly harmony (*tianhe* 天和), the third principle comprising Zhuangzi's concept of freedom, is the mechanism by which the measure of heaven carries itself forward. It is the outcome of the act of letting-be through forgetfulness:

> ... forgetting other men, they are taken to be men of heaven ... they are so because they have joined with heavenly harmony. If one who is enraged has no rage, then his rage is in fact no rage at all. If one who acts does so non-deliberately, then his acting is not acting at all. If one desires quiescence, then one must level-out one's *qi*. If one desires to be spiritual, then one must put the heart-mind into order. These are courses of action. If one wishes to be so, then one must go along with that which cannot be grasped; that which cannot be grasped belongs to the way of the sage.[8]

> ……忘人,因以為天人矣……唯同乎天和者為然。出怒不怒,則怒出於不怒矣;出為無為,則為出於無為矣。欲靜則平氣,欲神則順心,有為也。欲當則緣於不得已,不得已之類,聖人之道。

From the above, we can see that heavenly equality is to recognize that, on a fundamental level, all things partake in a singular cosmic circling of being whose center and outlying regions belong to the letting-be of Dao. Empty, still, and quiet, primal nothingness permits things to engage in self-reflection and self-cultivation for the purpose of recognizing that, in their grounding, they are all one. Sharing in the oneness of existence, the myriad things lose the need for a transcendental experience for at their meontological core, there is nothing present to transcend. They are imbued with the harmonious equality of Dao through and through, an imbuement whose source is the living possibility of nothingness. Gathering and pooling as they do, their endless changes and transformations trace themselves back to their root in the One, to the dark mystery of Dao.

The unknowability of Dao precludes it from being grasped by human cognition, so if our cognitive ability is rendered null and void, of what use are words? To attempt to speak of Dao, one must resort to non-words; to try and intuitively grasp its essence, one must conjoin with it as one spiritual essence to another. Dao resembles a mirage of potentiality whose darkness beclouds it when we approach, and whose profundity beclouds it when we attempt to pin it down with words. This is why Zhuangzi developed the technique of goblet words—words whose use are but temporary occurrences yet whose insight manages to touch the heart of all who hear them. We can thus pronounce goblet words succeed where normal words fail due to their knack for letting-be.

Freedom as letting-be is thus much more than ontic constraint. It is a letting-be that lets the nothingness of being follow its natural evolution. Wherein, the virtue of heavenly measure brings harmony to all things lies in its use of the non-mind of Dao. Using the non-mind of Dao, the lordship over right and wrong comes to pass, leaving things to their natural devices. Left to their own self-so-ness, the myriad things are thereby able to complete their allotted lifespans. Living out the timespans allotted them, years turn into non-years and life and death turn into an unbreakable circle of spontaneous self-transformation. This is the genuineness of their reality—what more can words add! The equanimity of the natural is thus a self-so equality that cannot be equalized through concepts such as right and wrong, and must be relinquished in order to preserve the integrity of our authentic experience of Dao:

> Remove compulsions of the will, unravel wrongdoings of the heart-mind, discard tangles of virtue, and clear away blockages to Dao. Honor and wealth, distinction and austerity, fame and profit; these six are compulsions of the will. Appearance and demeanor, beauty and reason, manner and intention; these six are false expressions of the heart-mind. Vice and desire, joy and anger, grief and happiness; these six are tangles of virtue. Turning away and taking in, adopting and offering, knowledge and skill, these six are blockages to Dao. When these four conditions and their six causes no longer sway the breast, we

will be upright. With uprightness we will be quiescent, with quiescence we will be illuminated; with illumination we will be empty, and with emptiness we will refrain from deliberate action yet nothing will remain undone.[9]

徹志之勃，解心之謬，去德之累，達道之塞。貴富顯嚴名利六者，勃志也。容動色理氣意六者，謬心也。惡欲喜怒哀樂六者，累德也。去就取與知能六者，塞道也。此四六者不盪胸中則正，正則靜，靜則明，明則虛，虛則無為而無不為也。

Heavenly differentiation, measuring, and harmony are hence three principles whose togetherness constitutes Zhuangzi's vision of cosmological freedom. Their cohesion and complementariness belie the notion that freedom stems from humanity alone. Indeed, in Zhuangzi's formulation, the human element fails to even factor into the equation; if anything, it is a hindrance in need of eradication.

Freedom *qua* nothingness thus symbolizes one's successful entrance to the fold of Dao. It is the ultimate reward for overcoming the limitations of our own humanity rather than being an implicit requirement of it. To be free is to live via the praxis of self-forgetting, speaking without words, and engaging things through mutual self-reflection and coexistence. In the act of letting-be, one disengages oneself from vain pursuits of material and intellectual profit, thus reflecting what is natural while pursuing the art of spontaneous living. This is the epitome of Daoist freedom. It is a modeling after the cycles and principles of Nature, of coming to realize that many of the perils faced in the course of human temporality are self-induced. If we can simply leave-be the things that drive a wedge between the world and us, then our lives can be lived without fear of being cut short.

Freedom, in other words, is simplicity and silence amidst a surrounding chaos. For those who are able to reach this ultimate realm of reality, no harm can befall them. Changing with the times as the seasons change with theirs, a person who is free in Dao harms no one and is harmed by no one. In this state of perfect unity, all dichotomies vanish, leaving only the possibility of nothingness from which the sprout of being can grow and be nurtured. If we cultivate the idea that nothingness is not a static state of non-existence but a milieu of potentiality, we will no longer have reason to fear it and can wander carefree, experiencing things as Dao experiences them. Before we can put wandering in freedom into practice, however, we must first understand what it means to be harmonious with things, and how such harmony not only focuses our freedom, which is always contingent upon it, but nourishes our life too.

Previously we examined how being useless led to life-prolongation and enrichment resulting in a form of phenomenological freedom, and how the various stages of forgetting serve as a prelude to cosmological freedom, but harmony is undoubtedly of even greater importance. Although the idea of heavenly harmony has been discussed to some degree already, if we wish to understand how harmony as a cosmological idea functions while one is experiencing freedom, further investigation is needed. Indeed, Zhuangzi's adoption of harmony as another representative principle of Dao was not accidental, especially given the role it plays in both uniting things while simultaneously cultivating them. This is crucial if we are to come to an understanding of how the sage can wander unburdened in the world, uniting the myriad things via heaven's measure, all the while displaying an appearance of simple mindedness and pristine virtue. Let us now turn to harmony and its relationship to nothingness.

Nothingness the Great Harmonizer

The key to successfully coming to terms with Daoist cosmogony is not to simply attribute it to a mysterious nothingness informing the universe; rather, nothingness is the material employed by Dao, the source of all creation, as well as the thread running through said creation. Whereas Dao instills in the things it creates a kernel of its own perfect virtue, the kernel of nothingness around which life takes hold acts as the great harmonizer of the universe. Nothingness, in other words, is the meontological oneness that balances the onto-cosmological oneness of Dao.

In order to discover an authentic knowing of the world that is even more primal than that shared between being and beings, our search should be conducted in such a way that it is not prone to the restrictions implied in freedom predicated upon the relationship of one thing to another. What we are in search of is a meontological freedom whereby what touches things is not the being of the One but the non-being of nothingness. For Zhuangzi, oneness is a metaphor for the cohesion things experience when following Dao, and in following Dao, they are left to their own devices. Dao, in its letting-be, thus makes room for nothingness to unfold in things, an unfolding that does not interfere in thing's pursuance of their life-path. Harmony in this sense is not just the letting-be of Dao, but the working of nothingness through Dao. Things work their way back to nothingness and, in so doing, preserve their integrity while enhancing their closeness to Dao. In other words, the harmonization of things via nothingness is not so much about reducing them to a singularity as it is about procuring a means to nullify destructive dichotomies in order to return to natural orders of balance. This is why the *Zhuangzi* writes:

> The people of ancient times who followed Dao used quietude to cultivate knowledge. With knowledge in them they did not act on its behalf, and this was called using knowledge to cultivate quietude. Knowledge and quietude thus took turns cultivating each other, and harmony and order emerged from their inborn nature.[10]

古之治道者，以恬養知；知生而無以知為也，謂之以知養恬。知與恬交相養，而和理出其性。

Natural order is perceived not in terms of hierarchy but balance. Balance, in turn, is seen not in terms of rectification and accommodation but equanimity and quiescence. Had the sages of old chosen to act according to the knowledge of the common man, such action would have led to strife and not harmony. That they acted in the spirit of heaven, the world knew only harmony and order. To compose oneself by sitting in forgetfulness is thus to transpose the inborn nature of Dao for one's own. Because the myriad things of the world order themselves along natural alignments of harmony, human knowledge falls by the wayside. Forgoing knowledge by composing the heart-mind is to embrace the empty tranquility of nothingness as the inborn nature of the universe. It is here where freedom dwells, and it is here where the sage returns and creates his abode. If we examine other early-period texts such as the *Huainanzi*, harmony is expressed using altogether different aphorisms. Take the following passage from the "*fanlun* 氾論" chapter of the *Huainanzi* as an example:

> In the *qi* of heaven and earth, nothing is greater than harmony. As for harmony, it blends *yin* and *yang*, divides day and night, and gives birth to things. In spring there is birth, in autumn completion, and it is in birth and completion that things necessarily obtain the essence of harmony.[11]

天地之氣莫大於和，和者，陰陽調，日夜分，而生物。春分而生，秋分而成，生之與成，必得和之精。

In his commentary to this passage, Gao You 高誘 noted that "as it is harmony, it thus gives birth to the myriad things 和, 故能生萬物." As for that which is the essence of harmony, Gao declared it to be none other than *qi*. Regardless of how they chose to illustrate the social climate of antiquity, texts explicating the nature of Dao all agree said antiquity was a time of still quietude, unperturbed by the vices of human knowledge. This abiding by the three principles of heaven was seen as one of perfect virtue, a state the *Zhuangzi* characterized as supreme unity (*zhiyi* 至一):

> The people of ancient times lived in a time of chaos and darkness, yet within this world they were able to attain quiescence and indifference. During that time, *yin* and *yang* were harmonious and still, ghosts and spirits were not troublesome, the four seasons held to their periods, the myriad things existed without harm, all living beings knew not of premature death, and while man had knowledge, he did not use it. This was called Supreme Unity. At that time, no one acted for anything and there was constant spontaneity.[12]

> 古之人，在混芒之中，與一世而得澹漠焉。當是時也，陰陽和靜，鬼神不擾，四時得節，萬物不傷，群生不夭，人雖有知，無所用之，此之謂至一。當是時也，莫之為而常自然。

Once again, we are presented with the idea that harmony will prevail in the world so long as humanity does not use knowledge to induce change or affect the natural balance between things. Forgetting one's place amongst things, the people of ancient times only thought of themselves as one being amongst a myriad of beings. Engaging the world with playful innocence, purposeful action remained unbeknownst to them and they lived spontaneously, mirroring Dao. This explains why wherever there is genuine life praxis, supreme unity is also found. Indeed, harmony as perfect unity is predisposed to a state of primal oneness such that the interaction of beings reflects not upon their state of being, but their inner nothingness. Such meontological harmony includes both the ontological nothingness of Dao and the ontic non-being arising from composing the heart-mind and sitting in forgetfulness. It should be noted that in terms of textual chronology, cosmological harmony has its precedent in the *Daodejing* where it says: "The myriad things rely on *yin* and embrace *yang*, taking the void of *qi* as their harmony."[13] With regard to this sentence, Lin Xiyi's commentary took it to mean: "As for the creation of the myriad things, they embrace and rely upon the *qi* of *yin* and *yang*. Moving with the principle of the void and emptiness, they achieve harmony."[14] We can hence argue that the early Daoist conceptualization of freedom was neither dependent on teleology of the will nor involved transcendence of one's desires, but was rooted in simply embracing the universal equanimity of Dao.

The presumed link between freedom and desire has proven to be a well-trodden theme in early Chinese thought, however, there remains an assumption that in linking these terms, the element of necessity interlopes therein. The problem with creating a triad between freedom, necessity, and desire, whereby necessity's bonding to desire is in need of overcoming if one wishes to attain freedom, is that it also recognizes desire as a conditioned necessity informing the authenticity of freedom, thus becoming a precondition for its own arising. Zhuangzi, interestingly enough, took the stance that things lose their freedom only when they view themselves as being bound to each other. How they released themselves from this mutual binding was to renounce the presence of their empirical selves and to do that, they require harmonizing with the oneness of Dao.

To introduce the concept of necessity as a prerequisite is to misconstrue the spirit of the *Zhuangzi*'s cosmological freedom—as a perfect unity with nothingness—because if transcending necessity were to directly result in freedom, it would imply that the grounding of one's being lies with one's self. This, in turn, would subsequently imply that the condition of our freedom is relative to the self-grounding we experience through being, not the authentic un-grounding afforded by Dao. To authentically un-ground ourselves in Dao—to take the meontological nature of Dao as our root—is to base our capacity for judgment in harmony and not in the notion of freedom. In harmonizing our knowledge of the world with the measure of heaven, we can thereupon view the world from the perspective of heavenly equality. Indeed, the *Zhuangzi* opens with a tale espousing precisely this—the great fish *kun* 鯤 transforming into the majestic bird *peng* 鵬.

When the cicada and turtledove later laugh at *peng* for needing to fly so high as it heads on its southern journey when they simply skip from branch to branch, Zhuangzi not only wanted us to bear in mind that all things, save for the sage, live with some kind of conditioned freedom, but that the key to attaining genuine freedom on a cosmological scale is to stop thinking of it as such, and regard it in terms of the harmony of things. Such harmony forms a collective presence whose purpose is to serve as a natural balance to the ontological nothingness of Dao. He who thinks along these lines can be said to possess kingly virtue, an attribute that the text describes thusly:

This is called the man of kingly virtue. He can see in darkness and hear in silence. Within such darkness, he alone can see dawn; within such silence, he alone can hear harmony. Thus although there are depths beyond depths, he is still able to discern things. Although there are spirits beyond spirits, he is still able to discern essences. Thus in his connection to the myriad things, he makes use of perfect nothingness to feed their needs. With the galloping of time he lodges in the large and small, the long and short, the near and far.[15]

此謂王德之人。視乎冥冥，聽乎無聲。冥冥之中，獨見曉焉；無聲之中，獨聞和焉。故深之又深而能物焉，神之又神而能精焉；故其與萬物接也，至無而供其求，時騁而要其宿，大小，長短，脩遠。

In reading this passage, it is hard not to notice that someone who possesses kingly virtue roams the world in perfect unity with it. His virtue unifies all things, as it is the virtue of heaven. Heavenly virtue, therefore, serves as a manifestation of the three heavenly principles discussed earlier. Being inwardly sagacious while outwardly kingly, the person of perfect virtue knows no bounds when it comes to his wandering. He takes day to be night and night to be day, chaos to be harmony and harmony to be chaos. In this way, all differences resolve themselves leaving only their meontic root. Mystery after mystery, the person who practices perfect unity sees only the constancy of their meontological essence. As a result, he dwells in the imperceptible and roams in the immeasurable. Thus he who uses kingly virtue as a means to fulfilling heavenly unity is the very personification of oneness with Dao.

But does this ability to personify the ultimate state of harmony also imply that the possessor of kingly virtue is free? Yes and no. Yes, in that only the sage or authentic person has accumulated enough of Dao's generosity to be adequately prepared to engage the world via forgetfulness and darkening of the conscious mind; no, in that anyone can be sagacious in their moral composition simply by adhering to the praxis of acting through non-deliberate doing, which is to engage things through letting-be. Forgetting and cultivating a mind that is dark hence serves two purposes: first, the act of forgetting keeps knowledge at arm's reach, preventing it from unduly influencing our discourse and lived-experience in the world; second, darkening the mind leads to still tranquility, a necessary trait if one is to observe the thread of nothingness that mysteriously ties all things together. From this a person comes to realize their inherent freedom through forgetfulness, and forgetfulness is the realization of still tranquility.

In a tone reminiscent of our previous discussion on time, rest comes to play an important role in Zhuangzi's definition of freedom. Resting in knowledge rather than allowing it to dictate courses of pursuance provides one with the opportunity to reflect upon the state of affairs in the world and adjust one's participation accordingly. Without a mind that is quiet and empty of the desire for personal aggrandizement, knowledge will eventually destroy its receptivity to Dao's harmonizing essence. This state of simplicity, which the *Daodejing* called *pu* 樸,[16] takes as its grounding not the will of consciousness, but the nothingness safeguarding Dao. In this way, the mind that is originary and genuine is the mind that acts by inwardly composing itself through the letting-be of rest. In restful quiescence, the heart-mind unites with the One and letting-go of its self, transforms into the non-mind of Dao. As the sage is one with Dao, his mind enlightens others while remaining dark and mysterious. It is through this resting that all things return to a state of quiet equilibrium, one in which they mutually cultivate one another, ensuring their continued freedom and longevity. Herein is seen Zhuangzi's answer to the need for the heart-mind to transcend its own nature of being and which is taken up in the text's commentaries, two of which will now be examined.

Guo Xiang's analysis of Zhuangzi's solution to any mind-freedom dichotomy is to read quietude and knowledge as coming together to form a principle of things existing for themselves:

> He who is calm and quiet will have knowledge that cannot be swayed; when one's knowledge is unswayable then one's nature cannot be lost. If one does not act on behalf of knowledge and believes it to be self-knowing, although he is aware of the myriad things around him, he remains quiet and self-assured. If one knows but does not act, then nothing will harm his quiescence; if in quietude one acts for oneself, then nothing can sway his knowledge. This can be called mutual cultivation. With these two engaged in mutual cultivation, harmony and principle separate. How can I speak of others![17]

恬靜而後知不蕩，知不蕩而性不失也。夫無以知為而任其自知，則雖知周萬物而恬然自得也。知而非為，則無害於恬；恬而自為，則無傷於知；斯可謂交相養矣。二者交相養，則和理之分，豈出佗哉！

From the above, it can be observed that harmony is the pivot to which the sage clings and the center from which Dao's self-so nature emerges. To be in harmony with the myriad things is thus to possess the capacity to walk two paths at once. The leap from harmony to freedom can occur because harmony both blends with, and takes into account, the ontological nothingness inherent to all things. In other words, harmony with the world is but another way of saying one has harmonized with Dao. As for what performs this harmonizing act, it is not being but nothingness, and each thing blends and morphs into the One because of it. Our emergence from and return to primal nothingness marks the start and end of temporality, as we have already seen, but it also delimits the extent of our freedom. Freedom, therefore, is the spontaneous potentiality found in nothingness, and in order to be aware of it, one must rid oneself of all trace of the discriminating mind and empirical-self, leaving behind a blankness to which nothingness is drawn. In light of this, the sage is free, not because of his existence in the world, which somehow gives him a sense of entitlement; rather, he is free in that he has perfected the meontological art of letting-be.

This is why Guo Xiang wrote that despite our possessing knowledge, we do not use it to engage the world. Having knowledge but choosing not to act upon it is to preserve the balance between things without disrupting the equanimity that brought such balance to the fore. If, on the other hand, one takes to action while practicing quietude of mind, doing so not for the purpose of profit or personal aggrandizement, such behavior will remain in accordance with the natural principle of things, leaving the harmony of the world unperturbed. However, with one nourishing the other, forming a recursive cycle, how can we discern their underlying principle? For Guo Xiang, this principle evolved from a cosmology of Dao to a principle of self-so-ness inherent to things themselves.

Indeed, Cheng Xuanying would also latch onto Zhuangzi's use of principle, though he tied it back to Dao and did not turn it into a law unto itself as did Guo Xiang. Cheng's commentary reads:

> Calmness is tranquility. The sage of ancient times used Dao to govern his body and the nation. He thus used the model of tranquility to cultivate his knowledge of genuine reality, employing it to not sway what exists beyond him. With his natural

disposition illuminated, knowledge was born. Knowing things mindlessly, he refrains from acting on their behalf. Having faith in his knowledge, he proceeds but does not arrive at a course of action. This is the knowledge of non-knowing, of knowing things without any knowledge of them. In this way, one comes to know without trying to know, and does not try to not know. Ultimately, one acts without trying to act and one does not try to not act and yet, use of this true knowledge is cultivated in quietude. If it were not like this, how could there be quietude! If one cannot be calm and tranquil, then how can we give birth to true knowledge? Without true knowledge, how can we cause such calm tranquility? It is, therefore, calmness that results in knowledge and so there can be tranquility. Knowledge aids tranquility and so becomes true knowledge, thus knowledge is found in calmness and each one cultivates the other. Herein is the harmony of Dao, existing in the minds of men, the principle of naturalness, and is shown in heavenly nature. It exists in me and that is all. How can I speak of others![18]

恬，靜也。古者聖人以道治身治國者，必以恬靜之法養真實之知，使不蕩於外也。 率性而照，知生者也；無心而知，無以知為也。任知而往，無用造為，斯則無知而知，知而無知，非知之而知者也。故終日知而未嘗知，亦未嘗不知，終日為而未嘗為，亦未嘗不為，仍以此真知養於恬靜。若不如是，何以恬乎！夫不能恬靜，則何以生彼真知？不有真知，何能致茲恬靜？是故恬由於知，所以能靜；知資於靜，所以獲真知。故知之與恬，交相養也。斯則中和之道，存乎寸心，自然之理，出乎天性，在我而已，豈關他哉！

Dao, being primordially empty and still, exudes a calm tranquility in all who follow it. If the sage is to prove valuable to others, be it on a level of personal engagement or that of the state, he must employ ways that are not valuable to himself. He emulates the newborn child, completes things by non-deliberate doing, and speaks with non-words. Using the knowledge of non-knowledge, the sage thus appears dim and unknowing, yet he is forever guided by Dao. His dimness is guided by the bright illumination of nothingness in such a way that the myriad things coalesce around him without knowing why. Their gathering is not the result of his sagacious wisdom, but his simplicity and ability to mirror the virtue of Dao. What the sage reflects, of course, is nothing and everything, the bright and the dark, the inner essence of things, and their outer character. Insofar as the sage is in harmony with Dao, his moral framework becomes representative of the heavenly principles permeating the universe. Given that heavenly harmony is the third principle needed to complete the attainment of cosmological freedom, and in light of the fact that such harmony is partially enacted through the sage, harmony is as much about virtuosity as it is about mutual conjoining:

> He who has an understanding of the virtue of heaven and earth may be called the Great Root or Great Ancestor, for he harmonizes with heaven. In dividing and promoting all under heaven, he harmonizes with others. Harmonizing with others is called the joy of humanity; harmonizing with heaven is called the joy of heaven.[19]

> 夫明白於天地之德者，此之謂大本大宗，與天和者也；所以均調天下，與人和者也。與人和者，謂之人樂；與天和者，謂之天樂。

Rather than view freedom as an inalienable right that must be bestowed on the superior and petty alike, Zhuangzi declared that freedom in Dao is based on our cultivation of the heavenly principles under discussion in this chapter. Understanding heavenly virtue is to know the root of all things, while understanding worldly virtue is to be their ancestor. In this way, there is no distinguishing the being of the sage's humanity from the oneness of his non-presence, for both his authentic and relational selves have conjoined in calling the Spirit Tower (*lingtai* 靈台) of Dao their storehouse. Perfecting his inner nature to be in line with the virtue of heaven, the sage roams the universe and wanders the four corners of the world, not to inculcate others in the arts of Dao, but to restore said arts to a world that lost them long ago.

The common person might be considered free on a secular level, but they will never know the cosmological freedom enjoyed by the sage unless they go through the steps outlined in this chapter and the one preceding it. All beings are free, irrespective of their station in life insofar as freedom flows from the bowels of nothingness. The question is how far freedom penetrates reality. To take things on the level of ordinary existence, as participating in a reality shaped and molded by epistemological norms, freedom will not extend beyond the shallowest of shallows. By availing ourselves of the life praxis espoused by Zhuangzi, however, humanity can not only penetrate the deepest depths of reality, but the notion of reality altogether. Of course, forgoing such normative frameworks as reality and language does not imply divorcing ourselves from their use; rather, Zhuangzi's philosophy is about placing our trust and lives in the cosmological processes stemming from Dao instead of those institutions devised by humanity. Freedom, then, is not something that comes and goes but is persistently and perpetually accessible to beings the world over. So long as Dao remains unharmed, freedom is assured.

Where this assuredness originates is in the harmony of ontological nothingness. To be free is to return to the One, and returning to the One is to blend with nothingness. Nothingness is the root of the One and being is its branches. We live our lives on the tips of those branches, never knowing where they might take us. Zhuangzi wished to awaken us from our complacency by repeatedly pointing out that we are but one amongst a myriad of beings whose time is incomprehensibly small next to the non-time of Dao. Our bodies are but clumps of earth lent to us by Dao, and whose power is only as great as the ground upon which we stand, when faced with a universe whose grounding is beyond groundedness as such. Ridding ourselves via forgetfulness of our continued attachment to names and designations is to hence look beyond their fleeting nature and be free of them.

The Great One's constancy is endless and in this endlessness freedom lurks for those willing to seek it out. Zhuangzi's preferred method of doing so was the act of wandering—one that may be literal or metaphorical. No matter the technique, wandering in the freedom of cosmic harmony with Dao is to wander carefree beyond the confines of temporal and spatial boundaries. It is a wandering that has neither beginning nor end, but becomes a form of spiritual existence in its own right. In this mindless, groundless wandering, even reality itself experiences an uprooting such that no single instance of it can be said to belong to the one experiencing it. This transience cannot persist if it is rooted in a particular being, or the world of beings for that matter, which would affix it with a hint of permanence; rather, the ephemerality of reality can only take its source in the perpetuity of nothingness. Only a quiescent, empty nothingness has the capacity to absorb and generate all potentialities and this is the source of nourishment for Dao. Carefree wandering is thus the epitome of Zhuangzi's cosmological freedom and serves as a mark of the highest state of existence human beings can experience, for it is premised upon returning to the One.

Freedom as Carefree Wandering

Unlike the lack of a specific word to delimit the terminology of Zhuangzi's idea of freedom, when it comes to the idea of wandering, and doing so in an unhindered manner, Zhuangzi already had a term at hand in the case of the former and invented one for the latter. The word *you* 遊, to wander or play, was used quite liberally in the *Zhuangzi* and yet, the term for a heart-mind carefree in disposition (*xiaoyao* 逍遙) was used most sparingly. Given the great disparity in their respective usage, it is clear that *you* is the more mundane form of freedom while *xiaoyao* represents the supramundane. We shall thus examine the peculiar idea of carefree wandering so as to uncover how it embodies and conveys Zhuangzi's formulation of cosmological freedom. This will not only serve as a fitting end to the present chapter, but nicely reflects the theme of this book—that Daoist cosmology is not based on hierarchically irreversible relationships but on Dao's symbiotically spontaneous creation realized through nothingness.

Wandering is an action whose non-deliberateness is seldom considered carefree or, for that matter, proving beneficial to one's condition. Carefree wandering is a sauntering in the unknown; it is a free-spirited meandering in nothingness. When we meander without knowing where we are headed or why, we return to a state of spontaneous equilibrium with our surroundings. To wander is thus to leave things undetermined such that our conscious will is blocked off, allowing our instinctual dance with Dao to commence. Faced with this situation, the outcome of our wandering creates itself while never deviating from being in accordance with our inborn nature; to be otherwise would be unnatural and in conflict with the oneness of all things. This is why the sage outwardly lives his life in playful ignorance and carefree bliss of the pursuit of names and distinctions prized by common people, while inwardly maintaining a constitution of quiet equanimity and mystery. To play for the pure joy of being playful is hence taken as being different from playing for the sake of attaining something; similarly, wandering in nothingness is not equal to wandering to pass time or to avoid something. The sage epitomizes the former, the petty person the latter. Regarding the sage, the *Zhuangzi* poetically referred to him as a "remote practitioner of the arts of Mr. Chaos."

This unusual expression arises as part of the response given by Confucius to his disciple Zigong 子貢 upon recalling an encounter he had with a gardener from the state of Jin 晉. The response by Confucius reads as follows:

He [the gardener] is a remote practitioner of the arts of Mr. Chaos. [Zigong], you know one thing of him but not the other. We govern what is internal but not what is external. He who has bright clarity and can enter plainness, who returns to simplicity through non-deliberate doing, whose body and inborn nature embraces his spirit and so wanders amidst the mundane world, in meeting such a person, would you not have been taken aback? Regarding the arts of Mr. Chaos, how are you and I qualified to know them![20]

彼假脩渾沌氏之術者也；識其一，不知其二；治其內，而不治其外。夫明白入素，無為復樸，體性抱神，以遊世俗之間者，汝將固驚邪？且渾沌氏之術，予與汝何足以識之哉！

In order to understand why Zhuangzi had Confucius say such things we need to look at a passage much earlier in the text wherein Confucius says: "They are men who wander beyond boundaries; I, however, am one who wanders within boundaries."[21] To wander beyond the boundaries of men is to roam in Dao; for the person who roams within said boundaries, they merely wander amongst other men. This is the onto-cosmological distinction between common and carefree forms of wandering. When we wander in the common sense of the word, we take our being as a receptacle from which other beings interact with us. This type of being-to-being encounter is not genuine, however, due to its forgoing of the complementary qualities of that which is naught. Carefree wandering is thus that which belongs to the open possibilities of nothingness; it is a mindless, bodiless journeying in the empty quiescence of Dao and is why Zhuangzi, through the voice of Confucius, made such remarks.

In Zhuangzi's eyes, Confucius was a man of the world and so could not escape his bondage to his relational-self. Unable to forget the phenomenal world and discard his own body, he was bound to a purposive wandering that toiled and exhausted his spirit. This is what Zhuangzi was alluding to when he said that Confucius wanders within boundaries while he and other Daoists wander beyond them. He who practices the arts of Mr. Chaos lives in simplicity; resting in non-deliberate doing, he experiences the complete and marvelous potentiality of the universe. In smashing his body, his will surrenders itself to his inborn nature and with his inborn nature intact, the essence of his former being attains spiritual freedom such that he wanders the world in oneness with Dao.

While Zhuangzi viewed Confucius as someone roaming the plains of the earth in order to espouse his virtue-centric doctrines, such ideals nevertheless belong to the world of humanity, not heaven. Had he adhered to the principle of heavenly measure to ground his ethics, Confucius would have been able to break free of it and wander beyond its boundaries. In all of this, what is of importance is the element of nothingness. Humanity cannot wander in the boundless infinity of Dao until the realization dawns on us that the myriad things are rooted in nothingness, and owing to this creative negativity, we can cultivate the *qi* of Dao while honing our practice of being usefully useless. To nurture oneself in the arts of chaos is thus to master the art of composing the heart-mind so as to return to and actualize the perfect virtue of Dao. Through his harmony with Dao, the sage becomes free and freedom is the key to mastering life. Confucius may have mastered the virtuous ways of the human heart-mind but he was far from mastering its spirituality:

> Confucius said: They are men who wander beyond boundaries; I, however, am one who wanders within boundaries . . . They see man's body as being the composition of different substances coming together in one form. They forget their liver and gall, their ears and eyes; over and over they end and they begin, not knowing head from tail. Peaceful and carefree they occupy themselves in what lies beyond the dust and dirt of the world, roaming carefree in the spirit of non-deliberate doing. How can they irritate themselves with such practiced etiquette so as to impress the views of common people's ears and eyes![22]

孔子曰: 彼, 游方之外者也, 而丘, 游方之內者也……假於異物, 托於同體; 忘其肝膽, 遺其耳目; 反覆終始, 不知端倪; 芒然仿徨乎塵垢之外, 逍遙乎無為之業。彼又惡能憒憒 然為世俗之禮, 以觀眾人之耳目哉!

For the common people of the world, there appears to be a clear delineation between things within the world and those beyond it. If such were the case, Zhuangzi's theory of cosmological freedom would be beyond the reach of humanity for the simple reason that his theory of freedom is spiritually grounded. Carefree wandering in freedom is not about transcending one plane of existence so as to enter another—our aimless roaming in nothingness forbids it—rather, to roam beyond the world of humanity is to meontologically extend ourselves such that we harmonize with Dao. Looked at in this way, there no longer exists any separation between the inner- and outer-world for they are one and the same. Herein lies the reason the *Zhuangzi* claimed that those who wander beyond the world of humanity forget their liver and gall, their ears and eyes, for in learning how to forget their bodies they must first stop viewing them as a collection of disparate parts. The liver and gall are no different from each other than they are from eyes and ears because they come from the same source in Dao.

The inevitable cycle of change experienced by things in the universe is yet another observation we can make regarding the above passage. Looking past the superficiality of our epistemologically driven reality is to take things for what they are. Things are not constant, however, as they undergo a myriad of transformations over the course of their lifetime. These minute changes come together to form large-scale changes, which are in turn reflected in the alternation of life and death. To be caught up in the minutiae of transformation is to lose sight of its source. Being immeasurable, Dao lacks the facticity of the being of man. When we speak of humanity's cosmological freedom in Dao, we are not declaring our being to be free; on the contrary, what makes us free is the harmony attained upon returning to our root. When the *xianren* (sagely immortals) alluded to in the above quotation focus their attention on that which lies beyond the dust and dirt of the world, they use their knowledge of the arts of Dao to grasp the significance of things instead of merely seeing their surface patterns. Zhuangzi thus took jabs at Confucius for building an ethical system dependent on the practice of ritual and the inculcation of artificial norms. It was his fixation on the patterning of social conduct that prevented Confucius from living a carefree life and embodying simplicity. These two characteristics are essential for one seeking the kind of freedom spoken of in Daoist texts such as the *Zhuangzi*.

Toiling their lives away in hardship and misery, the petty people of the world are neither free nor live a life of quiet stillness. Had they accepted the fact that their fate lies with heaven, they would not have struggled in futile resistance to the life-changing transformations that Dao induces in them. Given this and the fact that human social norms are unable to bring about change to that which is unchangeable or beyond influence (i.e., Dao), the best course of action to pursue is to rest in non-doing. Resting in non-deliberate doing is to engage in letting-be; it is to embody the traits of nothingness wherein the spirit is free to aimlessly wander within the realm of Dao. Thus the letting-be of non-doing is one of the highest ideals in all of Daoism and epitomizes Zhuangzi's idea of carefree wandering.

As non-deliberate doing is the epitome of the letting-be of carefree wandering, he who partakes in it can only be a sage, a person whose virtue is so close to that of Dao, the *Zhuangzi* referred to him as the "gatherer of authenticity" (*cai zhen* 采真):

> The perfect man of old borrowed benevolence from Dao, took lodging in righteousness, wandered carefree in the wastelands, took his meals in the careless and simple fields, and strolled in the garden of no bestowal. Carefree, he engaged in non-deliberate doing; plain and simple, life for him was easy. In not bestowing anything, nothing emerged. In ancient times this was called the wandering of he who gathers authenticity.[23]

> 古之至人，假道於仁，託宿於義，以游逍遙之墟，食於苟簡之田，立於不貸之圃。逍遙，無為也；苟簡，易養也；不貸，無出也。古者謂是采真之遊。

Non-deliberate doing is hence much more than the praxis of uselessness, it also pertains to distinguishing the authentic from the non-authentic. Zhuangzi's idea of authentic, however, was not formulated along lines of Western reason, but shaped itself with the components of virtue—righteousness and benevolence. Thus when we speak of Daoist virtue, we are actually pointing to non-virtue. A paradox, perhaps, yet we have already delimited the non-virtue of Dao as being the heavenly principles of equality, measuring, and harmony. When perfected, these aspects of heavenly virtue result in the subject's unadulterated freedom. The perfection of human virtue thus stands at the bottom of Zhuangzi's spiritual ladder and is followed by the virtues of heaven and Dao. The virtue of Dao, however, is the antithesis of heavenly virtue, for if the virtue of Dao were quantifiable, it would no longer be that of Dao. In other words, all manifestations of virtue stem from the nothingness of Dao's non-virtue, thus Zhuangzi's meontological cosmogony begins and ends with nothingness.

Nothingness is the beginning of things, the realm wherein they attain freedom, and is that which welcomes their return to the One upon the moment of their expiration. We do not do things in nothingness, we can only do nothing. Non-doing, therefore, is a doing for the sake of nothing. To learn the art of *wuwei* one must unlearn what one has learnt. Unlearning thus requires that we embody the traits of ontological nothingness (i.e., quietude, stillness, emptiness), and this can be accomplished through the non-doing of rest and by personifying uselessness. To be usefully useless is thus to harmonize with things and when things are harmonious, they mutually enrich one another. Enrichment via mutual non-doing is but one way heavenly virtue makes itself known to the world, and so the gatherer of authenticity does not seek out objective truth, but looks to the virtue of heaven for guidance on how to respond in any given situation. Letting matters unfold via their own terms by practicing non-deliberate doing and uselessly engaging the world, the sage wanders the world untouched by debates over this and that. Only with an epistemological vision of non-knowledge can the gatherer of authenticity cultivate a carefree state of mind, and only when his phenomenal self becomes the non-self of nothingness can he engage in aimless wandering.

Wandering, uselessness, and an unbound mind are the principal characteristics of one who has found perfect unity with Dao. Those petty men whose minds toil over the artificiality of names and reality are men whose knowledge is blocked up and whose virtue has been lost. Wherein their pettiness takes root is in their misguided quest to create a human ethics by seeking a solution for that to which no resolution is necessary. Humanity's attempt to hoard heavenly virtue does not result in freedom but in the trifling over what are essentially mutually complimentary opposites. Selfish hoarding does nothing to bring us closer to the root of our being, nor does it illuminate the error of our ways. Instead, what is needed is an ethics of letting-be, of returning to simplicity so as to compose our mind and forget the presence of our disingenuous selves.

All things undergo change, this is irrefutable. For the gatherer of authenticity, change represents authentic reality in that change is Dao's manifestation made real. However, Dao as the ultimate reality of the universe is not without its own authenticity, a non-authenticity that traces itself to ontological nothingness. This is why in rest the sage is able to notice all that passes him by. As he composes his mind to reflect the empty quietude of nothingness, he pays no heed to the dusty ramblings of the world. Reduced to a non-essence that blends with Dao, the aimless wandering of the sage takes after Dao's own endless drifting. Guided by the non-being of his authentic-self—a selfless self—the sage glides from place to place without so much as a worry or care for its purpose. Selfless, mindless, and bodiless, the gatherer of authenticity embraces nothingness as the authentic non-truth of reality, as the genuine progenitor of being, and as the only plane of existence whereby he can live according to his self-so nature. Unbounded by laws and social stipulations, moral norms, and the vices of emotions and loyalty, Zhuangzi's sage enjoys a freedom unbeknownst to the rest of humanity.

Carefree wandering thus translates into an aimless spirit whose journeying knows no bounds. Adapting to each and every situation as easily as water circumvents an obstacle, the sage relies on the freedom gained by the non-mind of Dao to traverse the universe. He traverses the universe not in a corporeal sense, but by way of an inner-intuition that belongs to the oneness of things without possessing or being possessed by them. The myriad things cannot own this spiritual essence for it is that of Dao and, as such, is the non-essence of nothingness. In other words, carefree wandering is an expression of the freedom common to the entire universe insofar as it is the harmony inherent to *yin* and *yang*, non-being and being, heaven and earth, all of which are meontologically rooted in Dao.

Conclusion

The incorporeal One is not a singular entity but an undifferentiated wholeness that is otherwise known as chaos. Chaos does not exist in time or space, hence the sage who returns to the One also returns to a time when wholeness prevailed in the universe. Dwelling in the tranquil silence of nothingness, the sage knows not of life and death, youth and old age, virtue and vice, for such knowledge would bar him access to the playground of Dao. He is free not from something, nor free to do something, but is free insofar as he no longer needs to be free. The freedom of non-freedom is thus more powerful than freedom because it is a self-forgetting of the need for a free self. Free selves cannot return to the One, nor can they enjoy the bliss of wandering in nothingness due to their continual clinging to the concept of freedom. Carefree wandering is, therefore, a non-wandering in non-freedom; it is not an escape from one's self but a returning to the source of the non-self in Dao. The source that is not a source is also the essence that is a non-essence; this non-essence grants us the freedom to wander carefree in nothingness, to no longer regard ourselves as human beings but as a spark of creation whose coming and going is unknowable and unstoppable. To accept this fate is to be free of the chains of our own humanity, however hard we might try to deny or cloak them in words of prophecy or science.

Zhuangzi was thus attempting to open our minds to his unique cosmogonist vision. His goal was not to indoctrinate an ethics of the goodness or evilness of the human heart but to get us to stop thinking in such dichotomies. His call was for an experiential partaking in the everydayness of things; to bear witness to the joy and miracle of their mundaneness. The ontology of the sage is not directed toward his human quality; rather, the sage is a metaphor for someone who lives in the natural world by living beyond it through an inner embracing of nothingness. Transcendence was not a term Zhuangzi used because for him, nothing needs to be transcended when all is united in the oneness of Dao. Likewise, there can be no hint of nihilism in Daoist cosmology for things at their core are already inlaid with nothingness. From the naught, creation occurs, and with creation things naturally return to their root. Given that humanity did not devise such a process, why should we fear it? If we overcome this fear we can attain harmony, and with harmony comes peace of mind and preservation of spirit. This was Zhuangzi's message, one whose profoundness was beyond compare and remains as valid as ever.

Conclusion

Zhuangzi lived in a tumultuous time, one where social cohesion had fallen into disarray and people no longer turned to heaven for consolation. Amidst all the hubbub, his beckoning for a return to more naturally inclined principles rang through the air like a clap of thunder. The challenge that modern scholars face when trying to elucidate the *Zhuangzi*'s cosmogony is that many of its themes are scattered throughout the text, making a coherent presentation difficult. This book, however, has brought these variegated issues together, showing that there indeed exists textual cohesion and consistency. In light of this, Zhuangzi's cosmology no longer presents itself as a collection of loosely related ideas but comes together to form an original and tightly coherent discourse. More specifically, this book has demonstrated that the three core concepts of Zhuangzi's cosmological philosophy—Dao, nothingness, and being—can be applied to other avenues of metaphysical discourse resulting in a unique form of spiritual thinking.

Our analysis began by identifying and justifying the cosmological framework of the *Zhuangzi*. These preliminary measures were necessary to fend off the imposition of any preconceptions due to the dominant nature of Western cosmogony. Having differentiated nothingness from non-being, and these two from Dao, what remained to be done was to layer them in such a way that Dao's propensity for creation would remain undisturbed. This was achieved by situating nothingness concurrently with Dao while non-being and being were given posterior positions. Given the ubiquitous appearance of nothingness, the next challenge was to preempt any claim that Zhuangzi's cosmology was a take on *creatio ex-nihilo*, or worse, nihilism. It was here that the positive aspect of nothingness came into play, and is why we referred to it as ontological. Not only that, but there existed the need to separate the cosmological function of nothingness from its ontic appearance in the world of everyday things. The role of being in this triadic framework thus became secondary in importance.

Indeed, Zhuangzi was not particularly interested in the ontological import of things and this was reflected in his cosmological discussion of the One.

The *Zhuangzi*, taken as a whole, is a text devoted to espousing the holistic nature of both the world and the cosmos. In working out how Dao, nothingness, and being come together as the One without cancelling one another out proved to be the least challenging endeavor encountered thus far. By proposing that the One serve as a combination of nothingness and ontological being, the *Zhuangzi* safely conjoined them into an undifferentiated whole without fear that doing so would deny nothingness its meontological constancy, or that being would become dispersed and hence unable to give rise to ontic beings. In this way, Zhuangzi's extension of ontological traits to the universe at large, as opposed to limiting them to the realm of human beings alone, ensured his cosmology would remain genuinely universal. Bringing all of these components together thus gave us a full picture from which to approach its more particular aspects and applications, such as the ways in which things profess to manifest themselves.

By saying that things manifest themselves out of the creative milieu of nothingness, we are not declaring they have the propensity to self-procreate; rather, all things emerge from the One and thenceforth exist in a state of oneness. The One from which all things arise in turn points to the inherent presence of Dao in them, for it is the latter that animates and sustains the former. On this point, particular care was needed to avoid any inclination that Zhuangzi's idea of oneness was somehow reductionist or monistic. It proved to be neither, for in saying that all things are One, Zhuangzi was making two claims: first, the unity of things comes from having a single source in Dao; second, the time during which they congregated as a collective whole was notable for its lack of distinguishing names or discriminations. Things were thus epistemologically amorphous yet phenomenologically distinct. The result was a cosmology whose philosophical import stood out amongst its peers for its ingenuity while proving attractive to those who had a disdain for human-centric models of living.

In knowing that things are mirage-like representations of the Thing lying at the top of their chain of signification, the *Zhuangzi* decried our need to accumulate such objects, including certain types of knowledge, for it regarded the amassing of things to be unnatural. To this end, what the text took as useful proved to be radically different from the typical social norms of the time. Usefulness was thus held to the measure of life-prolongation and any endeavor that led to the reduction of one's years or personal injury was discarded as useless. In other words, Zhuangzi took the concepts of useful and useless and flipped them upside down, creating the life praxis of useful uselessness. What is interesting to note is that this unorthodox way of viewing the world was modeled after naturally occurring examples such as the crippled man and the old tree. Additionally, the case of the clay vessel featured prominently in the discussion, not because said vessel held any particular material significance, but because its inner void could be tied to the nothingness connecting being to Dao.

Forgetting the outward appearance of things so as to grasp their inborn nature served as a lead in to the issue of freedom, a theme whose importance for Zhuangzi cannot be stressed enough. Not only was forgetfulness a prized characteristic of the sage, Zhuangzi extrapolated it to the world at large in order to demonstrate how, when things are comfortable with their station in life, they forget about notions of competition, deceit, honor, and so forth. Forgetting said human vices requires one to recall something else in their stead and for Zhuangzi, the only thing worthy of being recalled is Dao. Using the analogy of letting-be, what we learned was that on the one hand, binding forgetfulness to memory and the mind proved futile insofar as true temporality can only be experienced through the non-deliberate doing of rest; on the other hand, in order to attain freedom of a holistic nature, one must endure a series of encounters whereby the degree of forgetting becomes ever more cosmological in nature.

Through the letting-go of our attachment to names and other conventions it is best, Zhuangzi said, to forget them so as to harmonize with Dao. Once one has succeeded in joining Dao, freedom ensues. The challenge we face when discussing Zhuangzi's idea of freedom stems from the fact that it is not held to be a one-to-one relationship. In other words, one cannot claim oneself to be free from another thing; instead, one needs to think in terms of being free from one's relational-self. Using the three principles of heaven was one way by which freedom could be attained, while another involved the process of progressive self-forgetting. It is fitting that this book should end with a chapter on freedom as it also reflects the meontological nature of the One and its dependence on Dao for sustenance. Indeed, Zhuangzi's formulation of freedom offers a unique vision of the sage's connection to the world and universe at large. In taking the sage as an exemplar of what it means to be free, humanity is presented with a vision of freedom that still lies within its grasp in spite of its aloofness. All that is required is to let go of the world. Said differently, believing in Dao means one is free, while following Dao sets others free.

This book brings together the various cosmological themes of the *Zhuangzi* to create a cohesive discourse. In doing so, it not only presents his ideas on Dao, nothingness, and being in an accessible manner, it brings to the fore many aspects of Daoist cosmogony that have been overlooked or remain unknown. By illustrating the multifarious ideas of Zhuangzi's cosmological thought and the subtleties and profound richness of his arguments, we have not only seen the text in a new and inspiring light, we have also come to appreciate the deft handling with which the *Zhuangzi* was crafted. The *Zhuangzi* is, after all, not just a work of philosophy but one of sublime poetry.

Having said as much, there are implicit limitations to Zhuangzi's philosophy, a few of which we shall now discuss. Certainly, the most noticeable pertains to the question of accessibility to Dao. Due to the finitude of human life, comprehending that which is perpetual and unknowable through conventional tools of knowledge is not for the faint of heart. Indeed, in reading the *Zhuangzi*, it would seem that much of the text's arguments are directed toward the sage and not the common person. This, of course, has more to do with the *Zhuangzi*'s writing style than anything else; however, nowhere does the text espouse an elitist attitude or engage in mockery of those who have suffered physical or social harm. If anything, the *Zhuangzi* goes to great lengths to use as its moral exemplars individuals who would have suffered more extremely had they appeared in the work of Confucius, Mozi, Yang Zhu, and so forth.

Zhuangzi's satirizing of these schools was not without its purpose, but that is not so much a fault as a deliberate attempt to shock people out of their misplaced trust that any of these schools could lead to measurable improvement in the human condition. We saw how letting things be could bring about change, as could appearing useless and composing one's mind; but again, these methods appear to be directed toward those who are in a social or economic position to pursue what is surely a lengthy path of self-perfection and cultivation. They would certainly appear unattractive to the farmer or court official whose very survival depends on earning a wage. Does this imply that the *Zhuangzi* was calling for the cessation of activity so as to practice the arts of Dao? No, because that would be a form of purposeful activity. What the *Zhuangzi* was actually striving for was a natural, purposeless action that no longer depends on discriminations or social norms as a means to measure one's conduct.

One may go on and criticize Zhuangzi for being a relativist and skeptic but such faults fall beyond the scope of this project. Indeed, the rather narrow agenda of this book can itself be criticized for not offering a more comprehensive view of the *Zhuangzi*'s philosophical thought. While valid, the reasons for not doing so were given in the Introduction. To briefly recount them, we argued that presenting a comprehensive overview of the

Zhuangzi's thought would prove both unwieldy and philosophically ineffective. Rather than make such an attempt here, this book is but the first of three intended studies. Given classical Daoism is first and foremost a tradition of cosmology, without grasping the central themes of Dao, nothingness, and being, and how these in turn inform subsequent themes such as temporality, life praxis, and freedom, jumping straight into an analysis of Daoist ethics or epistemology would prove rather treacherous. We have, therefore, set such treachery aside for future conversations.

Notes

Introduction

1. Conor Cunningham holds the "logic of nihilism" responsible for turning Nothing into Something. My interpretation differs in that it views nothingness to be creational without altering its inherent nature. See Cunningham, xiv.
2. See Hartmann, 13–18.
3. For example, Bohm speaks of implicate and explicate orders through which the primary reality of the world as a whole is revealed. See Bohm, 20.
4. I have in mind the field of evolutionary ontology. See, for example, Smajs; Lowe 2006.
5. For more on Zhuangzi's lifetime and the evolution of the text bearing his name, see Chai 2008: 4–7, 15–18.
6. For more on the dating and classification of the *Zhuangzi* chapters, see Chai 2008: 7–14, 18–26. Additional readings on the textual history of the *Zhuangzi* are available in Angus C. Graham, "How Much of Zhuangzi did Zhuangzi Write?" *Studies in Chinese Philosophy and Philosophical Literature*. Albany: SUNY Press, 1990: 283–321; Liu Xiaogan. *Classifying the Zhuangzi Chapters*, Ann Arbor: University of Michigan Center for Chinese Studies Monograph, 1994; Harold Roth, ed., *A Companion to Angus C. Graham's Zhuangzi: The Inner Chapters*. Society for Asian and Comparative Philosophy Monograph. Honolulu: University of Hawai'i Press, 2002.

Chapter 1

1. All translations of Chinese materials are my own unless stated otherwise.
2. *Zhuangzi* chapter 22, "*zhibeiyou* 知北游." See Guo Qingfan, 759–60. Burton Watson follows the *Huainanzi* 淮南子 in amending the end of this passage from "及為無有矣，何從至此哉" to "及其為無無，至妙何從及此哉." See Watson, 244n14; for the *Huainanzi*, see Zhang, 138. Watson was perhaps influenced by Liu Wendian's 劉文典 *Zhuangzi* annotation, which reads: "*Wuyou* 無有 at the time was written *wuwu* 無無. Written as *wuyou* would have involved the previous passage's *youwu* 有無 which is incorrect. Chapter 2 of the *Huainanzi*

says: "I can grant the fact of nothingness but not the non-being of nothingness. As for the non-being of nothingness, how can one realize such wonderment!" It has thus been carried over to this passage. However, the "*daoying* 道應" chapter writes: "As for the non-being of nothingness, how can one realize such perfection!" Although the passage has a minor variance, it correctly writes *wuwu*." See Liu Wendian 1999: 610. Wang Shumin 王叔岷 also makes this observation. See Wang Shumin 1999: 841.

3. Chapter 25 of the *Daodejing* says: "There is something undifferentiated and whole that existed before heaven and earth. Silent and empty, solitary and unchanging, it is found everywhere yet remains free from danger, thus it can act as the mother of heaven and earth. I do not know its name and so call it Dao. Forced to give it a name, I call it Great." See Lou Yulie, 63. In the *Wenzi* 文子, a text whose authorship was thought to be spurious but is now considered to date to the Han dynasty, we see a similar description: "Laozi said: There is something undifferentiated and whole that existed before heaven and earth. It is only a formless resemblance, an abstruse profundity, solitary and indifferent, whose sound we cannot hear. Forced to give it a name, I call it Dao." See Wang Liqi, 1. For more on the *Wenzi*'s history, see Ding Yuanzhi 丁原植. *Wenzi Ziliao Tansuo* 文子資料探索. Taibei: Wanjuan Lou, 1999.

4. *Zhuangzi* chapter 22, "*zhibeiyou* 知北游." See Guo Qingfan, 760. Accused of plagiarizing the commentary of Xiang Xiu 向秀 (227–272 CE), Guo Xiang's (252–312 CE) commentary entitled *Zhuangzi Zhu* 莊子注 has survived in a variety of sources. References to it in this work will be to the page numbers of Guo Qingfan's 郭慶藩 edited collection of *Zhuangzi* commentaries, the *Zhuangzi Jishi* 莊子集釋. For more on Guo Xiang's role in the textual evolution of the *Zhuangzi*, see Chai 2008: 7–18. For more on Guo's life and writing, see Fang Yong, volume 1: 376–401.

5. See Shang Geling, "Embracing Differences and Many: The Significance of One in Zhuangzi's Utterance of Dao." *Dao: A Journal of Comparative Philosophy*, 1.2 (June 2002): 229–50.

6. See Fu Weixun "Creative Hermeneutics: Daoist Metaphysics and Heidegger." *Journal of Chinese Philosophy*, 3.2 (1976): 115–43. Fu's overall conclusion is that: "Zhuangzi's view of the relation between being and non-being can [thus] be understood in terms of the trans-ontological priority of the nameless non-being of non-being to the duality of non-being and being epistemologically differentiated and thus named."

7. Shang, 241.

8. Shang, 239.

9. *Zhuangzi* chapter 2, "*qiwulun* 齊物論." See Guo Qingfan, 79.

10. For more on this topic see Hansen, 265–306; Kjellberg; Shen, "Zhuangzi and the *Zhuangzi*" in Mou, 237–65; and Wong, 234–40.

11. *Zhuangzi* chapter 2, "*qiwulun* 齊物論." See Guo Qingfan, 80.

12. *Zhuangzi* chapter 22, "*zhibeiyou* 知北游." See Guo Qingfan, 760. Although Cheng lived in the Tang dynasty, the dates of his lifetime are uncertain. His commentary goes by the title *Nanhua Zhenjing Shu* 南華真經疏 and is typically paired

with Guo Xiang's in the role of "sub-commentary." Their combined commentaries are known as the *Nanhua Zhenjing Zhushu* 南華真經注疏 and appear in volume 13 of the *Zhonghua Daozang* 中華道藏. All references to Cheng's commentary are to the page numbers corresponding to Guo Qingfan's *Zhuangzi Jishi* 莊子集釋. For more on the life and writings of Cheng Xuanying, see Fang Yong, volume 1: 492–514.

13. See Tang Jun, 411. Lü Huiqing (1032–1111 CE) authored a commentary by the name of *Zhuangzi Yi* 莊子義 which has been preserved, albeit with textual variations, in the *Zhengtong Daozang* 正統道藏 and in Chu Boxiu's *Nanhua Zhenjing Yihai Zuanwei* 南華真經義海纂微. These two manuscripts, along with a third, the *E Zang Heishui Chengwen Xian* 俄藏黑水城文獻, have been reprinted in a modern edition under the name *Zhuangzi Yi Jijiao* 莊子義集校 edited by Tang Jun 湯君. References to Lü's commentary are to the page numbers of Tang Jun's text. For more on the life and writings of Lü, see Fang Yong, volume 2: 37–42.

14. See *Zhonghua Daozang*, volume 14: 365. Chu Boxiu (d. 1287 CE) is known not so much for his own commentarial prowess but for his *Nanhua Zhenjing Yihai Zuanwei* 南華真經義海纂微, an enormous work written in 160 *juan* 卷 (scrolls). At the time, it was the largest collection of complete *Zhuangzi* commentaries in existence. Chu's text is preserved in volume 14 of the *Zhonghua Daozang* as well as volumes 337 and 338 of the *Siku Quanshu* 四庫全書. All references to Chu's text are to the page numbers of the *Zhonghua Daozang* edition. For more on his life and writings, see Fang Yong, volume 2: 141–57. As for Chen Jingyuan (1025–1094 CE), like Cheng Xuanying he was an ordained Daoist priest and a prolific scholar who wrote commentaries to the *Zhuangzi* and *Daodejing*. Chen Jingyuan's lesser commentaries to the *Zhuangzi* are found in volume 15 of the *Zhonghua Daozang*. References in this book will be to Chen's principle commentary as preserved in Chu Boxiu's text. For more on the life and writings of Chen, see Fang Yong, volume 2: 83–105.

15. Fu Weixun made a point of saying that the term *ziran* is hardly used by Laozi and Zhuangzi and that it was Guo Xiang who turned it into a philosophical concept. Fu writes: "Guo Xiang went beyond Wang Bi in reaffirming *ziran* as one and the only one reality; Dao is simply brushed off as inessential or dispensable. The term *ziran* appeared five times in the *Daodejing*, four times in the *Zhuangzi*, and twenty-seven times in Wang's commentary on the *Daodejing*, but astonishingly twenty-eight times in Guo Xiang's commentary on the first two chapters of the *Zhuangzi* alone." See Fu, 128.

16. The character *qi* has many English connotations, the most common being: vital breath, vapor, force, and spirit. All are valid terms and can be used interchangeably, hence I will leave *qi* in its untranslated form.

17. *Zhuangzi* chapter 2, "*qiwulun* 齊物論." See Guo Qingfan, 51.

18. *Zhuangzi* chapter 6, "*dazongshi* 大宗師." See Guo Qingfan, 246. In chapter 37 of the *Daodejing* one finds a similar explanation: "道常無爲而無不爲." In the "*xinshu* 心術" chapter of the *Guanzi* 管子 there is: "正人無求之也，故能虛無。虛無無形謂之道." See Li Xiangfeng 2006: 759.

19. See Lou Yulie, 1.

20. For example, in chapter 14 of the *Daodejing*, Dao is described as invisible, inaudible, and imperceptible while in chapter 25 it is characterized as undifferentiated and whole, existing before heaven and earth.

21. The *Wenzi*, thought to be a forgery but now acknowledged to be an authentic text, was most likely written during the Warring States period but compiled in the Han. The only complete English translation is by Thomas Cleary entitled, *Wenzi: Understanding the Mysteries*. Boston: Shambhala, 1992. The complete *Huainanzi* has been translated by a team of scholars led by John Major entitled, *The Huainanzi: A Guide to the Theory and Practice of Government in Early Han China*. New York: Columbia University Press, 2010. Finally, the *Liezi* has been translated by A. C. Graham as *The Book of Liezi: A Classic of Dao*. New York: Columbia University Press, 1990.

22. See Wang Liqi, 52–53. On the idea that the formless is the beginning of the formed, we can cite two additional references: The first is in Wang Liqi's commentary to the passage just quoted where he cites the "*chuzhen* 俶真" chapter of the *Huainanzi*: 有有者，有無者，有未始有無者，有未始有夫未始有有無者……有未始有夫未始有無者，天地未剖，陰陽未判，四時未分，萬物未生，汪然平靜，寂然清澄，莫見其形，若光耀之間於無有，退而自失也，曰：子能有無，而未能無無也。及其為無無，至妙何從及此哉。See Zhang, 137–38. The second is in chapter 2 of the *Zhuangzi*, which we discussed earlier. Although these three texts have slightly different accounts, there is no denying they share a common understanding of the progenitor of things.

23. See Yang Bojun, 9–10. Zhang Zhan 張湛 (fl. 320 CE) in his commentary writes: "Form, sound, color, and taste are all suddenly-so in being born, they cannot give birth to themselves. Given they are not self-birthing, they thus take non-deliberate doing as their root. Taking non-deliberate doing as their root, they do not cling to one appearance nor depend on one flavor; therefore, they take the form of *qi* as their master, acting according to its movement. 形、聲、色、味皆忽爾而生，不能自生者也。夫不能自生，則無為之本。無為之本，則無當於一象，無係於一味；故能為形氣之主，動必由之者也。" A similar portrayal of Dao occurs in the *Wenzi*, which says: "Empty nothingness (*xuwu* 虛無) is the idea of tranquility, the ancestor of the myriad things. Putting these three to use, one can enter into formlessness; formlessness is also known as oneness . . . [oneness] is without form yet things having form are born from it. It is without sound yet all sounds emanate from it. It is without flavor yet all flavors are derived from it. It is without color yet all colors are produced from it. Therefore being is born from non-being and actuality is born from emptiness (*xu* 虛)." See Wang Liqi, 30.

24. *Zhuangzi* chapter 22, "*zhibeiyou* 知北游." See Guo Qingfan, 752.

25. See Wang Liqi, 30–31.

26. See Yang Bojun, 6.

27. *Zhuangzi* chapter 12, "*tiandi* 天地." See Guo Qingfan, 424. Guo Xiang comments on the idea that things arise from a formless One, saying: "The One is the beginning of being, a state of ultimate wonderment. As it is ultimate wonderment, it thus does not have the principle of formed things. Since things arise

from the One, they do not arise from nothingness. Hence Zhuangzi repeatedly said nothingness is the beginning of things, but how? In the beginning, things were yet to be born and yet they obtained life. Obtaining the difficulty of life, they were not endowed with nothingness from above, nor entreated with knowledge from below, for they suddenly and naturally obtained life. How could they seek life in what was already born and lose their self-born nature! 一者，有之初，至妙者也，至妙，故未有物理之形耳。夫一之所起，起於至一，非起於無也。然莊子之所以屢稱無於初者，何哉？初者，未生而得生，得生之難，而猶上不資於無，下不待於知，突然而自得此生矣，又何營生於已生以失其自生哉！"

28. *Zhuangzi* chapter 23, "*gengsangchu* 庚桑楚." See Guo Qingfan, 800. The "*jingshen* 精神" chapter of the *Huainanzi* argues that: "Long ago when there was neither heaven nor earth, there were only images and no forms. Being obscurely dark, vast and unclear, hazy and cavernous, none could know its gateway. 古未有天地之時，惟像無形，窈窈冥冥，芒芠漠閔，澒濛鴻洞，莫知其門." See Zhang, 719; Major, 240.

29. Chapter 40 of the *Daodejing* says: "Reversion is the movement of Dao; pliancy is the function of Dao. The myriad things of the world gain life from being, and being is born from non-being. 反者，道之動；弱者，道之用。天下萬物生於有，有生於無." See Lou Yulie, 109–10.

30. The *Zhuangzi* also referred to this gateway as the "Repository of Heaven" (*tianfu* 天府), the "Spirit Tower" (*lingtai* 靈台), and the "Dark and Mysterious Gate" (*yaoming zhi men* 窈冥之門). The *Daodejing* on the other hand preferred to call it the "Gate of the Mysterious Female" (*xuanpin zhi men* 玄牝之門).

31. See Zhou Qicheng, 364. Lin Xiyi (1193–? CE), whose style name was Juan Zhai 鬳齋, not only wrote commentaries to the *Zhuangzi* but to the *Daodejing* and *Liezi* as well, and each used the phrase "oral significance" (*kouyi* 口義) in their title. His commentary to the *Zhuangzi* is preserved in volume 15 of the *Zhonghua Daozang*, and while it is known by a variety of names (*Zhuangzi Kouyi* 莊子口義, *Zhuangzi Juanzhai Kouyi* 莊子鬳齋口義, *Nanhua Zhenjing Juanzhai Kouyi* 南華真經鬳齋口義), its modern edition uses the title *Zhuangzi Juanzhai Kouyi Jiaozhu* 莊子鬳齋口義校註. All references in this work are to the second edition (2009) of this text, edited by Zhou Qicheng 周啓成. For more on the life and writings of Lin, see Fang Yong, volume 2: 106–40.

32. "此所以明有之不能為有而自有耳，非謂無能為有也。若無能為有，何謂無乎." *Zhuangzi* chapter 23, "*gengsangchu* 庚桑楚." See Guo Qingfan, 802.

33. "故知止其所不知，至矣。孰知不言之辯，不道之道？若有能知，此之謂天府." *Zhuangzi* chapter 2, "*qiwulun* 齊物論." See Guo Qingfan, 83.

34. "其上不皦，其下不昧。繩繩不可名，復歸於無物。是謂無狀之狀，無物之象." *Daodejing* chapter 14. See Lou Yulie, 31. To this Wang Bi added: "One may wish to say it is non-existent but things complete their existence from it. One may wish to say it exists but its form cannot be seen. We thus say it is the form of the formless, the image of that which is no-thing. 欲言無邪，而物由以成。欲言有邪，而不見其形，故曰，無狀之狀，無物之象也." For more on Wang Bi's contribution to Chinese philosophy, see Wagner 2003b, 2000; Chai 2010.

35. *Zhuangzi* chapter 11, "*zaiyou* 在宥." See Guo Qingfan, 390.
36. *Zhuangzi* chapter 23, "*gengsangchu* 庚桑楚." See Guo Qingfan, 798.
37. The *Hengxian* was unearthed in 1994 and comprises 13 bamboo slips of approximately 500 characters. It is currently housed in the Shanghai Museum and was published as part of their bamboo-slip series edited by Ma Chengyuan 馬承源 entitled *Shanghai Bowuguan Cang Zhanguo "Chu Zhushu"* 上海博物館藏戰國楚竹書. See volume 3, (2003): 287–99. According to Liao Mingchun 廖名春 the character *huo* 或 should be read *yu* 域, an interpretation based upon the use of *yu* in *Daodejing* chapter 25 which reads: "域中有四大，而王居一焉." It is also found in the "*tianwen* 天文" chapter of the *Huainanzi*: "道始于虛霩，虛霩生宇宙，宇宙生氣，氣有漢垠." See Liao Mingchun, "Shangbo Cang Chu Zhushu *Hengxian* Xinshi 上博藏楚竹書恒先新釋," *Zhongguo Zhexueshi* 中国哲学史, Issue 3: 83–92. During his translation of the *Daodejing*, Richard J. Lynn also chose to adopt *yu* 域 over *huo* 或 such that he interprets *chengzhong* 域中 as 'within the realm of existence;' Rudolf Wagner, on the other hand, translates it as 'in the beyond' to convey the spatial connotation of the term. See Lynn 1999: 96; Wagner 2003: 202.
38. See Tang Jun 2009: 240.
39. *Zhuangzi* chapter 6, "*dazongshi* 大宗師." See Guo Qingfan, 234–35.
40. Regarding this "dilemma," James Behuniak proposes a two-step solution: first, allow the One of the Great One (*taiyi* 太一) to mean continuity while the One of chapter 42 of the *Daodejing* means particularity; second, regard the *Taiyi Shengshui* as cosmogony and chapter 42 of the *Daodejing* as cosmology. The difference thus becomes descriptive: the origin of the world versus the world at it exists. See James Behuniak, "Embracing the One in the *Daodejing*." *Philosophy East and West*, 59.3 (July 2009): 364–81. For more on the *Daodejing* in its bamboo-slip variant along with the *Taiyi Shengshui*, see Ames 2004; Henricks 2000.
41. Neville writes: "Does the movement from nothing to being (in its three stages) back to nothing take place within the process of time—a cosmological generation and return—or does temporal process itself arise with the emergence of being (at one of its stages)? The metaphors are temporalistic, and I suspect that it would be reading in a *creatio ex-nihilo* theory to interpret the movement from nothing to being and from being to nothing as transcending temporal process, as an ontological 'movement' rather than a cosmological one." See Robert Neville, "From Nothing to Being: The Notion of Creation in Chinese and Western Thought." *Philosophy East and West*, 30.1 (Jan. 1980): 21–34.
42. *Zhuangzi* chapter 23, "*gengsangchu* 庚桑楚." See Guo Qingfan, 800.
43. See Yang Bojun, 5–6.
44. *Zhuangzi* chapter 2, "*qiwulun* 齊物論." See Guo Qingfan, 79.
45. *Zhuangzi* chapter 19, "*dasheng* 達生." See Guo Qingfan, 632.
46. See Wang Liqi, 30.
47. *Daodejing* chapter 39. See Lou Yulie, 105–106.
48. The entire description is as follows: "小夫之知，不離苞苴竿牘，敝精神乎蹇淺，而欲兼濟導物，太一形虛。若是者，迷惑於宇宙，形累不知太初。"

彼至人者，歸精神乎無始而甘瞑乎無何有之鄉。水流乎無形，發泄乎大清。悲哉乎！汝為知在豪毛，而不知大寧." *Zhuangzi* chapter 32, "*lieyukou* 列禦寇." See Guo Qingfan, 1047.

49. Chapter 42 of the *Daodejing* conveys the same principle, albeit more simplistically: "Dao gives birth to the One, the One gives birth to two, two gives birth to three, and three gives birth to the myriad things. 道生一，一生二，二生三，三生萬物." See Lou Yulie, 117. The "*tianwen* 天文" chapter of the *Huainanzi* reflects this cosmogony when it says: "Dao begins with one. One [alone], however, does not give birth hence it divided into *yin* and *yang*. From the harmonious union of *yin* and *yang*, the myriad things were produced. Thus it is said: one produced two, two produced three, and three produced the myriad things. 道始於一，一而不生，故分而為陰陽，陰陽合和而萬物生。故曰一生二，二生三，三生萬物." See Zhang, 341; Major, 133.

50. The Jin dynasty thinker Pei Wei 裴頠 (267–300 CE) was the first person to use the term "collective being" (*qunyou* 群有). It appears in his *Treatise on Revering Existence* (*chongyoulun* 崇有論) and can be found in his biography in the *Historical Record of the Jin* (*Jin Shu* 晉書).

51. With regard the character *fan* 反, there are two combinatorial variations: the first is *xiangfan* 相反 which translates as "opposite," the second is *fangui* 反歸 which translates as "reversal." We are interested in the former, not the latter.

52. *Zhuangzi* chapter 2, "*qiwulun* 齊物論." See Guo Qingfan, 70.
53. *Zhuangzi* chapter 6, "*dazongshi* 大宗師." See Guo Qingfan, 268.
54. *Zhuangzi* chapter 21, "*tianzifang* 田子方." See Guo Qingfan, 712.
55. *Daodejing* chapter 40. See Lou Yulie, 109–110.
56. *Daodejing* chapter 16. See Lou Yulie, 36.
57. Lü's commentary, *Daode Zhenjing Zhuan* 道德真經傳, is preserved in the *Zhonghua Daozang*. See *Zhonghua Daozang*, volume 10: 321.
58. See the story of chaos at the end of chapter 7 in the *Zhuangzi*.
59. "人法地，地法天，天法道，道法自然." See Lou Yulie, 65.
60. *Zhuangzi* chapter 11, "*zaiyou* 在宥." See Guo Qingfan, 390.
61. We shall say more on this passage in chapter 6.

Chapter 2

1. *Zhuangzi* chapter 12, "*tiandi* 天地." See Guo Qingfan, 424.
2. Wang Bi in his "Introductory Remarks to the *Daodejing*" (*Laozi zhilue* 老子指略) echoes this idea: "Regarding the means by which a thing is born . . . it lies in their being born from that which is formless and from that which is without name. That which is formless and nameless is the ancestor of the myriad things." See Lou Yulie, 195.
3. The most obvious example is that of cook Ding but others abound: the wheel maker, the carver of bell stands, the belt-buckle maker, the catcher of cicadas, etc.

4. *Zhuangzi* wrote: "To use a signifier to show that a signifier is not signified is not as good as using a non-signifier to show that a signifier is not a signified." See *Zhuangzi* chapter 2, "*qiwulun* 齊物論." See Guo Qingfan, 66.

5. He wrote: "The sage takes right and wrong and mixes them together and in doing so, dwells in the balance of heaven." See *Zhuangzi* chapter 2, "*qiwulun* 齊物論." See Guo Qingfan, 70.

6. Wang Bi's "Introductory Remarks to the *Daodejing*" says: "All names are born from forms; there has yet to be a form born from a name. Having a particular name thus entails there must be a particular form, and given there is a particular form, there must be separation [between them]." See Lou Yulie, 199.

7. *Zhuangzi* chapter 2, "*qiwulun* 齊物論." See Guo Qingfan, 79.

8. *Zhuangzi* chapter 31, "*yufu* 漁父." See Guo Qingfan, 1031.

9. "物固有所然，物固有所可。無物不然，無物不可……道通為一." *Zhuangzi* chapter 2, "*qiwulun* 齊物論." See Guo Qingfan, 69. Wang Bi also spoke along these lines: "When things are born or achievements completed, there is nothing to which it [Dao] does not adhere." See Lou Yulie, 195.

10. *Zhuangzi* chapter 6, "*dazongshi* 大宗師." See Guo Qingfan, 283–85; 243–45.

11. Wang's original text reads: "夫欲定物之本者，則雖近而必自遠以證其始；夫欲明物之所由者，則雖顯而必自幽以敘其本." See Lou Yulie, 197.

12. For more on the centrality of harmony (*he* 和) in Daoism, especially in the context of the musical thought of *Xuanxue* 玄學 (neo-Daoism), see Chai 2009.

13. *Zhuangzi* chapter 22, "*zhibeiyou* 知北游." See Guo Qingfan, 752.

14. Lou Yulie, 27. Wang Bi explained this passage to mean: "Wood, clay, and mortar give us the three [i.e., the wheel, vessel, and room] but all of them attain their usefulness by way of nothingness. In other words, of those benefits derived from existence, all are dependent on their use of nothingness."

15. *Zhuangzi* chapter 22, "*zhibeiyou* 知北游." See Guo Qingfan, 741.

16. Brook Ziporyn argues such a distinction is indeed present and justifiable from an epistemological perspective: "It is an epistemological distinction that is being made between traces and what leaves them, where each thing is simultaneously the essential darkness, in its relation to itself as its own self-forgetting self-rightness, and at the same time a trace, which is just the same content as perceived from without, from a point of view not fit and comfortable with this content." See Ziporyn, 44.

17. *Zhuangzi* chapter 14, "*tianyun* 天運." See Guo Qingfan, 532.

18. "泰氏其外徐徐，其覺于于，一以己為馬，一以己為牛，其知情信，其德甚真，而未始入於非人." *Zhuangzi* chapter 7, "*yingdiwang* 應帝王." See Guo Qingfan, 287.

19. See Tang Jun, 152.

20. "萬物復情，此之謂混冥." *Zhuangzi* chapter 12, "*tiandi* 天地." See Guo Qingfan, 443.

21. Guo Xiang, in commenting on the passage quoted in note 87, wrote: "The true condition and muddied darkness [of the myriad things] is that which is traceless. 情復而混冥無跡也." *Zhuangzi* chapter 12, "*tiandi* 天地." See Guo Qingfan, 443.

22. *Zhuangzi* chapter 7, "*yingdiwang* 應帝王." See Guo Qingfan, 288. Additionally, the "*quanyan* 詮言" chapter of the *Huainanzi* states: "What people point at has its manifestation because it moves; what people observe leaves its trace because it acts. When movements have manifestations, they will be criticized; when actions have traces, they will be appraised. Thus the sage conceals his brilliance in the formless and hides his traces in non-deliberate doing." See Zhang, 1469; Major, 538.

23. *Zhuangzi* chapter 11, "*zaiyou* 在宥." See Guo Qingfan, 381.

24. "不形之形，形之不形，是人之所同知也，非將至之所務也." *Zhuangzi* chapter 22, "*zhibeiyou* 知北游." See Guo Qingfan, 746.

25. *Zhuangzi* chapter 12, "*tiandi* 天地." See Guo Qingfan, 445.

26. "夫堯舜帝王之名，皆其跡耳，我寄斯跡而跡非我也，故駭者自世." *Zhuangzi* chapter 11, "*zaiyou* 在宥." See Guo Qingfan, 375. Another example is the following: "The Odes and Rites are but stale traces of the former kings; if one is unsuitable for them, Dao will not move in vain. 詩禮者，先王之陳跡也，苟非其人，道不虛行." See *Zhuangzi* chapter 26, "*waiwu* 外物." See Guo Qingfan, 928.

27. Such mockery takes the following form: "Who can rid himself of achievement and fame, returning to place himself on the level of commoner men! His Dao flows but is not visible; he moves by residing in virtue, not dwelling in fame. Simple and commonplace, he would appear to have lost his mind. Destroying his trace and abandoning his influence, he does things for neither achievement nor fame. Hence he does not blame others and others do not blame him. The authentic person has no need for reputation. Why do you take such pleasure in it? 孰能去功與名而還與眾人！道流而不明，居得行而不名處；純純常常，乃比於狂；削跡捐勢，不為功名；是故無責於人，人亦無責焉。至人不聞，子何喜哉?" See *Zhuangzi* chapter 20, "*shanmu* 山木." See Guo Qingfan, 680.

28. *Zhuangzi* chapter 14, "*tianyun* 天運." See Guo Qingfan, 512. For more examples of how the trace of Confucius was summarily erased, see chapter 20, "*shanmu* 山木" (Guo Qingfan, 684), and chapter 28, "*rangwang* 讓王" (Guo Qingfan, 981).

29. *Zhuangzi* chapter 10, "*quqie* 胠篋." See Guo Qingfan, 344. Regarding the darkness of the sage, the "*quanyan* 詮言" chapter of the *Huainanzi* noted: "The sage dwells in the formless, moves in the traceless, and wanders in that having no beginning. He does not initiate things for the sake of good fortune, nor does he begin things to deal with misfortune. He remains in emptiness and nothingness, and moves when he cannot do otherwise." See Zhang, 1469; Major, 537. For a similar tale, see Wang Liqi, 177.

30. Ziporyn, 38.

31. Ibid., 39.

32. I say this as a counter-argument to Ziporyn who postulated: "Traces are the means by which knowledge and will come about, by which one thing cognizes another." Ziporyn, 36.

33. "夫堯實冥矣，其跡則堯也。自跡觀冥，內外異域，未足怪也。世徒見堯之為堯，豈識其冥哉." *Zhuangzi* chapter 1, "*xiaoyao you* 逍遙游." See Guo Qingfan, 34.

34. "絕跡易，無行地難." *Zhuangzi* chapter 4, "*renjianshi* 人間世." See Guo Qingfan, 150.

35. The story of woodcarver Qing and the cicada catcher can be found in chapter 19, "*dasheng* 達生" while that of the belt-buckle maker occurs in chapter 22, "*zhibeiyou* 知北遊."

36. The following works are a few examples of how the *Zhuangzi* has been seen in a mystical vain: Livia Kohn, *Early Chinese Mysticism: Philosophy and Soteriology in the Daoist Tradition*. Princeton, NJ: Princeton University Press, 1992; Jordan Paper, *The Spirits are Drunk: Comparative Approaches to Chinese Religion*. Albany, NY: SUNY Press, 1995; Robert Allinson, *Zhuangzi for Spiritual Transformation*, Albany, NY: SUNY Press, 1989.

37. For example, Robert Eno reads this story as an example of Zhuangzi's particularization of knowledge into either skilled or theoretical epistemological modes (see his "Cook Ding's Dao and the Limits of Philosophy" in Paul Kjellberg and Philip Ivanhoe, eds., *Essays on Skepticism, Relativism, and Ethics in the Zhuangzi*. Albany, NY: SUNY Press, 1996: 127–51; Lee Yearley interpreted the skill of cook Ding as stemming from a transcendental state of mind in which Ding's spiritualism embraces both heavenly and daemonic realms (see his "Zhuangzi's Understanding of Skillfulness and the Ultimate Spiritual State" in Ibid., 152–82; William Callahan stated that Ding was in fact putting forth a theory of political decision-making (see his article "Cook Ding's Life on the Whetstone" in Roger Ames, ed., *Wandering at Ease in the Zhuangzi*. Albany, NY: SUNY Press, 1998: 175–95); Michael Crandell translated the actions of cook Ding as a form of Gadamerian play (see "On Walking without Touching the Ground" in Victor Mair, ed., *Experimental Essays on Zhuangzi*. Honolulu: University of Hawai'i Press, 1983: 101–24); finally, Scott Cook took Ding's dance to be a literal dance of musical perfection invoking the spirits in a manner reminiscent of Confucian ritual (see "Zhuangzi and His Carving of the Confucian Ox" *Philosophy East and West*, 47.4 (1997): 521–53).

38. To date, Wu Guangming's analysis of the cook Ding story is the most competent. See his *The Butterfly as Companion: Meditations on the First Three Chapters of the Zhuangzi*. Albany, NY: SUNY Press, 1990: 301–59.

39. *Zhuangzi* chapter 3, "*yangshengzhu* 養生主." See Guo Qingfan, 117–19. Cook Ding is also mentioned in the "*qisu* 齊俗" chapter of the *Huainanzi*. See Zhang, 1165–66; Major, 416.

40. The *Mulberry Forest* is another name for a piece of music stemming from the time of king Tang of Yin (Shang dynasty), while the *Jing Shou* is a movement from a shamanic rain dance called the *Xian Chi*.

41. Wu Guangming went one step further: "Those musical pieces are unmistakably those of the spring, the rain, and the rising of life with the sun . . . the butcher's expertise is the skill that joins life and death, the spring and autumn, in the dance that rises with the rain and the sun." See Wu, 317.

42. Wu, 341.

43. For more on the role of spirit, see Wu, 319–20.

44. The Chinese character for dissect, split, and untie is *jie* 解 which can be broken down into the components of *jiao* 角, an animal horn, *dao* 刀, a blade or knife, and *niu* 牛, an ox or cattle. The ox's horn is thus an inherent representation of its own undoing. The implied symbolism is brilliant. Callahan, however, misreads such poetics as cook Ding's application of instructive knowledge to 'resolve' the ox into its component pieces. See Callahan in Ames 1998: 191.

45. A reference to the story of Nanguo Ziqi found at the beginning of chapter 2 of the *Zhuangzi*. We will discuss the theme of forgetting later in chapter 5.

46. We will take up the idea of rest in chapter 3 when we discuss Dao and temporality.

47. Watson translates *qi* 齊 as "fasting," however, I follow Cheng Xuanying who takes it to mean "composure": "In composing his true state of mind, after three days Qing suspended his need for reward and punishment, rank and title, profit and stipend, and so they could no longer enter his emotional territory 心跡既齊，凡經三日，至於慶吊賞罰，官爵利祿，如斯之事，並不入于情田." *Zhuangzi* chapter 19, "*dasheng* 達生." See Guo Qingfan, 659.

48. See Ibid., 658–60.

49. See the story of carpenter Shi in chapter 4 of the *Zhuangzi*.

50. This story also occurs in chapter 2 of the *Liezi*.

51. *Zhuangzi* chapter 19, "*dasheng* 達生." See Guo Qingfan, 639–41.

52. The term *chui* 捶 means to beat or pound; *gou* 鉤 is a hook or hook-like sword. Chapter 10 of the *Zhuangzi* says: "He who steals a belt-buckle shall be executed 竊鉤者誅." I am thus inclined to use belt-buckle over sword and refer to the craftsman by trade rather than by the product of his labors. *Zhuangzi* chapter 10, "*quqie* 胠篋." See Guo Qingfan, 350–51.

53. *Zhuangzi* chapter 22, "*zhibeiyou* 知北游." See Guo Qingfan, 760–61. This story also appears in the "*daying* 道應" chapter of the *Huainanzi*. See Zhang, 1271; Major, 465.

Chapter 3

1. *Zhuangzi* chapter 23, "*gengsangchu* 庚桑楚." See Guo Qingfan, 800.

2. See Ma Chengyuan, 288–89.

3. See Chen, 2004: 470. The "*daoyuan* 道原" chapter was uncovered in 1973 alongside several others in tomb number 3 at Mawangdui in present-day Changsha city, Hunan province, China. The site is famous because it also contained a silk manuscript version of the *Daodejing* that differs radically from previously known copies. A comprehensive study of the *Huangdi Sijing* was carried out by Chen Guying 陳鼓應 in 1995. All references are to the 2004 reprint of Chen's *Huangdi Sijing Jinzhu Jinshi* 黃帝四經今注今釋.

4. The text asks: "Of that born before heaven and earth, is it a thing? That which treats things as mere things is not a thing. Those things that issue forth

cannot precede other things, yet there were things already extant. Furthermore, there were things already extant before then too, and so on without end. 有先天地生者物邪？物物者非物。物出不得先物也，猶其有物也。猶其有物也，無已。" *Zhuangzi* chapter 22, "*zhibeiyou* 知北游." See Guo Qingfan, 763.

    5. We may refer to the story of Zhuangzi's wife dying and his explanation for why he ceased mourning her: "I thought back to the beginning of her being, when she had yet to be given life. Not having any life, she was also without form. Not yet having any form, she was also without *qi*. Amidst the vast and remote darkness, a change occurred and she had *qi*. When her *qi* changed, she then had a form. When her form changed, she was thus born. Today there has been yet another change and she is dead. 察其始而本無生，非徒無生也而本無形，非徒無形也而本無氣。雜乎芒芴之間，變而有氣，氣變而有形，形變而有生，今又變而之死." *Zhuangzi* chapter 18, "*zhile* 至樂." See Guo Qingfan, 614–15.

    6. Zhang, 245. Gao You 高誘, in his commentary to this statement, wrote that these characteristics describe "the appearance of that which is formless 馮, 翼, 洞, 灟, 無形之貌" hence I cannot agree with John Major's translation of *fengfeng yiyi* 馮馮翼翼 as "ascending and flying" and *dongdong zhuzhu* 洞洞灟灟 as "diving and delving" for they fail to viscerally portray a universe in the midst of creation, portraying it instead as one would a spiritual journey or creature of fancy such as a dragon or phoenix. See Major, 114.

    7. See Yang Bojun, 5–6.

    8. The story of the death of chaos occurs in chapter 7 of the *Zhuangzi*.

    9. I differentiate Dao time, cosmological time, and human measured time in this way: Dao time is the non-time of Dao and ontological nothingness, whereas cosmological time refers to the temporality of the One and the physical presence of the universe. Human measured time is the causal or durational time of humanity, divided into past, present, and future.

    10. *Zhuangzi* chapter 25, "*zeyang* 則陽." See Guo Qingfan, 917.

    11. *Zhuangzi* chapter 6, "*dazongshi* 大宗師." See Guo Qingfan, 252.

    12. "能知古始，是謂道紀." *Daodejing* chapter 14. See Lou Yulie, 32. Here the meaning of ancient beginning (*gushi* 古始) is identical with the great beginning (*taishi* 太始) seen in chapter 1 of the *Liezi*.

    13. See Lou Yulie, 32.

    14. *Zhuangzi* chapter 17, "*qiushui* 秋水." See Guo Qingfan, 584–85.

    15. *Zhuangzi* chapter 25, "*zeyang* 則陽." See Guo Qingfan, 885.

    16. *Zhuangzi* chapter 2, "*qiwulun* 齊物論." See Guo Qingfan, 100. For similar tales on the toil of human life, see *Zhuangzi* chapter 6, "*dazongshi* 大宗師." See Guo Qingfan, 242 and 262.

    17. "人法地，地法天，天法道，道法自然." *Daodejing* chapter 25. See Lou Yulie, 65.

    18. See *Zhonghua Daozang*, volume 14: 429. Lin Zi 林自, whose pen name was Yidu 疑獨 (Song dynasty, dates unknown) authored the *Zhuangzi Zhu* 莊子注 which survives in Chu Boxiu's text cited above, and in Jiao Hong's 焦竑 (1540–1620 CE) *Zhuangzi Yi* 莊子翼. References to Lin's commentary are to Chu Boxiu's text. For more on the life and writings of Lin Yidu, see Fang Yong, volume 2: 49–57.

19. *Zhuangzi* chapter 6, "*dazongshi* 大宗師." See Guo Qingfan, 260.
20. "莫壽於殤子，而彭祖為夭。天地與我並生，而萬物與我為一." *Zhuangzi* chapter 2, "*qiwulun* 齊物論." See Guo Qingfan, 79.
21. "且夫乘物以遊心，託不得已以養中，至矣." *Zhuangzi* chapter 4, "*renjianshi* 人間世." See Guo Qingfan, 160.
22. See Lou Yulie, 195.
23. *Zhuangzi* chapter 16, "*zhile* 至樂." See Guo Qingfan, 614–15.

Chapter 4

1. *Zhuangzi* chapter 26, "*waiwu* 外物." See Guo Qingfan, 936.
2. "故足之於地也踐，雖踐，恃其所不蹍而後善博也." *Zhuangzi* chapter 24, "*xuwugui* 徐無鬼." See Guo Qingfan, 871.
3. "宋人資章甫而適諸越，越人斷髮文身，無所用之." *Zhuangzi* chapter 1, "*xiaoyao you* 逍遙游." See Guo Qingfan, 31.
4. *Zhuangzi* chapter 1, "*xiaoyao you* 逍遙游." See Guo Qingfan, 36–40.
5. *Zhuangzi* chapter 2, "*qiwulun* 齊物論." See Guo Qingfan, 66.
6. *Zhuangzi* chapter 13, "*tiandi* 天地." See Guo Qingfan, 488.
7. *Zhuangzi* chapter 2, "*qiwulun* 齊物論." See Guo Qingfan, 45–46.
8. *Zhuangzi* chapter 7, "*yingdiwang* 應帝王." See Guo Qingfan, 309.
9. *Zhuangzi* chapter 2, "*qiwulun* 齊物論." See Guo Qingfan, 70. The phrase "going both ways" (*liangxing* 兩行) actually appears in an altogether different context, one regarding a keeper of monkeys. Its relevance here is no less diminished however.
10. *Zhuangzi* chapter 17, "*qiushui* 秋水." See Guo Qingfan, 577.
11. Chapter 48 of the *Daodejing* says: "損之又損，以至於無為，無為而無不為." See Lou Yulie, 128.
12. *Zhuangzi* chapter 5, "*dechongfu* 德充符." See Guo Qingfan, 186.
13. *Zhuangzi* chapter 23, "*gengsangchu* 庚桑楚." See Guo Qingfan, 773.
14. "夫大塊載我以形，勞我以生，佚我以老，息我以死。故善吾生者，乃所以善吾死也." *Zhuangzi* chapter 6, "*dazongshi* 大宗師." See Guo Qingfan, 242.
15. See Zhang, 791; Major, 259–60.
16. *Zhuangzi* chapter 4, "*renjianshi* 人間世." See Guo Qingfan, 176–77.
17. "匠石之齊，至乎曲轅，見櫟社樹……而幾死之散人，又惡知散木." *Zhuangzi* chapter 4, "*renjianshi* 人間世." See Guo Qingfan, 170–72.
18. "仲尼曰: 丘也嘗使於楚矣，適見㹠子……皆無其本矣." *Zhuangzi* chapter 5, "*dechongfu* 德充符." See Guo Qingfan, 209.

Chapter 5

1. *Zhuangzi* chapter 2, "*qiwulun* 齊物論." See Guo Qingfan, 108.
2. "有治在人，忘乎物，忘乎天，其名為忘己。忘己之人，是之謂入於天." *Zhuangzi* chapter 12, "*tiandi* 天地." See Guo Qingfan, 428.

3. "雖忘乎故吾，吾有不忘者存。" *Zhuangzi* chapter 21, "*tianzifang* 田子方." See Guo Qingfan, 709.

4. *Zhuangzi* chapter 19, "*dasheng* 達生." See Guo Qingfan, 662–63.

5. *Zhuangzi* chapter 21, "*tianzifang* 田子方." See Guo Qingfan, 709.

6. In his commentary to this passage, Cheng Xuanying had this to say: "As for the transformation of Dao, there is no time when it is suspended. Although my old self is lost and my new self is still present, this presence of existence has not been forgotten. As the old I has yet to begin to be a not-I, why are you fretting so! 夫變化之道，無時暫停，雖失故吾而新吾尚在，斯有不忘者存也，故未始非吾，汝何患也." *Zhuangzi* chapter 21, "*tianzifang* 田子方." See Guo Qingfan, 711.

7. *Zhuangzi* chapter 6, "*dazongshi* 大宗師." See Guo Qingfan, 272.

8. *Zhuangzi* chapter 6, "*dazongshi* 大宗師." See Guo Qingfan, 229–30.

9. *Zhuangzi* chapter 26, "*waiwu* 外物." See Guo Qingfan, 944.

10. As part of his commentary to the *Yijing* 易經, Wang Bi justified ontic forgetfulness using precisely this argument: "Thus if one preserves words, one cannot obtain the image; if one preserves the image, one cannot obtain the idea. Images are born of ideas and are thus preserved as images, but these images are not the images themselves. Words are born of images and are thus preserved as words, but these words are not the words themselves. Such being the case, if one were to forget the image, one could then obtain the idea; if one were to forget words, one could then obtain the image. Obtaining the idea lies in forgetting the image, and obtaining the image lies in forgetting words. 是故，存言者，非得象者也；存象者，非得意者也。象生於意而存象焉，則所存者乃非其象也；言生於象而存言焉，則所存者乃非其言也。然則，忘象者，乃得意者也；忘言者，乃得象者也。得意在忘象，得象在忘言." See Lou Yulie, 609.

11. *Zhuangzi* chapter 5, "*dechongfu* 德充符." See Guo Qingfan, 216–17. These lines occur in a passage involving two deformed men (Yinqi Zhili Wuchun 闉跂支離無脣 and Wengang Daying 甕㿻大癭) and the Dukes (Ling of Wei 衛靈公 and Huan of Qi 齊桓公) of their respective home states.

12. *Zhuangzi* chapter 5, "*dechongfu* 德充符." See Guo Qingfan, 217–18.

13. *Zhuangzi* chapter 4, "*renjianshi* 人間世." See Guo Qingfan, 150. The expression "sitting while the mind gallops" (*zuo chi* 坐馳) also appears in the "*lan ming* 覽冥" chapter of the *Huainanzi* which reads: "於遠方之外，是謂坐馳陸沈，晝冥宵明，以冬鑠膠，以夏造冰." See Zhang, 643; Mair, 218.

14. "故養志者忘形，養形者忘利，致道者忘心矣." *Zhuangzi* chapter 28, "*rangwang* 讓王." See Guo Qingfan, 977.

15. *Zhuangzi* chapter 27, "*yuyan* 寓言." See Guo Qingfan, 947.

16. *Zhuangzi* chapter 2, "*qiwulun* 齊物論." See Guo Qingfan, 43–45.

17. Wang Pang (1044–1076 CE) was a literary genius who succumbed to illness when he was only thirty-three, but not before producing commentaries to the *Zhuangzi*, *Daodejing*, *Analects*, and *Mencius*. His commentary to the *Zhuangzi*, entitled *Nanhua Zhenjing Xinzhuan* 南華真經新傳, has been preserved in volume 16 of the *Zhonghua Daozang* as well as volume 337 of the *Siku Quanshu*. All references to Wang's commentary are to the *Siku Quanshu* edition. For more on his life and writings, see Fang Yong, volume 2: 61–82.

18. See Tang Jun, 18.
19. See Zhou Qicheng, 13.
20. "真人之息以踵，衆人之息以喉." *Zhuangzi* chapter 6, "*dazongshi* 大宗師." See Guo Qingfan, 228.
21. *Zhuangzi* chapter 12, "*tiandi* 天地." See Guo Qingfan, 427–30.
22. *Zhuangzi* chapter 2, "*qiwulun* 齊物論." See Guo Qingfan, 79.
23. Interestingly, the phrase "non-mind" or "mindlessness" (*wuxin* 無心) is also used just three times.
24. *Zhuangzi* chapter 6, "*dazongshi* 大宗師." See Guo Qingfan, 283–84. This story also appears in the *Huainanzi*. See Zhang, 1282; Major, 468–69.
25. *Zhuangzi* chapter 21, "*tianzifang* 田子方." See Guo Qingfan, 718.
26. See for example the tale in chapter 18 when Zhuangzi's wife died and he clapped on a drum, singing.
27. *Zhuangzi* chapter 6, "*dazongshi* 大宗師." See Guo Qingfan, 285.
28. The character *zhai* 齋 appears in the story of bell stand maker Qing but without the *xin* 心 element, thereby changing the meaning from "composing the heart-mind" to "composing the self." The text reads: "When I am preparing to make a bell stand, I do not let it wear out my energy but compose myself in order to still my heart-mind. 臣將為鐻，未嘗敢以耗氣也，必齊以靜心." *Zhuangzi* chapter 19, "*dasheng* 達生." See Guo Qingfan, 658–59.
29. *Zhuangzi* chapter 4, "*renjianshi* 人間世." See Guo Qingfan, 147–48.
30. "志一，則心鑑定而思慮澄，廓然空虛而至道自集也." See *Siku Quanshu*.
31. Ibid.
32. Another name for Yan Hui.
33. The *guan* 管 is an ancient Chinese wind instrument made of bamboo and had six holes along its length. The *yue* 籥 is an ancient Chinese flute.
34. See *Zhonghua Daozang*, volume 14: 64.
35. *Zhuangzi* chapter 2, "*qiwulun* 齊物論." See Guo Qingfan, 46.
36. "故養志者忘形，養形者忘利，致道者忘心矣." *Zhuangzi* chapter 28, "*rangwang* 讓王." See Guo Qingfan, 977.

Chapter 6

1. *Zhuangzi* chapter 2, "*qiwulun* 齊物論." See Guo Qingfan, 63.
2. *Zhuangzi* chapter 2, "*qiwulun* 齊物論." See Guo Qingfan, 108.
3. Ibid.
4. "為是而有畛也……聖人懷之，眾人辯之以相示也." *Zhuangzi* chapter 2, "*qiwulun* 齊物論." See Guo Qingfan, 83.
5. See Guo Qingfan, 66. Zhuangzi's reference to horses occurs in chapter 2 and points to the treatise "White Horse is not a Horse 白馬非馬" by the logician Gongsun Long 公孫龍. In fact, Zhuangzi turned Gongsun's arguments on their head to demonstrate the irrelevancy of his sophistry.
6. *Zhuangzi* chapter 27, "*yuyan* 寓言." See Guo Qingfan, 950.
7. *Zhuangzi* chapter 27, "*yuyan* 寓言." See Guo Qingfan, 949.

8. *Zhuangzi* chapter 23, "*gengsangchu* 庚桑楚." See Guo Qingfan, 815.
9. *Zhuangzi* chapter 23, "*gengsangchu* 庚桑楚." See Guo Qingfan, 810.
10. *Zhuangzi* chapter 16, "*shanxing* 繕性." See Guo Qingfan, 548.
11. See Zhang, 1368; Major, 498. On a side note, a passage closely resembling this one occurs in the "*shangren* 上仁" chapter of the *Wenzi*: "和者，陰陽調，日夜分。故萬物春分而生，秋分而成." See Wang Liqi, 451.
12. *Zhuangzi* chapter 16, "*shanxing* 繕性." See Guo Qingfan, 550–51.
13. "萬物負陰而抱陽，沖氣以為和." *Daodejing* chapter 42. See Lou Yulie, 117.
14. "萬物之生，皆抱負陰陽之氣，以沖虛之理行乎其間，所以為和也." See *Zhonghua Daozang*, volume 11: 261.
15. *Zhuangzi* chapter 12, "*tiandi* 天地." See Guo Qingfan, 411.
16. Further examples from the *Daodejing* include: chapter 15, "敦兮其若樸;" chapter 28, "为天下谷，常德乃足，复归于朴;" chapter 32, "道常无名，朴;" and chapter 37, "化而欲作，吾將镇之以无名之朴，镇之以无名之朴，夫將不欲."
17. *Zhuangzi* chapter 16, "*shanxing* 繕性." See Guo Qingfan, 548.
18. *Zhuangzi* chapter 16, "*shanxing* 繕性." See Guo Qingfan, 548–49.
19. *Zhuangzi* chapter 13, "*tiandao* 天道." See Guo Qingfan, 458.
20. *Zhuangzi* chapter 12, "*tiandi* 天地." See Guo Qingfan, 438.
21. "彼，游方之外者也，而丘，游方之內者也." *Zhuangzi* chapter 6, "*dazongshi* 大宗師." See Guo Qingfan, 267.
22. *Zhuangzi* chapter 6, "*dazongshi* 大宗師." See Guo Qingfan, 267–68. A similar tale also appears in the "*dasheng* 達生" chapter. See Guo Qingfan, 663.
23. *Zhuangzi* chapter 14, "*tianyun* 天運." See Guo Qingfan, 519.

Bibliography

Allison, Robert. *Chuang-Tzu for Spiritual Transformation: An Analysis of the Inner Chapters*. Albany: SUNY Press, 1989.
Ames, Roger, ed. *Wandering at Ease in the Zhuangzi*. Albany: SUNY Press, 1998.
Ames, Roger, and David Hall, trans. *Daodejing: A Philosophical Translation*. New York: Ballantine Books, 2004.
Bohm, David. *Wholeness and the Implicate Order*. New York: Routledge, 1980.
Chai, David. *Early Zhuangzi Commentaries: On the Sounds and Meanings of the Inner Chapters*. Saarbrucken: VDM Verlag Dr. Muller, 2008.
Chai, David. "Musical Naturalism in the Thought of Ji Kang" *Dao: A Journal of Comparative Philosophy*, 8.2 (2009): 151–71.
Chai, David. "Meontology in Early Xuanxue 玄學 Thought" *Journal of Chinese Philosophy*, 37.1 (2010): 91–102.
Chai, David. "Meontological Generativity: A Daoist Reading of the Thing" *Philosophy East and West*, 64.2 (April 2014): 303–18.
Chai, David. "Zhuangzi's Meontological Temporality" *Dao: A Journal of Comparative Philosophy*, 13.3 (Sept. 2014): 361–77.
Chan Wing-Tsit. *A Source Book in Chinese Philosophy*. Princeton, NJ: Princeton University Press, 1963.
Chen Guying 陈鼓应. *Huangdi Sijing Jinzhu Jinyi* 黃帝四經今注今譯 (Modern Commentary and Annotations to the *Four Classics of the Yellow Emperor*). Taibei: Shangwu Yinshu Guan, 1995.
Chen Jingyuan 陳景元. *Nanhua Zhenjing Zhangju Yinyi* 南華真經章句音義 (On the Sounds and Meaning of the Chapters and Sentences of *Zhuangzi*). Volume 13 of *Zhonghua Daozang*.
Chu Boxiu 褚伯秀. *Nanhua Zhenjing Yihai Zuanwei* 南華真經義海纂微 (Admiring the Profound Sea of Meaning of *Zhuangzi*). Volume 14 of *Zhonghua Daozang*.
Cunningham, Conor. *Genealogy of Nihilism: Philosophies of Nothing and the Difference of Theology*. London: Routledge, 2002.
Du Daojian 杜道堅. *Wenzi Zuanyi* 文子續義 (Written Meaning of the *Wenzi*). See *Siku Quanshu*. For modern edition, see Wang Liqi 王利器.
Fang Xuanling 房玄齡. *Guanzi* 管子 (*Guanzi*). See *Siku Quanshu*. For modern edition, see Li Xiangfeng 黎翔鳳.

Fang Yong 方勇. *Zhuangzi Xueshi* 莊子學史 (Historical Study of the *Zhuangzi*). Beijing: Renmin Chuban She, 2008.

Froese, Katrin. *Nietzsche, Heidegger, and Daoist Thought: Crossing Paths in-Between.* Albany: SUNY Press, 2006.

Guo Qingfan 郭慶藩, ed. *Zhuangzi Jishi* 莊子集釋 (Collected Annotations to *Zhuangzi*). Beijing: Zhonghua Shuju, 1997.

Guo Xiang 郭象, Cheng Xuanying 成玄英. *Nanhua Zhenjing Zhushu* 南華真經注疏 (Commentary and Annotations to *Zhuangzi*). Volume 13 of *Zhonghua Daozang*. For modern edition, see Guo Qingfan 郭慶藩.

Hansen, Chad. *A Daoist Theory of Chinese Thought: A Philosophical Interpretation.* New York: Oxford University Press, 1992.

Hartmann, Nicolai. *New Ways of Ontology*. Translated by R. C. Kuhn. Chicago: Henry Regnery Co., 1953.

Henricks, Robert. *Laozi's Daodejing: A Translation of the Startling New Documents Found at Guodain*. New York: Columbia University Press, 2000.

Heshang Gong 河上公. *Daode Zhenjing Zhu* 道德真經註 (Commentary to *Daodejing*). Volume 9 of *Zhonghua Daozang*. Modern edition entitled *Laozi Daodejing Heshang Gong Zhangju* 老子道德經河上公章句. Beijing: Zhonghua Shuju, 1993.

Hou Wailu 侯外廬. *Zhongguo Sixiang Tongshi* 中國思想通史 (A General Intellectual History of China). Beijing: Renmin Chuban She, 1995.

Huang Shouqi 黃壽祺 et al., eds. *Zhouyi Shizhu* 周易譯注 (Annotated Commentary to *Zhouyi*). Shanghai: Shanghai Guji Chubanshe, 2009.

Jiang Cheng 江澂. *Daode Zhenjing Shuyi* 道德真經疏義 (Annotations on the Meaning of *Daodejing*). Volume 9 of *Zhonghua Daozang*.

Jiang Yu 江遹. *Chongxu Zhide Zhenjing Jie* 沖虛至德真經解 (Explanations to *Liezi*). Volume 15 of *Zhonghua Daozang*.

Kang Zhongqian 康中乾. *Youwu zhi Bian: Wei-Jin Xuanxue Benti Sixiang zai Jiedu* 有無之辨: 魏晉玄學本體思想再解讀 (Discriminating between *you* and *wu*: The Metaphysical Thought of Wei-Jin Xuanxue Reconsidered). Beijing: Renmin Chuban She, 2003.

Kjellberg, Paul, et al., eds. *Essays on Skepticism, Relativism, and Ethics in the Zhuangzi*. Albany: SUNY Press, 1996.

Li Daoping 李道平, ed. *Zhouyi Jijie Zuanshu* 周易集解纂疏 (Collected Explanations and Compiled Annotations to *Zhouyi*). Beijing: Zhonghua Shuju, 2006.

Li Xiangfeng 黎翔鳳, ed. *Guanzi Jiaozhu* 管子校注 (Examination of the Commentaries to *Guanzi*). Beijing: Zhonghua Shuju, 2006.

Li Yao 李約. *Daode Zhenjing Xinzhu* 道德真經新注 (A New Commentary to *Daodejing*). Volume 9 of *Zhonghua Daozang*.

Lin Xiyi 林希逸. *Nanhua Zhenjing Kouyi* 南華真經口義 (Oral Significance of *Zhuangzi*). Volume 13 of *Zhonghua Daozang*. For modern edition, see Zhou Qicheng 周啓成.

Lin Xiyi 林希逸. *Chongxuzhide Zhenjing Yanzhai Kouyi* 沖虛至德真經鬳齋口義 (Yan Zhai's Oral Significance of *Liezi*). Volume 15 of *Zhonghua Daozang*.

Lin Xiyi 林希逸. *Daode Zhenjing Kouyi* 道德真經口義 (Oral Significance of *Daodejing*). Volume 11 of *Zhonghua Daozang*.

Liu Wendian 劉文典. *Huainan Honglie Jijie* 淮南鴻烈集解 (Collected Explanations to *Huainanzi*). Beijing: Zhonghua Shuju, 1989.

Liu Wendian 劉文典. *Zhuangzi Bu Zheng* 莊子補正 (Corrections to *Zhuangzi*). Hefei: Anhui Daxue Chuban She, 1999.

Lou Yulie 樓宇烈, ed. *Wang Bi Jijiao Shi* 王弼集校釋 (Collective Examination of the Annotations of Wang Bi). Beijing: Zhonghua Shuju, 1999.

Lowe, E. *Four-Category Ontology: A Metaphysical Foundation for Natural Science*. Oxford, UK: Oxford University Press, 2006.

Lü Huiqing 呂惠卿. *Zhuangzi Yi Jijiao* 莊子義集校 (Collective Examination of the Meaning of *Zhuangzi*). Preserved in Chu Boxiu's 褚伯秀, *Nanhua Zhenjing Yihai Zuanwei* 南華真經義海纂微. For modern edition, see Tang Jun 湯君.

Lü Huiqing 呂惠卿. *Daode Zhenjing Zhuan* 道德真經傳 (A New Commentary to *Daodejing*). Volume 10 of *Zhonghua Daozang*.

Lu Deming 陸德明. *Zhuangzi Yinyi* 莊子音義 (On the Sounds and Meaning of *Zhuangzi*). Preserved in his *Jingdian Shiwen* 經典釋文. See *Siku Quanshu*.

Lu Xisheng 陸希聲. *Daode Zhenjing Zhuan* 道德真經傳 (Commentary to *Daodejing*). Volume 9 of *Zhonghua Daozang*.

Lynn, Richard J., trans. *Classic of the Way and Virtue: A New Translation of the Tao-te Ching of Laozi as Interpreted by Wang Bi*. New York: Columbia University Press, 1999.

Ma Chengyuan 馬承源, ed. *Shanghai Bowuguan Cang Zhanguo Chuzhu Shu* 上海博物館藏戰國楚竹書 (Chu State Bamboo-slip Texts from the Warring States Period in the Collections of the Shanghai Museum). Volume 3. Shanghai: Shanghai Guji Chuban She, 2003.

Mair, Victor, ed. *Experimental Essays on Chuang-tzu*. Centre for Asian and Pacific Studies: University of Hawai'i Press, 1983.

Major, John, et al., eds. *The Huainanzi: A Guide to the Theory and Practice of Government in Early Han China*. New York: Columbia University Press, 2010.

Mou Bo, ed. *History of Chinese Philosophy*. New York: Routledge, 2009.

Munro, Donald, ed. *Individualism and Holism: Studies in Confucian and Daoist Values*. Ann Arbor: University of Michigan Press, 1985.

Qian Xizuo 錢熙祚, ed. *Yinwenzi* 尹文子. Volume 6 of *Zhuzi Jicheng* 諸子集成 (Collective Works of the Masters). Beijing: Zhonghua Shuju, 2006.

Roth, Harold. *Original Tao: Inward Training and the Foundations of Taoist Mysticism*. New York: Columbia University Press, 1999.

Shang Geling. *Liberation as Affirmation: The Religiosity of Zhuangzi and Nietzsche*. Albany: SUNY Press, 2006.

Siku Quanshu 四庫全書 (The Complete Library of the Four Treasuries). Electronic version.

Slingerland, Edward. *Wuwei as Conceptual Metaphor and Spiritual Ideal in Early China*. Oxford, UK: Oxford University Press, 2003.

Smajs, Josef. *Evolutionary Ontology: Reclaiming the Value of Nature by Transforming Culture*. New York: Rodopi, 2008.

Tang Jun 湯君, ed. *Zhuangzi Yi Jijiao* 莊子義集校 (A Collective Examination of the Meaning of *Zhuangzi*). Beijing: Zhonghua Shuju, 2009.

Tang Yijie 湯一介. *Guo Xiang yu Wei-Jin Xuanxue* 郭象與魏晉玄學 (Guo Xiang and Wei-Jin *Xuanxue*). Beijing: Beijing Daxue Chuban She, 2000.

Tang Yijie 湯一介, ed. *Wei-Jin Xuanxue Yanjiu* 魏晉玄學研究 (Research into Wei-Jin *Xuanxue*). Wuhan: Hubei Jiaoyu Chuban She, 2008.

Tang Yongtong 湯用彤. *Wei-Jin Xuanxue Lungao* 魏晉玄學論稿 (A Sketch of Wei-Jin *Xuanxue*). Shanghai: Shanghai Guji Chuban She, 2005.

Wagner, Rudolf. *The Craft of a Chinese Commentator: Wang Bi on the Laozi.* Albany: SUNY Press, 2000.

Wagner, Rudolf. *A Chinese Reading of the Daodejing: Wang Bi's Commentary on the Laozi with Critical Text and Translation.* Albany: SUNY Press, 2003a.

Wagner, Rudolf. *Language, Ontology, and Political Philosophy in China: Wang Bi's Scholarly Exploration of the Dark.* Albany: SUNY Press, 2003b.

Wang Bi 王弼. *Daode Zhenjing Zhu* 道德真經註 (Commentary to *Daodejing*). Volume 9 of *Zhonghua Daozang*. For modern edition, see Lou Yulie 樓宇烈.

Wang Liqi 王利器, ed. *Wenzi Shuyi* 文子疏義 (Annotations on the Meaning of *Wenzi*). Beijing: Zhonghua Shuju, 2009.

Wang Pang 王雱. *Nanhua Zhenjing Xin Zhuan* 南華真經新傳 (A New Commentary to *Zhuangzi*). See *Siku Quanshu*.

Wang Shumin 王叔岷. *Zhuangzi Jiaoquan* 莊子校詮 (Complete Examination of *Zhuangzi*). Taibei: Zhongyang Yanjiu Yuan Lishi Yuyan Yanjiusuo, 1999.

Wang Xianqian 王先謙, ed. *Zhuangzi Jijie* 莊子集解 (Collected Explanations to *Zhuangzi*). Beijing: Zhonghua Shuju, 1999.

Wang Youru. *Linguistic Strategies in Daoist Zhuangzi and Chan Buddhism: The Other Way of Speaking.* London: Routledge, 2003.

Wang Youru, ed. *Deconstruction and the Ethical in Asian Thought.* New York: Routledge, 2007.

Watson, Burton, trans. *The Complete Works of Chuang-tzu.* New York: Columbia University Press. 1968.

Wong, David B. *Natural Moralities: A Defense of Pluralistic Relativism.* New York: Oxford University Press, 2006.

Yang Bojun 楊伯峻, ed. *Liezi Jishi* 列子集釋 (Collected Annotations to *Liezi*). Beijing: Zhonghua Shuju, 2007.

Zhang Shuangli 張雙棣, ed. *Huainanzi Jiaoshi* 淮南子校釋 (Examination of the Annotations to *Huainanzi*). Beijing: Beijing Daxue Chuban She, 1997.

Zhonghua Daozang 中華道藏 (Chinese Daoist Canon). 49 Volumes. Beijing: Huaxia Chuban She, 2004.

Zhou Qicheng 周啓成, ed. *Zhuangzi Yanzhai Kouyi Jiaozhu* 莊子鬳齋口義校註 (Examination of the Oral Significance of Yan Zhai's Commentary to *Zhuangzi*). Beijing: Zhonghua Shuju, 2009.

Ziporyn, Brook. *Penumbra Unbound: The Neo-Taoist Philosophy of Guo Xiang.* Albany: SUNY Press, 2003.

Index

Beginning / Great Beginning (*shi* 始 / *taishi* 太始), xvi, 1, 4–5, 11–12, 14–15, 18–24, 26, 28, 30, 32, 34–35, 37, 67, 69, 70, 73–75, 77–81, 84–85, 110, 122–123, 160, 163, 165, 178n22, 178n27, 181n49, 183n29, 186n5, 186n12

Belt-buckle maker, xv, 48–49, 59, 61–62, 103, 181n3, 184n35, 185n52

Birds, 88, 97, 154

Bohm, David, xi, 175n3

Carpenter Shi, 58, 99–100, 102, 104, 185n49

Change (*bian* 變) / Transformation (*hua* 化), 4, 6, 9, 11, 13, 25, 27–29, 33, 37–38, 40, 43, 46, 48–49, 52, 60–61, 69, 72–74, 76–79, 81–82, 85, 87–88, 91–92, 98, 102–103, 107, 110–112, 123, 130–131, 133–134, 136, 140, 144, 146, 149–150, 153–154, 156, 164, 166, 172, 186n5, 188n6

Chaos (*hundun* 渾沌), xv, 24, 47, 55, 66–69, 73, 80, 94, 150, 153, 155, 161–163, 167, 181n58, 186n8

Chen Jingyuan 陳景元, 8, 177n14

Cheng Xuanying 成玄英, 7, 80, 117, 129, 145, 157, 176n12, 177n14, 185n47, 188n6

Chu Boxiu 褚伯秀, 8, 177n13, 177n14, 186n18

Cicada catcher, xv, 48–49, 59–61, 136, 154, 181n3, 184n35

Clay vessel, xvi, 39–40, 92, 97, 171, 182n14

Cook Ding (*paoding* 庖丁), xv, 48–57, 60–62, 94, 115, 127, 131, 181n3, 184n37, 184n38, 184n39, 185n44

Composing the heart-mind (*xin zhai* 心齋), xvi, 56–57, 104–105, 108–109, 119–120, 131–134, 142, 146–147, 152–153, 156, 163, 166, 172, 185n47, 189n28

Confucius, 11, 29, 41, 43, 45, 59, 102, 120, 127, 129–130, 132, 134, 161–164, 172, 183n28

Constancy (*chang* 常) / Unchanging (*bu bian* 不變; *bu hua* 不化), xi, 5, 27–28, 43, 63, 67, 71–81, 84, 93, 103, 109–111, 123, 126, 143–144, 153, 155, 160, 164, 170, 176n3

Creatio ex-nihilo, xiv, 1, 30, 169, 180n41

Cui Zhuan 崔譔, xiii

Darkness (*ming* 冥), 16, 31, 43–48, 70–73, 81, 85, 97, 103, 119, 149, 153, 155, 182n21, 183n29, 186n5

Dead ash (*si hui* 死灰), 120–123, 126, 130

Death, xiii–xvii, 5, 11–18, 26, 46, 51–55, 60–62, 65, 70–74, 80–83, 98–99, 112–116, 123–126, 143–146, 149, 153, 164, 167, 184n41, 186n8

Dirt / Soil, 26, 54, 88, 101, 163, 164

Fish, 88, 97, 113–115, 154
Forget / Forgetfulness (*wang* 忘), xvi, 5, 17, 26, 29, 37, 47, 52, 56–57, 72, 76–78, 81, 103–133, 136–137, 140, 142, 145, 146, 148, 150–156, 160–167, 171, 182n16, 185n45, 188n10
Form (*xing* 形), xii–xiii, 1, 2, 10, 12, 14, 16–26, 32–33, 41, 44, 62, 66, 69, 72, 74, 75, 77, 92, 98, 102–103, 116–117, 121, 125–129, 141, 143, 178n23, 179n34, 182n6, 186n5
Formless (*wu xing* 無形 / *wei xing* 未形), 1, 2, 10–24, 30–33, 41, 44, 67–69, 73, 176n3, 178n22, 178n23, 178n27, 179n28, 179n34, 181n2, 183n22, 183n29, 186n6
Four Classics of the Yellow Emperor (*Huangdi Sijing* 黃帝四經), 19, 67–68
Freedom, xvi–xvii, 23–28, 60, 75, 82–83, 87–89, 98, 105–108, 111–113, 118–120, 126–129, 137, 139–167, 171, 173

Gate of Heaven (*tianmen* 天門), 15, 21, 66, 72, 179n28, 179n30
Goblet Words (*zhi yan* 卮言), 147, 149
Great One gives Birth to Water (*Taiyi Shengshui* 太一生水), 20
Guo Xiang 郭象, xiii, 3–11, 16, 33, 42–48, 80, 116, 145, 156–157, 176n4, 176n12, 177n15, 178n27, 182n21

Harmony (*he* 和), xvi, 17, 28–29, 40, 48–52, 55–61, 72, 75–78, 99, 103, 108, 111, 129, 136, 139–140, 144, 148–160, 163–168, 182n12
Hartmann, Nicolai, xi, 175n2
Heaven / Heavenly (*tian* 天), xii, xvi, 2, 5, 11–16, 19–23, 29, 34, 49–62, 68–69, 77–82, 86, 91–92, 95–96, 101, 109, 112–114, 125–128, 131–134, 139–141, 145–152, 155, 158–159, 163–169, 171, 176n3, 178n20, 179n28, 179n30, 182n5, 184n37, 185n4
Heavenly Principle (*tianli* 天理), 56–57, 61–62, 139–140, 144, 155, 159, 165
Heavenly Differentiation (*tianni* 天倪), 140, 144–147, 150
Heavenly Measure (*tianjun* 天均), 140, 145–149, 163
Heavenly Harmony (*tianhe* 天和), 140, 148, 151, 159
Heng 恆 / *Hengxian* 恆先, 18–21, 66–70, 180n37
Huainanzi 淮南子, 12, 57, 68, 98, 152, 175n2, 178n21, 178n22, 179n28, 180n37, 181n49, 183n22, 183n29, 184n39, 185n53, 188n13, 189n24
Huizi 惠子, 88–91

King Hui of Liang 梁惠王, xiii
King Tang of Yin 成湯, 184n40
King Xuan of Qi 齊宣王, xiii
King Wei of Chu 楚威王, xiii
King Wenhui 文惠君, 49, 54–56, 62

Laozi 老子 (*Daodejing* 道德經), xvi, 2–4, 10–13, 16, 19–20, 23, 27–29, 33, 37–43, 72–73, 79–81, 84, 91–92, 153, 156, 176n3, 177n14, 177n15, 177n18, 178n20, 179n29, 179n30, 179n31, 179n34, 180n37, 180n40, 180n47, 181n49, 181n55, 181n56, 181n57, 181n2, 181n6, 185n3, 186n12, 186n17, 187n11, 188n17, 190n13, 190n16
Liezi 列子, 12–14, 21, 69, 134, 178n21, 179n31, 185n50, 186n12
Life, xiv, xvi–xvii, 5, 11–15, 18, 22–27, 30, 46, 49, 52–55, 60–62, 70–74, 77, 80–82, 85, 91, 96–102, 109, 112–113, 123–126, 133, 145–151,

Index / 197

160–167, 171–172, 178n27, 179n29, 184n41, 186n5
Life / Self-Cultivation, xvi, 50, 56–59, 96, 101–103, 112, 128, 146–148, 156, 159, 172
Life Praxis, 24–25, 48–58, 62, 87, 92–104, 107, 112–113, 117, 125, 137, 150–159, 165, 171–173
Lin Xiyi 林希逸, 15, 122–124, 153, 179n31
Lin Yidu 林疑獨, 79–80, 133–136, 186n18
Lose One's Self (wu sang wo 吾喪我), 51, 59, 110, 121, 125, 131
Lose One's Companion (sang qi ou 喪其耦), 121–123
Lü Huiqing 呂惠卿, 7, 19, 27, 42, 122–124, 177n13

Mind / Heart-Mind (xin 心), 8, 10, 16–17, 25–30, 34, 37, 49–57, 60–61, 70–72, 76, 79, 82–85, 97, 104, 107–142, 148–149, 156–158, 161–163, 166–168, 171
Mindless / non-Mind (wuxin 無心), 23–24, 58, 119–120, 123–127, 133, 136–137, 140–142, 149, 155–158, 160, 162, 166–167, 183n27, 184n37, 189n23

Naturalness / Self-So Nature (ziran 自然), 6–11, 29, 37–38, 44, 51–54, 58, 75, 78–80, 89, 96–97, 103, 109–113, 123, 126–131, 134, 145–150, 157–158, 167–172, 177n15, 178n27
Nanbo Zikui, 71–72
Nanguo Ziqi, 37, 57, 99, 120–123, 185n45
Nihilism, xi–xii, xiv–xv, 5–6, 17, 18, 26, 48, 65, 83, 84, 86, 108, 117, 142, 168, 169
Non-Deliberate Doing (wuwei 無為), 12, 26, 29, 58, 76, 86, 90, 103, 126, 148, 155, 158, 161–166, 171, 178n23, 183n22

Non-Words (wu yan 無言) / Forget words (wang yan 忘言), 16, 114–115, 147–150, 158–159, 188n10

Qi 氣, 9, 14, 18–21, 54, 57, 67–69, 85, 124–126, 132–136, 140, 148, 152–153, 163, 177n16, 178n23, 186n5

Ran Xiang 冉相氏, 77, 79
Repository of Heaven (tianfu 天府), 16, 179n30
Return (fan 反), xv, xvii, 6, 8, 10, 15–17, 22–31, 37–39, 43, 47–48, 53–54, 57, 62–65, 68–72, 76, 79–88, 95, 104, 107–118, 121, 125–126, 130–131, 136–137, 143–146, 152, 156–157, 160–169, 180n41, 183n27
Rest, xv, 9, 29, 35, 55–56, 65, 74–78, 81, 85, 98, 119, 122, 156, 162–167, 171

Sage, xvi–xvii, 8, 16, 20–21, 24–25, 31–33, 37, 40–47, 53, 60, 72–74, 77–82, 85–86, 91, 96–99, 103, 111–123, 126, 131, 136, 140–142, 145–172, 182n5, 183n22, 183n29
Shang Geling, 4–5, 176n5
Sima Biao 司馬彪, xiii, 121
Simplicity (pu 樸), 18–21, 59, 66–69, 105, 125, 150, 156–158, 162–166
Sitting in Forgetfulness (zuo wang 坐忘), xvi, 37, 126–132, 136–137, 142, 146, 152–153
Sitting while the Mind Gallops (zuo chi 坐馳), 119, 134, 188n13
Speech / Words (yan 言), 7, 41–42, 46, 50, 54, 62, 70, 90, 93, 108, 114–115, 120, 141, 146–149, 167, 188n10
Spirit (shen 神), xvi, 17–19, 22–24, 29, 41–42, 50–61, 67, 102, 118–155, 160–168, 177n16, 184n37, 184n43, 186n6
Spirit Tower (lingtai 靈台), 159, 179n30

The Thing, xi, xv, 30–48, 52, 62, 66, 68, 70, 73–75, 89, 103, 114, 122
Time / Non-Time, xv–xvi, 9, 11, 14, 21, 23–24, 28, 33–34, 40, 43, 50, 53, 60, 65–86, 89, 110–114, 122, 124, 128, 136, 144, 153, 155, 160, 167
Trace (*ji* 跡) / Traceless (*wuji* 無跡) xiii, xv–xvi, 11, 30–36, 40–48, 62, 78, 82, 109, 113–119, 130, 182n16, 182n21, 183n22, 183n26, 183n27, 183n29, 183n32
That Which Leaves the Trace (*suoyi ji* 所以跡), 41–44, 46–47, 130
Tree, xvi, 45, 58–60, 74, 87, 90–104, 135–136, 146, 171

Ultimate / ultimacy, xi, 2, 22, 38, 43–44, 67, 72, 178n27
Useless / uselessness, xv–xvi, 58, 60–62, 86–104, 107–108, 112, 117, 125, 137, 151, 163, 165–166, 170–172

Virtue (*de* 德), xvi, 2, 7, 9, 13, 15, 19, 23–24, 28–29, 32, 38, 40–42, 55, 62, 66, 83, 96–97, 109, 112, 114, 116–117, 132, 143, 145–146, 149, 151, 153–155, 158–159, 163, 165–167, 183n27

Wander, 26, 41, 43, 45, 53, 55, 60–61, 72, 83–84, 90, 107, 113, 137, 140, 143, 146, 150–151, 155, 159–167, 183n29
Wang Bi 王弼, 10–11, 37, 73, 84, 177n15, 179n34, 181n2, 182n6, 182n9, 182n14, 188n10,
Wang Pang 王雱, 121–122, 132, 188n17
Withered wood (*gao mu* 槁木), 59–61, 87, 95, 120–123, 126, 130
Wenzi 文子, 12–14, 23, 176n3, 178n21, 178n23, 190n11
Woodcarver Qing, 48, 56–58, 60, 184n35

Xiang Xiu 向秀, xiii, 176n4

Yan Hui 顏回, 29–30, 37, 127, 128–132, 134, 142, 189n32
Yijing 易經 (Book of Changes), 10, 188n10

Zhuangzi's wife, 84, 186n5, 189n26
Zigong 子貢, 161–162
Ziporyn, Brook, 47, 182n16, 183n30, 183n31, 183n32

www.ingramcontent.com/pod-product-compliance
Lightning Source LLC
Chambersburg PA
CBHW030652230426
43665CB00011B/1063